W9-DAO-057

THE TERRORIST CONJUNCTION

To Paul, Marylick
Mary
and all their tribe
a small contribution
To The understanding of the
several causes of the two
main forms of Terrorism
affectionately

Alfred Guerreroﾘ
06-02-2007

THE TERRORIST CONJUNCTION

The United States, the Israeli-Palestinian Conflict, and al-Qā'ida

ALFRED G. GERTEINY

Foreword by Jean Ziegler

PRAEGER SECURITY INTERNATIONAL
Westport, Connecticut • London

Library of Congress Cataloging-in-Publication Data

Gerteiny, Alfred G.
    The terrorist conjunction : the United States, Israel, the Palestinians, and Al-Qaida / Alfred G.
Gerteiny ; foreword by Jean Ziegler.
       p. cm.
    Includes bibliographical references and index.
    ISBN 978–0–275–99643–7 (alk. paper)
    1. Terrorism.   2. Terrorism—Religious aspects—Islam.   3. Arab-Israeli conflict—History.
    4. United States—Foreign relations.   I. Title.
    HV6431.G47   2007
    363.325–dc22   2007005897

British Library Cataloguing in Publication Data is available.

Library of Congress Catalog Card Number: 2007005897
ISBN-13: 978–0–275–99643–7
ISBN-10: 0–275–99643–3

First published in 2007

Praeger Security International, 88 Post Road West, Westport, CT 06881
An imprint of Greenwood Publishing Group, Inc.
www.praeger.com

Printed in the United States of America

The paper used in this book complies with the
Permanent Paper Standard issued by the National
Information Standards Organization (Z39.48–1984).

10 9 8 7 6 5 4 3 2 1

Contents

Foreword

BARBARITY AND ITS MIRROR

The Terrorist Conjunction: The United States, The Israeli-Palestinian Conflict, and al-Qā'ida is a brilliant analysis, innovative and profoundly original, of one of the most frightful yet evasive phenomena of our time: the devastating acts of armed terrorists. How is it possible to analyze in rational terms a political, military and ideological poisoning whose roots are buried in the darkest irrationality?

Professor Gerteiny has done so admirably.

A celebrated international specialist in the relations between the West and the Muslim Arab and African worlds, he has produced an impressive scientific study with a perception of the Muslim people rare among his American and European colleagues.

Born in Cairo, he received a solid education at the French Jesuit College, before pursuing graduate studies in Paris, The Hague, and New York. As a youth, he was exposed to various cultures. The fascinating multiculture of Egyptian society between 1940 and 1950 opened for him an historic horizon both vast and vibrant.

The great majority of organized terrorist groups currently in operation against the West and its allies is of Muslim Arab origin. Gerteiny understands the frustrations and motivations, both conscious and subconscious, that impel their actions.

The bloody terrorism practiced by global organizations and local groups, mainly of aforesaid Muslim Arab origin, has given rise in the West, to a perverse variation: the terrorism of the state, practiced by the United States in Afghanistan and Iraq and by Israel in Palestine and Lebanon.

Islāmist barbarity is reflected in Bush and Olmert's barbarity and vice versa.

Regis Debray sums up the situation thusly: "The choice is between an exasperating empire and an insufferable Medievalism."[1]

Precision is, at this point, necessary: I use the term "Islāmist" because it has entered the Western and Arab worlds' lexicons, for it would be injudicious to inculpate Islām, or the *Qur'ān* as a whole for the mindless massacres of children, women, and men, and we trust that the fundamental obsession with theocracy will be overcome by reason.

In its endless war on global terrorism, a phenomenon which knows no restrictions in the normative sense, the current United States government has unilaterally rescinded basic norms of international law by endorsing the concept of preventive war, violating the Charter of the United Nations and condoning torture on a grand scale.

I recall an autumn afternoon in Manhattan: the special Chairman of the Human Rights Commission on Torture, Theo van Bowen, was speaking before the General Assembly of the United Nations. It was Wednesday, October 27, 2004. The audience listened in a subdued state of shock and horror as he enumerated meticulously the torture techniques used by the occupying power in Iraq and Afghanistan, against both war prisoners and mere suspects—sleep deprivation for long periods of time; confinement in cages where captives could neither stretch out nor could barely stand or sit; transfer of detainees to secret prisons in states where the most atrocious methods of mutilation are practiced; sexual violation and humiliation; sham executions; intimidation by attack dogs; and more.

The American president can now decide at his discretion which of the detainees captured by the American authorities are to benefit from the Geneva Conventions and their additional protocols as well as the established principles of humanitarian rights and which will be "legally" surrendered to the whims of their jailers.

In the September 19, 2006, *International Herald Tribune*, Paul Krugman poses an interesting question, providing his own answer:

> Why is the Bush administration so determined to torture people?

> To show that it can. The central drive of the Bush administration—more fundamental than any particular policy—has been the effort to eliminate all limits on the president's power. Torture, I believe, appeals to the president and the vice president precisely because it's a violation of both law and tradition. By making an illegal and immoral practice a key element of U.S. policy, they're asserting their right to do whatever they claim is necessary.

Krugman echoes Gerteiny's own words:

> Bush finally found some things he wants Americans to sacrifice. And those things turn out to be our principles and our self-respect.

The Terrorist Conjunction subtly documents the neo-imperialism of the Bush regime. But this neo-imperialism was not born solely of a reaction to the frightful crimes committed by the al-Qā'ida murderers of September 11, 2001. In the United States, imperialism already had a history of applying its own definition of what is lawful.

It's here and only here that I must criticize Gerteiny: he fails to analyze the historic roots of President Bush's neo-imperialism.

According to Bob Woodward, Henry Kissinger, now 83, is one of Bush and Cheney's principal advisors.[2]

In 1957, Kissinger published his doctoral thesis under the title: *A World Restored: Metternich, Castelreagh and the Problems of Peace, 1812–1822*.[3] Here he developed the imperialist credo which he later applied to the period from 1969 to 1975, when a member of the National Security Council and from 1973 to 1977, as secretary of state. His central theme: Multilateral diplomacy produces only chaos. Strict adherence to the people's rights to self-determination and United States sovereignty does not constitute a guarantee for peace. Only a planetary power possesses the material means and the capability of swift global intervention in times of crisis. This power alone can impose peace.

During a recent conference at the Center for Strategic Studies at the University Institute of High International Studies in Geneva, Dr. Kissinger brilliantly analyzed the deadly conflict in Bosnia. As I listened to him, doubts began to rise in me. Could he be right?

For twenty-one months, Sarajevo had been bombarded and surrounded by the Serbs: 11,000 dead, tens of thousands wounded, mainly civilians—the majority, children. Yet there was total inability on the parts of the United Nations and Europe to bring the murderers of Milosevic to justice, until one day, in June, 1995, when the American president made the decision to bombard the Serbian artillery posted around the Sarajevo basin, to force the Dayton meeting, and finally, to impose peace in the Balkans through military might.

As the dysfunctions of multilateral diplomacy were made manifest, one could see that Kissinger's theory wasn't altogether ludicrous. During the decade of 1993–2003, forty-three low-intensity wars (fewer than 10,000 dead per year) have ravaged our planet. The United Nations hasn't managed to prevent a single one. Kissinger's imperialist theory has become the dominant ideology of the United States.

A hypothesis is implicit in Kissinger's statement: Moral force, the desire for peace and the efficacy of an empire's social organization are superior to those of all the other uses of power; but it is precisely this hypothesis that has been systematically contradicted by American politico-military action in Iraq, at Guantanamo and Bagram.

Another theme key to Gerteiny's book is that of the causal link between the misery endured by billions of human beings and the terrorist reaction to that misery.

Daily, 100,000 people die of hunger or as a consequence of it. Every seven seconds a child under ten dies of hunger. Every four minutes, someone loses his sight because of a lack of Vitamin A.[4] We are talking here about 852 million human beings who are permanently undernourished and mutilated by hunger.

All this, in a world overflowing with abundance. At the current rate of agricultural production, the planet can easily feed 12 billion human beings, that is, double the global population.[5] Conclusion: This daily massacre by hunger is not inevitable. Behind each victim is an assassin. Thus, the present world order is not only murderous. It is also absurd.

Jean-Jacques Rousseau wrote: "Between the weak and the strong is freedom which oppresses and law which liberates." To counteract the disastrous consequences of the politics of liberalization and obsessive privatization practiced by the masters of the world, the General Assembly of the United Nations has created a new and justiciable, human right—the right to be fed.

All human rights are universal, interdependent, and indivisible. Obviously, there is no question of comparing political and civil human rights with economic, social, and cultural rights. The decision to make justiciable this right to be fed was born of evidence summarized by Bertolt Brecht: "*Ein whalzettel macht den Hungrigen nicht satt.*" ("The voting ballot does not feed the hungry.")

The right to be fed today is being defeated across the vast lands of Asia, Africa and Latin America.

Although certain Islāmist terrorist organizations recruit their leaders from the prosperous classes of Sa'ūdi Arabia and Egypt, the vast majority of those committing suicide bombings and attacks against civilians originates from the poor districts of Casablanca and Cairo, the sordid slums of Karachi and of Gaza.

Gerteiny has spoken with force: Any victory over terrorism must begin with victory over humiliation, misery and hunger.

From time immemorial, people have risen in rebellion. Is al-Qā'ida a liberation movement, one seeking the emancipation of mankind? Obviously not!

In Israel, Michail Warschawski is one of the most influential leaders of the "Peace Now" movement. He has experienced prison in his own country, because of his impressive lucidity and acts of courage; and his literary achievements—*On the Frontier*, and *Toward the Abyss*, published by La Fabrique, Paris, are much admired in Europe. He is the cofounder in Jerusalem of the "Alternative Information Center" and of the review, *News from Within*. Recently, with Leila Shaid, the Palestinian Representative in Brussels, he offered a series of conferences in France's suburbs. Upon his return, he described to me the confusion and chaos he encountered there and the revelation that thousands of young Muslims—boys and girls—in his audience believed that Islāmist terrorist groups were authentic liberation movements.

It is tragic that they are so misguided, because what do these movements actually accomplish?

The amputation of thieves' hand; the stoning of suspected adulteresses; the reduction of women to infrahuman being; the rejection of democracy; the most abominable intellectual, social and spiritual regression . . . Is this the *Shāri'a*?

Since 1967, the persecuted people of Palestine have endured a military occupation that is particularly ferocious and cynical. Who today are the most vicious Palestinian resistants facing a colonial Israeli regime founded on state terrorism? They are the creatures of that occupation—the militants of Hamas and Islāmic jihād, men and women who, should they ultimately triumph, would plunge the multireligious and multiethnic Palestinian people into a most horrifying fundamentalism.

Since the start of the Russian aggression in 1955, 17 percent of the Chechen population has been massacred by Moscow's assassins. Russian troops are committing atrocities with total impunity—detainee torture ending in death; arbitrary arrests and nightly executions; outright disappearances of young men and the extortion of money from families wanting only to recover the battered bodies of their children.

But who are the most effective adversaries of the minions of President Putin? Doubtless, it's the Wahhabis—Jordanians, Saudis, Turks, Chechens—successors of Schamil Basjew, based in Boiviki, in the mountains to the South.

Is Wahhabism liberating? I think not. If, by chance, it becomes implanted at Grozny, it's the Chechen people who will bear the yoke of an appalling theocracy. The recent history of the Maghreb, of Africa too, is bloodied by the murderous repressions of such leaders as Nabil Sahraoui, a.k.a. Mustapha abu Ibrahim, Amara Saïf, a.k.a. Abderrazak el-Para and Abdelaziz Abbi, a.k.a. Okada el-Para.

Islāmist terrorism feeds upon the structural violence and the system of permanent warfare that are at the foundation of the American empire, giving meanings to its logic and somehow legitimizing it.

Light years separate the jihādists from the legitimate fighters for a planetary social justice. Destruction, vengeance, madness, and death constitute the vision of jihādism, while the dream of the children of Jean-Jacques Rousseau, Maximilien Robespierre, Thomas Jefferson and Benjamin Franklin seeks the utopia of liberty and the pursuit of universal happiness.

The irrational violence of the jihādists is a reflection of the barbarity of the cosmocrats. Only a surge toward true democracy can vanquish this double folly.

A liberated collective conscience is the precious conquest of enlightenment. It is the only fuel capable of generating the tsunami that can sweep the empire clean of its shame.

The forces of freedom trace back to the American and French revolutions at the close of the eighteenth century—the rights and liberties of men and women, universal suffrage, revocable delegated authority. These weapons are available; whoever seeks change must use them without delay.

Mankind is duty-bound by a moral imperative; Emmanuel Kant has defined it in these terms: "Let no action of yours be ordained but by your own will – you'd want this to be a universal law."[6] Indeed, Kant always dreamed of "a world of a different essence" ("*Eine Welt von ganz anderer Art.*")[7]

Restoring popular sovereignty and reopening the way toward the universal greater good is the modern world's most cogent imperative.

Gerteiny's excellent work will contribute powerfully to this end.

Jean Ziegler
(translated from French by Elizabeth Gerteiny)
Special United Nations Rapporteur on the Right to Food, Professor
of Sociology at the University of Geneva, Switzerland, and author of
L'Empire de la honte (Editions Fayard, Paris, 2005)

Preface

I have, over decades of teaching and lecturing on the Middle East and on the issue of terrorism, always stressed the inherent conjunction of the overwhelming influence of pro-Zionist organizations—both Jewish and Evangelical—on U.S. policies concerning the crucial conflict over Palestine, and on the catastrophic growth of violent religious fanaticism, here and elsewhere, particularly its confusion with legitimate patriotism and nationalism. I have always stressed the enormous positive social, cultural, and scientific contributions of Jews, Christians, and Muslims to Western civilization and to global human progress; and I never failed to underline the wide gap in perspectives on the Middle East and on the plight of the Palestinians under Israeli occupation, between the extremist Zionist, and the profoundly constructive and humane attitude of liberal Jews everywhere. Similarly, I remain unequivocally discriminating as concerns progressive Muslims and islāmist politics and obscurantism.

Even when America was still enjoying relative security behind its oceanic shields, I argued that Washington's blind partiality toward an expansionist, and not always humane, Israeli state will, of necessity, ignite vengeful terrorist reaction on American and European targets, and will further corrupt the tenuous relations between a resurgent and misguided militant islāmism and the West, adding to Israel's vulnerability, while driving Christians and Christianity out of their original geographic cradle.

The festering enmity between Israel, the Palestinians, and its neighbors, the unending emigration of Christians from the Middle East, the attacks on U.S. embassies and assets, and particularly the ignominious use of American civilian airliners in the criminal attacks on the New York World Trade Center, and also on the Pentagon, have sadly confirmed other observers' and my own well-founded assumptions.

It is, indeed, these unfortunate developments, and the inordinately counter-productive, arrogant, and aggressive foreign policy of George W. Bush that have ultimately compelled me to write candidly in this analytical book. I have done so, more in sorrow than in anger, to stimulate a needed debate on the issue.

Indeed, I find that the American media, despite its claim of being free, is paralyzed by an obsession with the bottom line and by fear of economic retribution; its reporting and analysis of the fundamental causes of Palestinian and islāmist terrorism have failed to contribute to a fair understanding of the issues.

U.S. politicians' hunger for funds to finance their perpetual political campaigning and to preserve their privileges and lucrative grip on power, coupled with ethnocentric bias and ignorance of Middle Eastern realities have added to the confusion.

My book—*The Terrorist Conjunction: The United States, the Israeli-Palestinian Conflict, and al-Qā'ida*—is the result of years of introspection and analysis; it was written in the hope that it might stimulate a productive dialogue on the seminal causes of terrorism and result in a fairer assessment of how to deal with it.

My interpretations, arguments, judgments, and recommendations, indeed my candor in addressing intimidating issues relative to the seminal causes of contemporary transnational terrorism—be it driven by nationalism or by apocalyptic vision—will undoubtedly offend friends and readers committed to the defense of Israel and shock many others by their political incorrectness.

There will indubitably also be the usual detractors and publicists who will intentionally misconstrue and manipulate my analysis and choice of words, in order to persevere in obfuscating any challenge to the harmful and counterproductive political *status-quo* they cunningly advocate.

I fully expect and welcome these reactions, for they are intrinsic to the needed open debate called for by scholars around the world—following the publication of Professors Mearsheimer and Walt's probing and thoroughly researched article, "The Israel Lobby," on March 23, 2006, in the *London Review of Books*—on the significance of the pro-Zionist lobby's ability to affect American policy in the Middle East.

My criticism of the U.S.–Israeli policy nexus in the Middle East is offered humbly and with good intentions; it seeks to promote a healthier environment for reaching a just peace between two savaged peoples—the Palestinians and Israelis—both with legitimate rights and grievances, by exposing some of the more vexing factors in the ominous, dark cloud spreading over relations between the Muslim world and the West.

In the final analysis I am, and remain the only individual responsible for the content, judgments, and conclusions herein contained.

Alfred G. Gerteiny
Fairfield County, CT - USA

Acknowledgments

I am deeply thankful to so many—my children, family, friends, and colleagues—for the encouragement, help, and support they provided, while I was writing this book; particularly to:

Nell K. Murry, for her wise suggestions, and for reviewing and editing the manuscript;
Professor Stanley Elwood Brush, for his valuable remarks on the Muslim faith;
Professor David DeGrood, a noted philosopher for his critical inputs;
Praeger Security International, and its Senior Editor, Hilary D. Claggett, for the opportunity to publish a book on a very sensitive subject;

and to:

Professor Jean Ziegler, for contributing a "Foreword" with a European perspective, and Elizabeth Gerteiny, the poet who superbly translated it from the French;

I am particularly indebted to
Chandra Niles Folsom,
a daring, witty writer and journalist,
for her invaluable editorial and research assistance in writing this book.

Introduction

Terrorism is a pathology of the human mind that has eluded all therapeutic attempts. Human beings are, in fact, the only animals endowed with the capacity of consciously using terror as a coercive psychological weapon and otherwise, in sadism.

Terror is a weapon routinely practiced in all spheres of human endeavor; nations do not hesitate to use terror in war when they determine that it would accelerate victory or prevent defeat. Governments practice it to enforce arbitrary laws and also pretextually, in periods of emergencies, as an indispensable means to insure security. Organizations and individuals, too, often use terror tactics to reach their goals; and so do religious leaders when they wish to frighten their flock into greater submission to their faith's interpretation of God's will and in fulfillment of his design on earth.

The terrorist attack on the Israeli Olympic team during the 1972 Munich Olympiads, jolted American popular complacency about their own security more than any of the many other previous terrorist incidents; but being geographically shielded by two wide oceans, their concern with security remained limited to international travel. Thus the Munich incident failed to lead the nation into a significant reappraisal of its foreign policy in the Middle East, erroneously blaming terrorism on anti-Semitism, rather than on nationalist considerations.

Following Munich, the raised awareness of terrorism proved rewarding to "terrorism experts" and consultants, as government and corporations sought their services. It stimulated specialized research, studies, and related technological development, as well as employment opportunities in the field of terrorist prevention.

Most of the government funded programs, however, were inspired by experiences gleaned from the Israelis; they focused primarily on intelligence gathering and under-cover operations, on military preparedness and judicial enactments and on political and economic coercion to combat or interdict the phenomenon. But the Israeli model, though probably the best of its kind, was only a stop gap—half a century of reciprocal violence and terror between Israelis and Palestinians prove it!

A sound and long-lasting solution must involve the elimination of the grievances that stimulate this violence, that is, as long as the grievances are legitimate; it is in this area, that actual research is most acutely needed. And studies and research must lead to action, such as humane policy modification and sympathetic diplomatic intervention; these constitute a better strategic investment than all the methods used in the terrorizing Israeli antiterrorism model.

It has taken years after the al-Qā'ida-inspired September 11, 2001, terrorist use of U.S. commercial airliners against conspicuous civilian and military targets within the continental United States, to finally stimulate more courageous research and writing on the seminal causes of Middle East-inspired terrorism. But this too has thus far failed to shake Washington policymakers out of their comfortable, unwavering pro-Israel frenzy.

After a brief discussion of the various uses and expressions of violence and its relationship to power, I have attempted to dissect the anatomy of terrorism, differentiating between state, nonstate and antistate terrorism and between the "reactive" terrorism associated with national liberation struggles and its "ideological" or "theopolitical" cousin. I have then turned to the discussion of the seminal causes of both Palestinian and transnational islāmist terrorism, before analyzing the consequences of neocons international political agenda.

I argue, that except when carried out aimlessly by anarchists—in which case, it has an ephemeral character—terrorism will persist as a weapon as long as its seminal causes are present and fuel it; furthermore, terrorism does not incubate in a vacuum; therefore, while physical interdiction is *a priori* necessary, understanding its fundamental causes and genuinely attempting to address the grievances behind them are ultimately the most logical responses to all forms of transnational terrorism.

Indubitably, the prevailing transnational terrorist activities are directly related to conditions in the Middle East, particularly to Israeli truculence, to its territorial annexations, and to decades of inhumane occupation, seemingly tolerated, if not acquiesced to, by the United States. This terrorist orientation, I argue, is related to several factors; these include active support of dictatorships in the area, while claiming to promote democratic ideals; unprecedented American political, military, financial and diplomatic support of Israel despite its noncompliance with UN resolutions; the seeming identical geostrategic goals of Israel and the United States in the Middle East; the U.S.-led and so far disastrous illegal invasion of Iraq, and the corollary failure to pacify and democratize a tribalist Afghanistan. I have, therefore, deemed it crucial in this brief monograph to focus on these and closely related issues because they are intimately related to Palestinian "reactive" terrorism and to the wider-reaching vengeful islāmist jihādism that feeds on it. It is from this conjunction of factors that I have distilled this book's title.

The Palestine–Israel conflict and the difficult problem it poses to the international community has two interrelated aspects; one is political and national, the other theological and emotional. In its extremist manifestation, the religious aspect of the conflict has assumed primordiality. Thus one may posit that the conflict over Palestine and Jerusalem is a conflict of divine messages—or of selective theological interpretations—and not only from the Muslim side of the equation.

Strangely, however, the theological aspect of the conflict, particularly its terrorist component, based, as it is, on a message presumably delivered in biblical times and on another delivered in our Christian era, implies either the existence of a schizophrenic divinity, or of at least two competing gods.

Western readers are generally familiar with the lore of the Old and New Testaments; however, they remain unfamiliar with the apparent fact that these two Testaments constitute the primary sources for Islām's *Qur'ān*. Thus, my particular effort to explain and differentiate between the pertinent, salient theological interpretations and world views of conservative popular Islām and of its islāmist, extremist off-shoot. My hope is to have succeeded in suggesting that it is not Islām, *per se*, but its extremist variant that is contributing to the promotion of the ongoing terror-inspiring "conflict of civilizations."

In the United States, unlike in Europe, the terrorism inherent in the military occupation of Palestine and the ethnic cleansing taking place there is generally ignored. Only the better publicized acts of terrorism of the Palestinian nationalists and jihādists seem to affect the American people's psyche. The prevalence of this moral disequilibria has led me to sadly describe, in some brevity, the brutality and horror of Israeli occupation. And, in order to comprehend—without condoning it—the psychology that prompts young and otherwise intelligent persons to practice morbid kamikazeism, I have attempted to interpret the possible spiritual or poetic emotions inspiring the "suicide-bomber."

My last chapter is devoted to a somewhat sardonic rebuke of the Bush administration's response to terrorism and particularly of its ideological component as expressed in the strategic blueprint elaborated by the Project for the New American Century—the doctrine of preemption, the need for America to answer its imperial calling by imposing its worldview globally, the need to control Middle Eastern oil sources, the need to remove Saddam Hussein and the need to establish a permanent presence in the Gulf region, a *sine qua non* to the permanent security of Israel.

1 ———————————————————————————

On Political Power, Legitimacy, and Violence

"Irrepressible violence is man recreating himself"—*Jean-Paul Sartre*

We are in the habit of thinking of power as brute force. Power, however, is an abstraction; it may refer to responsibility, authority, knowledge, influence, strength, wealth, energy, vigor, or simply determination. More sociologically, it is the ability and genius to produce, marshal, manage, control, project, and use energy in any of its forms with a view to creating, improving, preventing, spoiling, or destroying. It can be said, therefore, that power is akin to the two faces of God—good and evil— as conceived in so many original Asian belief systems and to a divinity's nature and multifarious manifestations as in African tradition.

Power can be sought, it can be created, imposed, shared, extended, transferred, abused, subtracted, or otherwise manipulated by one or more individuals, by collectivities, institutions, societies, or by states. Its application influences all aspects of life and existence—domestic, physical, intellectual, moral, spiritual, sexual, commercial, economic, financial, political, national, international, geopolitical, military, mechanical, electrical, magnetic, and so on. Its perception is relative and interpretative. Nature too, through its innumerable phenomena, expresses power beneficently or destructively. Thus the impact of weather or geology, in any of their forms, influences life and events, even moods and dispositions in ways we are all too familiar with and seek with relative success to control.

Power is exercised in the biological realm as well, by particles, amoebae, microbes, viruses, parasites, germs, and other organisms, and conversely, by chemical and pharmaceutical products; they all vie for dominance and fight for it within and all around us. The insect, animal, and vegetal communities also possess and use it much the way humans do to survive or prevail.

Violence is the misuse of power, physically or otherwise; as Hannah Arendt put it, "Violence is the most flagrant manifestation of power."[1] Violence is, unfortunately, part of the human condition. All animals use violence out of fear and to defend or feed themselves, but never out of selfishness, greed, or meanness; these traits are the exclusive purview of the human mind, the most constructive, as well as the most destructive, intangibility on earth. It has been said that man is a political animal, but he is also an economic one. And both politics and economics instigate violence. History attests to the marvelous creativity of the human species, but also to the devastating results of its violence toward both animate and inanimate existence. The pages of history are stained with the blood of inhumanities. Violence, in its multifarious expressions, has infected all human institutions, even those conceived to control, minimize, or eliminate it. Even religions, which as political and economic power centers, have disfigured their intent with imagination, corruption, and violence. In their attempt to promote goodness, or under its cover, they have often, through manipulation, discrimination, and the threat of divine wrath, spread terror, scrambled psyches, killed, enslaved, maimed, and robbed.

This brief essay shall be concerned with terrorism, not only as the unavoidable expression of the ultimate power of the powerless—of those whom Franz Fanon called "The Wretched of the Earth," and Albert Camus, "The Dominated Man"—but also with its provocateurs, the more egregious, terrorizing violence of the elite represented by the arrogant state. For, with some exceptions, the former's violence has historically been expressed in reaction to that of the latter. In fact, human organization, being what it is, cannot exist without it. In this endeavor, the essay shall also seek to debunk the notion of the total innocence of states victimized by terrorism, and *ipso facto*, of the exclusive assignment of guilt to those who rise against them. The intent here is not to whitewash, excuse, or condone nonstate violence, particularly terrorism, but to attempt to understand its constitutive factors and explain objectively that which fuels it, and to propose humane means to address and neutralize it. With this in mind—assuming that it is agreed that terrorism is not the exclusive weapon of the ruled, and that the state, under the cover of legitimacy, also uses it in pursuit of its ends—it may be rational to suggest that state terrorism deserves greater reprobation.[2] Indeed, legitimate order can act illegally, or certainly unjustly. Yet the state justifies its violence, legitimate or not, as a duty required by public or national security, or as the case may be, on the basis of constitutional, religious, cultural, or ideological imperative. Individuals or groups through the judicial process, through civil disobedience, or in extremis, may challenge the justification violently. But absent legitimacy, the challenge is expressed at the risk and peril of the challenger. It may also be challenged by another state through diplomatic representations, through international jurisprudential mechanisms and institutions, or ultimately, by violent armed confrontation. In any case, state violence may be judicious or injudicious, just or unjust. Nonstate violence is technically never legitimate since legitimacy is the privilege of the state, but it can, nevertheless, be justified. The nature of the violence, its intensity, or proportionality, may determine whether it is appropriate and respectful of human rights, or inappropriate and condemnable.

States are political entities possessing legal status and capacity within the community of nations. As such, at least in theory, their dealings with other states are conditioned by an international code of behavior, practice, rules, protocols, and laws. Diplomacy is the means by which ordinary relationships between and among states is entertained; these take place by way of embassies and consulates. War, or the use of violence in international relations, is "the pursuit of diplomacy by other means."[3] It is a means of last resort, and The Laws of War and several international conventions too, regulate its conduct.[4] Laws also regulate the relationship of a state, as occupier of a foreign land, with the people of that land, as well as with their national and private patrimony. The use of political violence by a state against its own population, or against subject people, may be legal within the territorial confines of that state and of a territory under its jurisdiction, but unlawful in the context of international norms and conventions. State violence against segments of its own population, or against a subject population, may seek to silence opposition through terrorizing violence; in that case, it is guilty of state terrorism. Indeed, a state may enact laws ordaining the use of violence and repression for what is usually called "raisons d'état." This violence is technically legal, but may be in violation of civil and human rights and International Law and conventions. National Security is always invoked to justify even the most hideous of political crimes; the Nazis' Genocide is a case in point. Less egregiously, the "Homeland Security Act" promulgated in reaction to the September 11, 2001, tragedy, under the George W. Bush administration, has been criticized by human rights groups as a virtual blank check for state violence. Jurists who drafted some of its elements—concerning the rights of prisoners from the armed intervention in Afghanistan—had the presumptive arrogance to say that the Geneva Convention on the Treatment of Prisoners of war was "quaint" and "obsolete." Other elements of the Act violate the constitutional rights of U.S. citizens and the human rights of immigrants. The determination of the obsoleteness of the Convention, and the reasons given for the curtailment of certain guaranteed rights and liberties under the Constitution, terrorizing as they are, were justified by the need to prosecute the "Global War against Terrorism." In its totality, the Act possesses legal status within the territorial jurisdiction of the United States, but raises serious questions as to its lawfulness in the context of International Law; it opens a Pandora's Box of determinations by enemy states as to its applicability to U.S. military and civilian prisoners in a conflict. The congressional modification of the Act, following a Supreme Court decision, does little to eliminate that eventuality.

Political violence by individuals and groups against the state are less common; they seem to occur when reasonable methods are impracticable under the law, or when they have been exhausted. Insurgencies, revolts, and uprising seldom develop unless tyrannical conditions or repression are extremely grievous and long-standing, and when calls for redress are neglected, ignored, or punished. The use of violence by insurgents or captive people against a state is, but for some exceptions, the result of despair, and because of the danger they represent, a means of last resort. It is in fact, suicidal in nature. When nationals use violence against the state, the terms insurgency, insurrection, or revolution may apply depending on the nature of its organization and the amplitude of its adherence. Revolt and uprising seem to refer more specifically to violence by subject people against the authority of an alien state. When this violence is directed intentionally or randomly against the civilian population of the enemy state, or against that of its allies, then one or more of the terms terrorism, transnational, and international terrorism may apply. The causes that lead people to use violence against a state are numerous and complex and they vary from case to case.

It is a universal democratic notion that sovereignty resides in the people; in democracies, sovereignty is legally bestowed upon the elected government, which then exercises the powers delegated to it for the common good. In parliamentary systems, the elected government, in accordance with procedures peculiar to a state's traditions or constitution, may be recalled should it act in ways antithetical to the will of a majority of the electorate; or it may resign as a result of a "no confidence" vote cast in the parliament. In constitutional, presidential systems, the people can freely express disappointment and disapproval of the conduct and policies of the sitting president, but unless an impeachable offense has been committed, must generally wait for the appropriate scheduled election to decide whether or not to continue the president in office.

Generally, in authoritarian states, the leader, however unpopular, remains at the helm unchallenged until power is wrested from him or her through defeat in war, or through extra-judicial means such as assassination, insurrection, revolution, putsch, or coup-d'état. While in power, such potentates rule absolutely and often violently, ruthlessly, and terrorizingly, with virtually no checks and balances. Violence is a by-product of power, indeed, according to C. Wright Mills, its ultimate expression[5] ; wherever power exists, violence, its inseparable shadow, looms threateningly. Violence expresses itself when power fails to persuade or enforce, or when it becomes corrupt; violence is the corrupt face of power. In the relations among nations, be they in times of peace or war, the power factor assumes a paramount determining character, imposing its will and shaping outcome, often regardless of equity and justice. Indeed, "might makes right" irrespective, unfortunately, of merit or fairness. As such, it is often responsible for causing what Jean-Paul Sartre has called the "mad fury" of subject peoples.[6]

Violence is used to coerce, scare, punish, humiliate, control, and paradoxically, even to enforce justice, or as a means to survive. Free human beings do not readily submit to coercion unless their loved ones' way of life and their personal existence, serenity, sanity, and safety are threatened. Reasonably, only when all possibilities of reaching a settlement have been exhausted, should violence be contemplated; even then, its use must conform to established norms of humaneness and to the principle of proportionality.

War is sometimes unavoidable. When a war is in response to a real threat to national security, it is referred to as a "just war." But it is a war of aggression when selfish interests motivate it, when its objective is domination, or when its rationale is frivolous or trumped up. Military doctrine states that war's objective is expeditious victory through overwhelming force and with the fewest sustained casualties. To this end, its prescription demands that all necessary means be put at the service of victory. Tactically, it asserts that the enemy's resolve is more expeditiously breached when the will of its civilian population is broken. But when war seeks submission of the enemy by terrorizing its population, it is a violation of the Laws of War and should fall under the rubric of international terrorism, even if terror is used as a means to minimize casualties.

Power is the twin of authority, violence its alter ego and terror its illegitimate child. In its own way, this notion is implied in the phrase "*si vis pacem para bellum*" ("If you want peace prepare for war"). War is the most overt violence a state can perpetrate on another; it involves killing, murder, spying, poisoning, ravaging of assets, lies, deception, propaganda, and often torture and terror. In the pursuit of victory, the end, sadly, seems to justify the means, no matter its legality.

The arsenal of warfare is vast and diversified; it is not limited to conventional, chemical, biological, nuclear and thermonuclear weapons and the means to produce and deliver them, but includes brainwashing and psychological propaganda; real and bogus threats of annihilation; assassination; espionage, and blockade. Psychological violence disorients and induces terror; it wounds and scars hearts and minds as grievously as physical violence. It pervades all spheres of life—political, ideological, social, economic, literary, and artistic. Though torture is outlawed, it is not unusual. Belligerents at war seek to terrorize, starve, maim, kill, and break the will of the enemy's armed forces and civilian population. War is a dehumanizing and devastating game nations play; its rules and laws are enshrined in international conventions and its crimes—sadly only those of the defeated—prosecuted in specialized tribunals. Victory is achieved through superior military methodology and manpower, intelligence, training, hardware, science, skills, and valor. Without the victor's understanding, magnanimity, compassion, and generosity in victory, the humiliation and suffering of the hapless vanquished nation translates into resentment and hatred, and this breeds revenge and more war. The history of nations is replete with wars, violence, and terror, and it is well nigh impossible to find a state that bears no such guilt. State violence is often inwardly directed. In multiethnic and bipolar societies, intolerance and bigotry often lead to violence against, and persecution of, minorities, particularly when they resist integration and practice endogamy. In quietist societies, out of fear of retribution, intolerance and bigotry are usually endured without murmur. Inwardly directed violence is more common under authoritarian rule and in dictatorial and totalitarian regimes, but it can also infect democratic governments absent pedagogic, political, judicial, and social vigilance. The perception of a threat to the state; to national identity; and to culture, traditions or faith triggers paranoia, confusion, and hatred. It stimulates the instinct of self-preservation and this, in turn, translates into irrational, senseless violence. Inwardly directed state violence can be obvious, but it may also be perniciously subtle; its expression may be psychological or physical, and it can be proactive or deadly passive. States have used violence against their own dissident citizens, but more often against aliens and subject people without provocation.

Insurgencies and movements of national liberation have no international status and therefore no legitimacy. Without international status and recognition, assistance in a struggle against a government is problematic. What then is legitimate order and who enjoys it? Legitimacy is vested in the state, which is represented by a government. Government either results from indirect popular consensus, or as a result of a putsch or of some dictatorial diktat. Once established and commanding authority, a government is ordinarily granted recognition by the Community of Nations, or at least has to be dealt with by it. It then assumes legal authority, power of enforcement, and diplomatic capacity. A government's mission under rational norms, is to insure—objectively and indiscriminately—through the dispensation of justice, the general well-being of the people and the pursuit of security, progress, and prosperity. In democratic states, its authority is specific and limited, is derived from the people through periodic, scheduled elections and is exercised in their name and at their pleasure. Ideally, it operates in conformity with standards set by a constitution, and it enforces laws enacted by the people's representatives. Civil society cannot function peacefully and in an orderly fashion, nor can progress and prosperity flourish without mutual respect, tolerance, self-discipline, and justice. Likewise, relations within the international community are regulated by international conventions, agreements, treaties, and laws and proceed through representatives selected by the member states. These relations seek to insure prosperity, commerce, security, harmony, justice and peace between and among nations. In order to enforce these goals, the legitimate and proportional power of coercion is used for the benefit of the community.

Of course, civil society can exist under an authority illegitimately acquired and exercised autocratically or under a monarchic or hereditary system, and may in some cases benefit by it, so long as it does not perpetuate itself against the will of the governed. Occasionally, authoritarian rule is unavoidable for the correction of abuse, to make needed radical changes quickly and even for the restoration of civil liberties. Without checks and balances it is possible that greater efficiency may be obtained, but at the expense of fairness and justice, as evidenced by the history of authoritarianism, totalitarianism, dictatorship, and colonialism, where in many instances, tyranny promoted order, development, and progress. History also teaches us that the fall of such regimes does not necessarily culminate in fair and just government, as administrative culture, anchored practices, and political expediency can bring about retribution, vengeance, and other abuse.

The issue of what is and what is not legitimate in the political arena, is a thorny one, because the law of the "fait accompli" often prevails; the party in effective control of the instruments of government, even if it is objected to by the governed, or by the international community, is in fact legitimate and has to be dealt with. Yet a popular insurgency against it or the assassination of a leader—criminal as the act may be—could be welcome and considered legitimate by other states that perceive it as politically convenient. Likewise, an uprising against a foreign occupier, though legitimate under International Law, is unlawful under the laws of the occupier and is so judged by its allies. Violence against the occupier's civilian population, however, is reprehensible, and depending on its nature and whether it is systematic, may fall under the rubric of terrorism. In recent history, uprisings and acts of violence carried out by national liberation movements against dictatorial regimes, or against nazi, communist, apartheidist, or zionist rule, have been so labeled by sitting authorities. Yet other governments and people may have viewed them as legitimate and even given them support.

Justified or not, political violence is not the exclusive purview of the state; it is practiced by individuals, by organizations and groups and is, where practiced, unlawful. Insurgencies and national liberation movements are ordinarily born in response to subjugation or tyranny. As in any well-conceived struggle, there is a strategic or ultimate objective with tactical means to achieve it. The most common strategic objective in insurgencies is independence from an occupier, or the overthrow of a government where legal means to change it is unavailable or virtually impracticable. The tactics include infiltration of government agencies, political persuasion, assassination, terrorism, sabotage, and even coercion and retribution on uncommitted fellow nationals. National liberation movements arise in extremis in order to gain independence from foreign or ethnic domination and abuse, be it the result of war, or colonization. Lacking the power of their abusers, their tactical means are primarily psychological. They seek to intimidate, harass and even terrorize the occupier agents and its settlers; to cripple their economic life by sabotage, and in situations where despair prevails, or when ideology or religious fanaticism are involved, to maim and kill through means deemed underhanded and criminal. Their strategic objective is total independence from the usurping power; sovereignty over the national patrimony. But the movements can also have, or develop, ulterior ideological objectives.

Beside insurgencies and movements of national liberation, terrorizing violence can become the instrument of other organizations. These organizations are generally motivated by religious fanaticism, ideology or racism; but economic, political, or other practical and legitimate issues add dimension to the cause and increase tangible appeal. The strategic objective of ideology and religion-based violence is anchored in an often unattainable idealism. Nevertheless, irrational as it may seem to objective observers, it resonates magnetically on the minds of susceptible and emotional individuals. The violence used by such movements is prone to being as extreme as the irrationality that motivates it. Later, we shall dissect the anatomy of these main categories of nonstate violence in the context of our concern with terrorism.

In most cases, politically motivated nonstate terrorism is a weapon of last resort; it is unlawful and condemned by national and international law. It is usually practiced in despairing hopelessness against the powerful. It seeks to shock them into realizing their own vulnerability and therefore, their common humanity.

Dehumanized and rendered worthless, indeed psychically dead, the oppressed come to view their life as meaningless, valueless, and futile. With such a mind-set, they translate its physical aspect into an ultimate vengeful weapon, one as crushingly compelling as that of their oppressor, and as if to dramatize their own human frailty, impose with violence, their hunger for life and liberty in a manner reminiscent of their oppressor's egotistical insouciance. To the freedom fighter, death is proactive. Its power and energy stem from a macabre selflessness and a creative willfulness which translates into organizational skill and astounding daring not unlike that of the "Navy Seal" on a suicidal military mission. Thus the "powerless," psychically crippled by his condition, artfully crafts his sinister, unorthodox brutality with the same indifference to life as that of his oppressor. To paraphrase Virgil, psychic death and misery provide the powerless with unorthodox lethality. Hence the weak derive power from their oppression, and express it, per force, in dissimulation and stealth, through inhumane and unconventional means.[7] As the expression of his dehumanization, it is stunningly shocking, indomitable, and, ultimately, possibly devastatingly "cleansing" as Franz Fanon succinctly expressed it. The degree of the violence of the oppressed is exponentially related to the length and nature of the oppression he endures, and its intractability to the countermeasures he meets.

This violence is rarely aimless, and though illegal, it is in fact, a cry in the wilderness begging attention to legitimate needs. Weaker nations can easily be defeated militarily, but the human will of a collectivity can seldom be. A defeated and subjugated people, in fact or in perception, ultimately derive surprising truculence from confrontation with their formidable adversary, and humiliated, are unlikely to surrender. History attests to the fact that living becomes an unbearable chastisement to those whose dignity, rights, and hopes appear definitively denied. Self-immolation, martyrdom, and selfless and senseless temerity become a spiritually redemptive and dignified end to a raped humanity. In this context, the symbolism inherent in the admixing of the oppressed's spilled blood with that of his oppressor—as in suicide bombings—shockingly savage, and terror-inspiring as it may be, appears as an act of transubstantiation of their mutual dehumanization.

Terrorism is a term that begs to be defined; it is often used as propaganda to defame a political opponent, to inhibit political dissidence, or to justify counter-violence and repression. The label "terrorism" is susceptible to exploitation and its determination will often continue to be a matter of politics or of interpretation. States seeking to justify their own repressive measures, or their inordinately disproportionate reactions to dissent, insurgencies and rebellions have also used it loosely. It is imperative that a judicious and unbiased analysis be undertaken to evaluate activities officially labeled terrorism. The clandestine, improvised, random violence often used by political desperados is obviously senseless, unlawful, and inhumane when it is directed against innocent civilians, and this, even when its ultimate objective is legitimate. When it is organized, sustained, and dramatic, it deserves the label of terrorism. But the dramatic background that distinguishes the unconventional fighting methods of terrorism from other acts of political violence is always evident. It lies in the inability of a subjugated nation to express its grievances through a corporate media that is moved only by sensationalism and profit, and in its helplessness before the disproportionate arsenal and capacity of the oppressor. While diverse factors otherwise motivate terrorism, the main rationale, or at least one of them, is that a terrorized civilian population might pressure the state into restoring its tranquility by negotiating a settlement that satisfies the terrorists' minimal aspirations. These seem to be major operating factors in many insurgencies and wars of national liberation. Refusal by powerful authorities to communicate with the perpetrators; the harsh repression unleashed against dissidents' families and people; the callousness shown toward their grievances and the indifference of the media to their plight exacerbate despair, further radicalize rebels, lead them to harden their resolve and often provide them with justification to find allies and recruits. The usually disproportionate nature of state reaction to terrorist violence—no matter how barbaric—is counterproductive and only prolongs the agony of both parties. Resolution of some hostage-taking situations in nonpolitical issues, through flexibility and expert negotiations, prove this point.

The illegal and reprehensible means of terrorism perpetrated clandestinely against the overwhelming military and political power of the state, however, are not exclusive to dominated people. Beyond colonialism and imperialism, whose oppressive and terrorist character is legend, states—even democratic ones—have used terror-producing propaganda and violence in regular warfare in order to accelerate their objectives. Regrettably, the victor always gets away with it, while the vanquished nation pays. The terrorizing announcement of a massive bombing, for instance, has a demoralizing effect on a civilian population's will to support a war. Among the recent cases in point are the Nazi London Blitz; the Allies massive and indiscriminate fire bombings of German cities; the fire bombing of Japanese cities; the nuclear attacks on Hiroshima and Nagasaki during World War II, as well as the use of defoliation agents and the carpet bombing during the Vietnam War. An additional case in point is the celebrated "Shock and Awe" goal of the bombing campaign over Iraq before the official declaration of that strategy at the beginning of the 2003 war. Clearly, the legitimate state at war is often as guilty of terrorism as the political nobody. By including in the definition of terrorism, warfare seeking enemy compliance through psychologically devastating means and the use of massive bombings of civilian cities, we mean to raise a controversial but important issue that needs scrutiny.

The celebrated terrorism expert, Brian Michael Jenkins, has touched upon the issue in an article published in a 2004 *Christian Science Monitor*, but his interpretation is somewhat exculpatory:

> Wars may involve acts of terror, but every act of extreme violence is not terrorism. The Nazi's "final solution," the London Blitz, the atomic bombs on Hiroshima and Nagasaki, fall in the category of genocide or war crimes, or are simply viewed as part and parcel of brutal, total war; they are not categorized as terrorism. Hitler wanted to physically eliminate all Jews, not terrorize them. Aerial bombardment, until

recently, was imprecise. Do collateral casualties constitute terrorism if not the product of deliberate strategy? Probably not. But to say that an act fits better in the category of war crimes than terrorism, does not lessen our need to condemn it.

He continues:

What sets terrorism apart from other violence is this: terrorism consists of acts carried out in a dramatic way to attract publicity and create an atmosphere of alarm that goes far beyond the actual victims. Indeed, the identity of the victims is often secondary or irrelevant to the terrorists who aim their violence at the people watching. The distinction between actual victims and a target audience is the hallmark of terrorism and separates it from other modes of armed conflict. Terrorism is a theater.

This is precisely our point; the examples we have cited, while being war crimes, suggest also an intermediate binary objective: to destroy the enemy's strategic assets and to terrorize his people with a view to bringing about an accelerated surrender. Also, it is obvious that European Jews were sufficiently terrorized by the rise of Nazism to have emigrated so hastily in such large numbers before the onset of the war and the Holocaust. "Kristall Nacht" was definitely an act aiming to terrorize the Jewish population. And the motivation behind the aerial bombardments—the London Blitz,[8] the fire storm bombings over Hamburg, Dresden, Köln, Essen, and other German cities,[9] and the nuking of Hiroshima and Nagasaki—was clearly to break the will of the enemy through terror.[10] Did we then care about the identity of the multitudes that perished, or were maimed in these terror bombings? There is no denying that these were indeed "acts carried out in a dramatic way to attract publicity and create an atmosphere of alarm that goes far beyond the actual victims," in order to accelerate unconditional surrender. This also was the aim of the "Shock and Awe" bombing in the war against Saddam Hussein.

Despite attempts, particularly in the twentieth century, to make wars less barbaric, the increased massive brutality that modern science has bestowed on weapons has rendered them even more terrorizing and dehumanizing. War is, in the words of Gloria Emerson, "a debasing enterprise that inflicts misery, physical harm and psychological trauma on innocent civilians and soldiers of all sides; nothing noble about it!" Throughout history, concern about war's barbaric nature, its terrorizing impact on innocent civilians and children, and its devastating consequences have preoccupied philosophers, ethicists, human rights activists, and international jurists. In the seventeenth century, Hugo Grotius, the father of modern international law, published *On the Law of War and Peace* in an attempt to systematically regulate and harmonize relations among nations and minimize conflicts and illegitimate aggressions.[11] But few recall his name, let alone his book. Since then, the League of Nations Charter, that of its successor, the United Nations, and several conventions, treaties, and declarations, notably The Hague and Geneva Conventions and the Nuclear non-Proliferation Treaty,[12] have added to Grotius's noble intent. These documents imposed universal rules and constraints on war and the conduct of warriors, and on such issues as the treatment of prisoners and of civilians and on their national patrimony under occupation. Despite these treaties and declarations, wars and their consequences have grown increasingly more devastating and terrorizing.

Anatomy and Physiology of Contemporary Terrorism

"Terrorists ... are neither ordinary criminals, nor recognized state actors, so there is no international or domestic law dealing with them."—*Douglas R. Burgess, Jr.*

An ultimate objective of the United Nations is to produce a universal, comprehensive agreement in order to establish systematic procedures to mitigate and bring to an end insane political violence by addressing its constitutive causes. But broadly speaking, the lack of consensus at the UN on the definition of terrorism hinders the efficient application of the "1998 International Convention for the Suppression of Terrorist Bombings" and its successor, "1999 International Convention for the Suppression of the Financing of Terrorism" and other such agreements.

The disagreements stem from the fact that the term "terrorism" has become politicized to suit selfish national interests, thereby inhibiting concerted intelligent approaches to minimizing its occurrences, let alone eliminating it. Thus terrorism continues to be undefined and its taxonomy nebulous. The need for a universally agreed-upon definition and objective taxonomy cannot be overemphasized; it must meet the security requirements of the industrialized world, as well as the sensitivities and perspectives inherent in the history of the emerging nations and their sociopolitical conditions. There must be a consensus on the particular causes that lead people and organizations to resort to terrorism in order to insure practical solutions to enhance world security. Without such consensus, appropriate responses, based on the widest possible cooperation from the international community, will remain problematic. Terrorism will persist and remain a curse on the civilized world.

The differences in opinion as to what causes and constitutes terrorism are due primarily to the peculiar historical backgrounds of colonizer and former colonized states; to powerful and dependent ones; to policies and attitudes concerning national liberation movements; to the means of addressing them and, of course, to the methods these movements use in their struggle to achieve their often legitimate goals. Nations that have emerged from colonial situations, and nations that, for one reason or another, did not participate in the elaboration of International Law, feel the need to review its terms in order to give them a more universally responsive character—reflecting also, their own particular needs, conditions, and interests. International Law has primarily been the child of European and "Eurogenic" states. Accordingly, the emerging non-Western nations insist that political violence, in the context of national liberation, however illegal, be distinguished from the more irrational ideological terrorism.

So far, definitions advanced by the powerful states have been less sensitive to that approach and more concerned with devising means to interdict and fight terrorism. Interestingly, however, while great powers have reservations on that issue—some more than others—they do support and regularly finance third-party political violence when it suits their own strategic ends. The history of great powers' reactions to political violence perpetrated by dependent nations reflects a traditional refusal to acknowledge their own contributions to its cause. The prevalent, indiscriminate practice by some powerful nations of rejecting the concept of negotiation with terrorists attests to that fact. Indeed, in cases of violence concerned with movements of national liberation, or those triggered by other legitimate grievances, the nonnegotiation is at least as much of a cause of exacerbating terrorist violence as negotiations with ideologically driven terrorist organizations. The ostensible reasons for nonnegotiation are threefold: Negotiating with terrorists may give them legitimacy, may contribute to their appeal, and may enhance the prestige of antistate violence generally.

At the end of World War II, terrorism directed against colonial powers ceased and good relations ensued only after negotiations finally satisfied the insurgents' legitimate rights. Conversely, violent attempts to repress insurgencies have historically prolonged the parties' mutual agony. Where victory over the insurgents— Amerindians, Armenians, Kurds, Vietnamese, etc.—remained an implacable goal, it was never attained except through brute force and, yes, genocide. Often, of course, terrorism is in the eye of the beholder, as terror can be caused or perceived in what may be called *passive violence*. Thus Saddam Hussein perceived the United Nations long-term, coalition-inspired economic embargo, U.S. assistance to Shī'ites and Kurdish insurgents, and the constant, provocative coalition over-flights and bombings, and Iraqi flight restrictions, as primarily American terrorism. And so does the Fidel Castro administration perceive the Cuban exiles' leadership as an American-sponsored terrorist organization, because it has responsibility for the devastating result of the U.S.-imposed, long-term economic sanctions and embargo.

Passive terror can also result from draconian laws and judicial procedures imposed by an authoritarian regime to curtail the freedom needed for the enjoyment of normal daily life. Special security measures enacted by democratic governments during states of emergency, in order to insure national security, may also cause terror in certain communities. The need, therefore, for more honesty and objectivity in all aspects of international and transnational violence, is pressing. Whether the violence is perpetrated by anarchists; by extremists and ideologues; by the alienated, the dominated and the dispossessed; or whether it is a result of devastating despair caused by passive-aggressive domination, a consensus on the nature of terrorism, its taxonomy and the means to respond to its different types and motivations, must be reached.

Quite apart from these considerations, terrorism as a label must be exclusively reserved for political violence directed against civilians, regardless that it is caused by legitimate grievances, in order to compel political change, silence opposition, or to coerce political submission.

Governments, even democratic ones, often seize the impact of a security crisis on society to enact undemocratic laws, to launch policies that would otherwise be unthinkable, or to wage war. Reichsmarschall Hermann Goering's cynical comment, quoted in G. M. Gilbert's book on the Nuremberg Trials, exemplifies the world leaders' common use of "national security" as subterfuge in stimulating and coercing popular support in such matters; though his statement refers to war particularly, it does, we feel, have a more universal propagandistic application: "Why, of course, the people don't want war," Goering shrugged:

> Why would some poor slob on a farm want to risk his life in a war when the best that he can get out of it is to come back to his farm in one piece. Naturally, the common people don't want war; neither in Russia nor in England nor in America, nor for that matter in Germany. That is understood. But, after all, it is the *leaders* of the country who determine the policy and it is always a simple matter to drag the people along, whether it is a democracy or a fascist dictatorship or a Parliament or a Communist dictatorship."

> "There is one difference," I pointed out. "In a democracy the people have some say in the matter through their elected representatives, and in the United States only Congress can declare wars." (sic.)

> "Oh, that is all well and good, but, voice or no voice, the people can always be brought to the bidding of the leaders. That is easy. All you have to do is tell them they are being attacked and denounce the pacifists for lack of patriotism and exposing the country to danger. It works the same way in any country."[1]

More recently the new British Anti-terrorism Act has raised serious apprehensions about the way the new law can affect free speech. Under the proposed British law, police may arrest an individual for "conduct which gives encouragement to the commission, preparation or instigation" of terrorist acts, as well as "conduct which gives support or assistance to individuals who are known or believed to be involved in terrorism-related activity." Mr. Blair insists the law would not be used to curb free speech, but even members of his own party have balked over language designed to punish the "glorification" of terrorism.

"Glorification is so broad," said Shami Chakrabarti, director of the British human rights group Liberty. "You can be found guilty of encouraging terrorism even when you had no such intention."[2]

In the United States, the psychological trauma triggered by the tragic terrorist events of 9/11/2001 is a case in point. It provided the Bush administration with the opportunity to put into action an aggressively militarist foreign policy. This policy is based on a blueprint prepared by the Project for The New American Century, 2000, and *titled* "Rebuilding America's Defenses—Strategy, Forces and Resources for a New Century.[3] " The terrorist attack on U.S. soil provided the requisite stimulus for its initial implementation: The war against the Taliban in Afghanistan, necessitated by Kabul's refusal to apprehend the leaders of the al-Qā'ida and to dismantle its infrastructure; the subsequent invasion of Iraq, hasty, illegal and uncalled for, potentially destabilizing to the Middle East and counterproductive in the struggle against terrorism, the quasi declaration of war against the "Axis of Evil" implied in the 2002 President's State of the Union Address, and the evident U.S. collusion in the 2006 Israeli retaliatory war on Lebanon.

The causes of terrorist violence are many; they are related to the particular character and nature of a terrorist organization's—or terrorist state's—objectives. Arguably, some violence—cruel and illegal though it may be—is triggered by legitimate reasons and grievances; other terrorist activities are motivated by irrational or ideological reasons; to these may also be associated legitimate grievances. Different strategies, therefore, must energize reactions to different types of terrorism.

Generally speaking, given the lack of international consensus on taxonomy and on targeted strategic responses to terrorism, what is reasonably referred to as terrorism is organized, indiscriminate, extreme violence directed, ordinarily, by a nonstate political entity against the people and assets of a state for political or ideological reasons. Ordinarily, the violence is more concerned with the psychological impact of the attack and the sensational news it engenders, than with the physical damage and human carnage it inflicts on the targeted society. These are incidental means of seeking sensational publicity for the cause. Their value, in the case of one kind of terrorism, lies in the desire to stimulate conditions leading to a modification of a particularly intractable, or abusive policy, or it can simply be, as we shall discuss later, an act of defiance, despondence, and despair.

In the case of an ideologically or irrationally driven movement, the sensationalism inherent in the terrorist act may have multiple objectives; among these are, certainly, the enhancement of the cause and its subsequent attraction for suicidal recruits, chaos, anarchy, etc.

Be that as it may, the United States Government has its own political reasons for rejecting the lesser world's argument on the need to differentiate between types of terrorism. The two-yearly lists that the State Department issues—one citing organizations that conduct terrorist violence and the other naming what it calls "Sponsors of Terrorism"—suggest that it is far from changing course. This does not bode well for a definitional agreement given the divergent perceptions concerning the root causes of terrorism. The lists obviously reflect a political determination based on whether the violence perpetrated by an organization was directed against American interests, or those of an allied nation, irrespective of motivational causes. Because this practice implies complicity with the enemy of the terrorist organization, it has invited vindictive redirection of violence against American interests by islāmists exploiting U.S. bias in favor of Israel in the Palestinian tragedy.

Anyway, the responsibility of designating terrorist organizations and states supporting them should be vested in an impartial international organization, such as the United Nations Security Council or Interpol. This would remove any semblance of nationally-based arrogance or partiality in ongoing intractable conflicts.

Terrorist violence is normally carried out by educated young women and men who volunteer to give up life, family, and dreams for a cause they consider vital.

In grievance-based terrorism, the volunteers are often desperate and hopeless individuals, some of whom may be holding a grudge or seeking revenge against an oppressive state; but they can also be eschatological fanatics or ideological extremists. Their ranks will always be filled as long as the grievances that inspire their insanity are ignored.

On the other hand, the terrorism stemming from ideology and theopolitics finds its recruits among extremists, converts, and fanatics lured by narrow intellectual vision, or eternal felicity. Success in confronting this type of terrorism requires a multipronged approach beyond judicial pursuit, preventive security measures, and the use of military violence. Its basic causes must also be addressed in close cooperation with influential moderate elements from within the religious or political community of the terrorist.

Indeed, the assumption that a "war on terrorism," with all its logistical implications—mobilization and deployment of the military and reservists, the setting-up and training of special civil defense organizations, their deployment throughout the nation's vulnerable sites and the investment in sophisticated technology, etc.—is psychologically unnerving, sociologically damaging, and financially and politically onerous. It diverts otherwise needed investments, while being virtually ineffective in insuring any nation's security, as can be witnessed by events in the United States, the United Kingdom, Israel, the Russian Federation, and elsewhere.

Of all the important concepts taught in military doctrine, only that of "surprise" is crucial to terrorist operations. Their success requires neither heavy administration nor expensive arsenals and none of the cumbersome logistics, equipment, and paraphernalia required by a conventional army. They can be swift, need minimal investment, and are, therefore, very cost-effective relative to their devastating human, physical, and psychological toll.

Furthermore, terrorists use sensational viciousness to put a heavy strain on democratic values and institutions. This leads to errors of judgment and to overreaction that are then easily manipulated by the terrorist organization for its own benefit. Witness the hasty, needless, and counterproductive aggression against Iraq; the strained relations it caused within the Atlantic alliance and other friendly nations; the maltreatment and abuse of prisoners at Abu Ghreib and Guantanamo; the related violations of International Law and Conventions and the impact these events have had on our reputation and prestige around the world.

All this has led to tens of thousands of innocent deaths and casualties in Iraq and Afghanistan and to the further radicalization throughout the Muslim world.[4] It has also created a climate of disquietude at home as the realization sinks in that sophisticated military power, technology and training are unsuited to the fight against terrorism. What a price to pay compared to the few thousand dollars invested by the al-Qā'ida and the few exalted zealots it immolated.

For states to deal with transnational terrorism is juridically very complex, because its determined and insane violence ordinarily stems from legitimate grievances, it is carried out by outlaws confident of the legitimacy of their cause, and it takes place outside the framework of International Law. Consequently, it is problematic, according to International Law Professor and Nobel Peace Laureate René Cassin, for international societies to apply to them the same international legal sanctions as those prescribed for uniformed personnel under the relevant conventions. But this also raises troubling questions about whether or not the activities of other nonuniformed, violent resistance forces—such as the minutemen during the American Revolution, or the maquis during the Nazi occupation of France—against an oppressor, or occupying country, are terrorist in nature.

Guerillas or freedom fighters would seem to be a more fitting definition for national liberation struggles, even when they use terrorizing violence, so long as civilians are not targeted, while the rubrics of terrorist and terrorism per se should be reserved for violence motivated by ideology and theology. In both cases, however, some governments have determined that international conventions concerning the conduct of war and the treatment of its prisoners are irrelevant in the context of the "war on terror," evidence the counterproductive treatment of detainees at Guantanamo, at Abu-Ghreib and in Egyptian, Israeli, and other gulags. Obviously, the guerillas/terrorists—given their legal marginalization, their nonstate status and their inherent relative powerlessness—also consider the 1907 International Convention of The Hague and that of the Red Cross of 1949, as irrelevant, and that any violence in pursuit of their "legitimate" goal is a right.

In discussing the crucial importance of an international compromise on a definition of terrorism, Douglas R. Burgess Jr., in *The Dread Pirate Bin Laden*, emphasizes the need for "a framework for an international crime of terrorism. The framework," he writes, "should be incorporated into the U.N. Convention on Terrorism and should call for including the crime in domestic criminal law and perhaps in the jurisdiction of the International Criminal Court."[5] In this context, he draws on the history of piracy which, he writes, "reveals startling, even astonishing parallels to contemporary international terrorism [and when] viewed in its historical context... emerges as a clear and powerful precedent."[6]

Both, he continues, began as instruments of states motivated by needs "identical to those of [Queen] Elizabeth [who, in the 16th Century, by granting pirates "letters of marque," viewed "English pirates as adjuncts to the royal navy] 'to harass the enemy, deplete its resources, terrify its citizens, frustrate its government and remain above the fray.'"[7] In this context, he observes, the United States did likewise during the cold war, manufacturing "its own enemy by training, funding, and outfitting terrorist groups in the Middle East, Afghanistan and Central America..."[8] The 1856 Declaration of Paris which defines the crime of piracy as "any illegal act of violence and detention, or any act of depredation committed for private ends" may hold the crux of a new legal definition of international terrorists because both represent "private war for private ends."[9] Because transnational terrorism is a crime against humanity, terrorists, Burgess suggests, may be referred to as *hostis humani generis* (enemies of the human race), just as Roman Law categorized their predecessors and historical twins, the pirates. As such, a permanent, specialized, international judicial authority, perhaps patterned after Interpol, would be better suited to interdict terrorist bases and cells and apprehend their agents wherever they may be, rather than the prevailing reactive, hastily organized, and controversial ad-hoc military coalitions.

Indeed wars—legitimate or not—are violent interactions between sovereign national states, not between states and individuals; transnational terrorism, even when motivated by legitimate grievances, is a crime committed by nonsovereign organizations and individual outlaws against sovereign states.

Terror as a tactic is not exclusive to terrorism per se, for like terrorism, war does include terror among its arsenal of psychological components as a means to a strategic end. War's objective, too, may be legitimate and just, or illegitimate and unjust; it is "just" when carried out in legitimate self-defense and as a last resort; otherwise, it is "unjust" and in this case, its perpetrators are liable to international judicial pursuit as "war criminals." Technically, war must be prosecuted in strict conformity with internationally sanctioned, appropriate laws and customs. These laws and customs prohibit bombing of urban centers and regulate the treatment of civilian populations under occupation; the mistreatment of civilians by the occupying authorities represents a war crime under the Fourth Geneva Convention. This convention also regulates the treatment of prisoners-of-war by their captors. The acquisition and annexation of territories in war is also illegal. Evicting, or causing conditions under occupation leading to civilian emigration and to their replacement with the victor's nationals, constitutes genocide and is punishable by the War Crimes Tribunal. Oddly, terrorizing the enemy's civilian population through bombardments, propaganda or other means is not viewed as terrorism per se, but as war crimes.

Putting aside terror as a tactic in warfare, terrorism expresses itself in many ways in different circumstances; consequently it behooves one to distinguish amongst what is properly "Domestic Terrorism," "International, or Transnational Terrorism," and "Terrorist Violence" used in the context of national liberation, and nihilist, irrational and ideologically motivated terrorism.

The term terrorism, as it is used today, is understood to mean sudden, seemingly mindless, political violence perpetrated against the people and assets of a state by a powerless, nonstate entity.[10] Exaggerated fear or paranoia is the tactical objective of terrorism; and while its strategic objectives vary from one case to another, it is generally self-evident and practical in nature. Terrorism seeks to bring about change by extra-judicial means when ordinary avenues for dialogue are denied by a powerful and determined state, and when hope for redress is virtually nil.[11] States however are usually in denial about the causes of terrorism and ascribe it instead to "evil doers," to "enemies of freedom," or to other self-exculpating reasons. While such ascriptions may indeed be contributing factors, branding them as the main factors motivating all terrorists is but a rationalization for the violence carried out by states in their struggle against the perpetrators.

The objective of all types of terrorism therefore, is not simply indiscriminate mass killing motivated by engrained, sociocultural bias, by hatred of freedom or by some other irrational "evil." Yet this simplistic interpretation continues to be proclaimed by the G.W. Bush administration. The label, "Axis of Evil," assigned to *non grata* states, masks its aggressive foreign policy and further contributes to blurring issues and exacerbating international discord and its terrorist component. Indiscriminate, spectacular violence—not unlike such acts perpetrated in international war—is often a means of last resort toward a perceived just practical end. Thus war, under the best of circumstances, is the legal use of military violence by the powerful state to attain a political objective—legitimate, or not—when diplomacy fails; terrorism is the illegal use of violence in order to create in the targeted state, a general climate of sustained, unnerving fear and paranoia, in order to achieve a legitimate, or illegitimate, political objective.

DOMESTIC POLITICAL TERRORISM

The U.S. Justice Department defines domestic terrorism as terror perpetrated by "groups or individuals who seek to further their political goals wholly or in part through activities that involve force or the threat of force." Domestic terrorism, however, has two different expressions; specialized literature classifies the first one as "anti-establishment" or "anti-state" terrorism and the second as "state" or "establishment" terrorism. In the United States, domestic terrorism refers to crimes or criminal intentions by militant right and leftwing organizations such as the American Nazi Party, the National Socialist Skinheads, the World Church of the Creator, the Ku Klux Klan, the radical Black Power, the Jewish Defense League, and like groups. Ideological, economical, religious, racist, or other aberrant, extremist or fanatical notions motivate their violence.

Domestic terrorist organizations exist in practically every country in the world and of course in the United States; thus France has terrorism associated with Corsican nationalist liberation bands, as well as with the mutually violent islāmist and Zionist terrorist gangs; Spain too, suffers from islāmist terror and from terrorism perpetrated by the Basque Liberation Movement, Euskadi Ta Askatasuna (ETA); the United Kingdom has endured Irish terrorism and is now confronting its own home-grown islāmist. Other countries, the former Yugoslavia, the former Soviet Union, Turkey, Sa'ūdi Arabia, Egypt, Pakistan, India, Indonesia, Columbia, ad infinitum, have to cope with their own domestic terrorism.

Quite a part from what is usually referred to as domestic terrorism, the terrorist scourge manifests itself socially as well; it exists in homes throughout the world. Abusive spouses, parents, or progenies perpetrate it. In schools, bullies—teachers and students alike—terrorize young and old; even in churches, impressionable people are often subjected to mental terrorism by the fanatical or unscrupulous spiritual authority figure.

Antiestablishment terror litters human history. Organizations, gangs, and even individuals have practiced it through the ages: the Sicarii zealots of the first century carried out an unrelenting campaign of terror against the equally terrorizing Romans and those who collaborated with them; during the seventh century, the Islāmic *Khāriji* in Mesopotamia and North Africa were no less their equal, and in the course of the eleventh and twelfth centuries, the *Hashshāshīn* systematically and ritualistically terrorized and slaughtered other Muslims and so on. The pejorative term "mafia," once the name of a Sicilian organization, is now currently ascribed to various organized criminal groups that terrorize merchants and businessmen, forcing them to pay periodic tribute or "protection" fees to hold on to their trade; other organized gangs use terror as well for economic gain.

But terrorism is often in the eye of the beholder. Thus the "minutemen," celebrated in America as quintessential patriots and heroes, were termed terrorists by the British Colonial establishment, as were the Irish-American Fenian Brothers, who, in the nineteenth century, planted explosive devices in and around London. The Spanish sponsored what is known in French History as *La Fronde des Princes* that used terror against Cardinal Mazarin's administration under Louis XIV. The *maquisards*, during the occupation of France in World War II, were invaluable freedom fighters for the Allies, but terrorists to the Germans. Many recent guerilla leaders—Menachem Begin, Yitzhak Shamir, Fidel and Raoul Castro, Ché Guevara, and Yasser Arafat—reviled terrorists to their enemies, enjoy iconic status among their own people. Individual terrorists too, such as Robin Hood and Zorro, reputed for terrorizing the rich and powerful, have achieved admiring legendary status in popular folklore. But the "weathermen" in the United States; *baaden-meinhoff* in the Federal Republic of Germany; the "red brigade" in Italy; the "red army" in Japan, and so many other organized, basically nihilist, ideological, or fanatical religious terrorist organizations have failed to enjoy such iconic distinction.

The second type of domestic terrorism—"State" or "Establishment" terrorism—is the practice of inhumane violence by a state when it imposes its views and yoke on some or all of its subjects.[12] States possess vast, exclusive authority and power and the means to coerce and dominate people. *La Terreur* (the [state of] terror) that characterized a period during the French Revolution is believed to have been the first time that the term was ever officially used in connection with domestic state terrorism. Establishment terrorism, however, is as old as the history of organized society, and its practice constitutes an indelible shameful stain on all nations.

Insuring public security has historically constituted the *raison d'état* behind the state's practice of domestic violence; but so have other claimed imperatives— the need to preserve a way of life, culture, ethnic or racial purity; to uphold morality; to punish unbelievers, heathens, and apostates; or to impose a religion, cult, or ideology. Catholic fanaticism led to the terrorism of the Spanish Inquisition; Protestant Puritanism in America sowed terror through its witch hunts; Judaism responded with its own terror to Baal worship in Canaan and so did Islām against some of its sects throughout the Muslim world. Ideology and exalted nationalisms, apartheidism, nazism, fascism, stalinism, McCarthyism, maoism, talibanism, islāmism, and zionism are but some of the recent terrorism-producing "nationalisms."

Beginning with the reign of Tiglath-Pileser, ca. 1000 B.C., "terror was [a] factor contributing greatly to Assyrian [military] success. Their exceptional cruelty and ferocity was also a calculated policy of terror, probably the earliest example of organized psychological warfare."[13] Recorded descriptions of terrorizing cruelty by a state can be found in archaeological inscriptions dating back to the apogee of the Assyrian Empire in the seventh century B.C. These report with pride that Shennacherib, Assurbanipal's grandson, boasted of his destruction of his political opponents saying, "I tore out the tongues of those who plotted against me before slaying them . . . I smashed many to death with the statues of their gods . . . I cut their corpses into pieces and fed them to dogs, pigs and vultures. . . ."

More recently—particularly since the emergence of totalitarianism in the twentieth century—science, technology, and developments in the fields of medicine and social psychology have contributed to the variety and refinement of the tyrannical state's arsenal of terror. In the area of Human Rights, despite important elaborations in International Law and the ratification of several specialized international conventions, the practice of terrorism by states continues to be a fact of life. In the Soviet Union, the GPU and the N.K.V.D. terrorized people, as did the SS in Hitler's nazi Germany and Mussolini's "brown shirts" in fascist Italy. In post–World War II, in modernizing Muslim states such as Egypt, Iraq, and Syria, the *mokhābarāt* are much feared; in *Wahhābi* Sa'ūdi Arabia and other islāmist states, the *mu'tawiūn* or "moral police" are ubiquitous, and many Tahitians remember *tonton macoute* with terror. At one time or another, many governments have used terror against their people. For example, the government in the former Soviet Union and its satellites; most governments in Latin America, particularly those of Argentina, Chile, Paraguay, and Nicaragua; governments practically everywhere in Africa—from Egypt to Morocco, from Mauritania to Congo, and from Sudan through Zimbabwe to South Africa; and in Asia, the governments of Turkey, Myanmar, Iran, Uzbekistan, and others all the way to China and North Korea have been guilty of the practice.

Indeed, the flagrant custom of state terrorism is not limited to dictatorships and authoritarian regimes. It is part and parcel of the political arsenal of practically every state, and even the most celebrated democracies have used it, albeit often passively or discretely, to control or deal with undesirable and bothersome elements in their societies. In the United States, putting aside the violence of its history—genocide against the American natives and the deculturation and violence inherent in slavery—intimidation and violence by domestic terrorist organizations were, until recently, allowed to take place despite a glorious Constitution guaranteeing life, liberty, and the pursuit of happiness to all. After the Civil War, the Ku Klux Klan perpetrated with impunity, some of the most inhumane atrocities, particularly on black Americans, terrorizing them well into the twentieth century. During the McCarthy period, innocent liberals and leftists were accused of being "fellow travelers" and jailed, terrorized, or persecuted by the government. In the United Kingdom, the British government tolerated, until recently, a reciprocal mutilating terror between Catholic Republicans and Protestant Loyalists in Northern Ireland. In Israel, our admired "closest ally" and "only democracy in the Middle East," both Labor and *Likud* Governments entertain the Kafkaesque concept that terrorizing draconian laws, curfews, kidnapping, assassinations, theologically inspired settler-violence and disproportionate military responses to freedom-seeking, terrorist Palestinian insurgents, guarantee their enjoyment of democracy in the "promised land."

INTERNATIONAL AND TRANSNATIONAL TERRORISM

The International Community has been grappling painfully with the need for a comprehensive convention on International Terrorism since 1972, following the daring terrorist attack on the Israeli Olympic team in Munich, Germany. While not the first instance of international (actually transnational) terrorism,[14] this massacre, occurring as it did in the course of the Olympiads—a major symbol of international peaceful competition—stimulated the urgent need for the United Nations to confront the issue.

In the 1990s, with the fading of the cold war and the simultaneous ephemeral *détente* between Palestinians and Israelis following the Oslo Accords, the pace of negotiations accelerated, and the United Nations succeeded in adopting several fundamental principles concerned with establishing general international standards regarding terrorism. In 1994, the "Declaration on Measures to Eliminate International Terrorism" established a "comprehensive legal framework" that covered many aspects of International Terrorism. And in 1998 and 1999, two other conventions were successfully negotiated by the member states: the "International Convention for the Suppression of Terrorist Bombings," and the "International Convention for the Suppression of the Financing of Terrorism." In fact, twelve legal instruments have already been agreed upon by the General Assembly of the United Nations, and a thirteenth, the "International Convention for the Suppression of Acts of Nuclear Terrorism" was finally approved in May 2005.[15] This latter convention includes definitions of acts of nuclear terrorism and covers a broad range of possible targets, including nuclear power plants and nuclear reactors. Although widely welcomed as an important contribution to the international legal framework governing terrorism and nuclear security, the agreed-upon treaty text leaves much to be desired.[16] Indeed, it sidesteps defining terrorism, whether it is exercised by nonstate organizations or groups, or by states possessing thermonuclear and other weapons of mass destruction, even if only for defensive purposes; it also does not define or distinguish between "terrorists," and "freedom fighters." The failure to agree on these definitions is due, according to Douglas R. Burgess Jr., to the fact that like pirates, "terrorists [hold] a strangely hybrid status in the Law. They are neither ordinary criminals, nor recognized state actors, so there is no international or domestic law dealing with them."[17] While this determination has value from a legal point of view, the failure stems more pertinently from divergent perspectives based on historical, cultural, and geopolitical considerations.

Two perspectives confront one another. One perspective is generally held by former hegemonic and colonial nations and by eurogenic ones such as the United States and Australia, that enjoy and exercise wide political and economic influence over vast geopolitically important regions of the planet. Among these nations are the traditional great powers that possess a large arsenal of thermonuclear weapons and are endowed with the all-important veto right in the United Nations Security Council. These nations reject any definition of terrorism that may restrict their freedom to use their formidable weapons of mass destruction, yet insist that antistate terrorism—even if it is perpetrated in pursuit of a legitimate objective such as national liberation—be included in the definition.

In contradistinction, the other perspective is held by nations that have, in the course of the last several decades, emerged from colonial subordination or are otherwise newcomers on the international scene. Because of the humiliating memory of colonial domination and the concomitant historical struggle they waged for their independence, a struggle that included "unorthodox" fighting methods against the formidable power that controlled their destiny, they feel a visceral empathy with the plight of subordinate peoples desperately fighting asymmetric wars in pursuit of their national liberation. They also continue to be highly suspicious of the great powers' legal positions that seem to reduce their own hard-won independence and sovereignty. This hypersensitivity translates into, and permeates, their political and legal perspectives.

So the matter of definition continues to dog the Community of Nations[18] as one side argues that a convention with a nonspecific definition is better than none, that the issues of war and foreign occupation are already governed by Customary International Law and Convention, and that the comprehensive treaty on terrorism should complement and refine, not encumber them. In response, the other side insists that the issue is crucial, because of the inherent right of dominated nations to counter—violently if necessary—pernicious state terrorism and foreign domination. They also insist that the eventual comprehensive convention on international terrorism must address and define the terrorism associated with conventional war. Thus the scope of the applicability of the convention, the question of intent, the inclusion or exclusion of state terrorism, and of people fighting for their liberation will continue to handicap the Community of Nations in its determination to eradicate both international and transnational terrorism.

Curiously, while as noted, the "1998 International Convention for the Suppression of Terrorist Bombings" and the "1999 International Convention for the Suppression of the Financing of Terrorism" do not offer a definition of the term "terrorism," the former, in Article 3, presents a caveat concerning the status of the actual perpetrator of a terrorizing act; it states that in order for the Convention to apply, the perpetrator must either fall under the jurisdiction of, or be a national of, a state other than the one where the crime is committed. This implies that the Convention would not apply, for instance, to the islāmist Britons who perpetrated the massacres in the London public transportation system in July 2005, even if their objective were the establishment of a universal Islāmic caliphate, or if their crimes were inspired by foreign extremist Muslim clerics. It would not apply either, to Frenchmen of Algerian descent who perpetrated the series of terror bombings in Paris during the 1980s and 1990s, nor to the truck bombers, who in 1995, destroyed the Oklahoma City Federal Building killing scores of people, even if the perpetrators were inspired by international anarchy. Arguably, this raises questions as to whether or not violent nationalist acts such as those carried out by the Irish Republican Army against the British, by Chechens against the Russians, and even by insurgent Palestinian terrorists under Israeli occupation constitute terrorism under Art. 3, since the perpetrators in these instances are all under the jurisdiction of the very systems they are fighting.

An eventual definition of terrorism by the United Nations will also have to distinguish between "international" and "transnational" terrorism. The international qualification should be reserved for an appropriate aggression carried out by agents of a state,[19] or carried out with the active support of a state against another state, its properties, or nationals, whether perpetrated on the victim state's territory or anywhere else. The alleged Libyan conspiracy to explode the Pan Am plane over Lockerbie and the Air France plane over Algeria are cases in point. The transnational term should be used to describe only the terrorist activities that are carried out by nonstate organizations that are not recognized as sovereign under International Law; or by independent individuals or groups. The determination of the responsibility of a state on whose territory a terrorist attack takes place against persons or property of another state depends on its reaction to the occurrence. Was it accessorial to the attack? Did it provide assistance or asylum to the perpetrators? Did it ignore demands to pursue the attackers? Or did it actively cooperate in the attempt to apprehend and punish them? The massacre of Israeli Olympic athletes in Munich, hijackings such as that of the S.S *Achille Lauro*, truck bombings similar to the first attempt at bringing down the World Trade Center, the 9/11 al-Qā'ida airborne suicidal attacks, the attacks against the American embassies in East Africa, and the March 11 bombing of the train in Madrid, are classic examples of transnational terrorism, because the perpetrators were foreign individuals and organizations and not sovereign states.

International terrorism can, of course, occur in tandem with transnational terrorism when a state conspires with or consciously permits active terrorists to operate with impunity from, or on, its territory and refuses to cooperate with the victimized state in the matter. The host state then becomes guilty of indirect, or of contributory passive aggression. This may, indeed, constitute a *casus belli* as it did when, following the al-Qā'ida attacks of 9/11, Talibani Afghanistan ignored U.S. demands to assist in pursuing, apprehending, and extraditing the al-Qā'ida established in its country. Nevertheless, going to war is a serious matter and evidence of "contributory" terrorist aggression must be irrefutable; war must not be waged on a hunch, on rumors, circumstantial evidence, or on ideological ground, lest it become unjustified aggression. The 2003 war against the Iraqi regime was clearly unjustified; its premises were baseless if not glaringly manufactured.

Broadly speaking, terrorism thus is the illegal as well as the illegitimate practice of carefully targeted, symbolic, extreme terror-seeking violence directed at soft civilian assets and populations. Terrorism is, as we have discussed, natural to insurgencies as it is to extreme ideologists, religious fanatics, and nihilists. Just like ordinary wars, it is violence based on conviction that seeks retribution and redress. Unlike regular warfare in which violence is both expected and theoretically regulated, it is a process in which particular occurrences are unexpected. Because its economic and psychological impacts are so exponentially disproportionate to the investment in weapon, money, and effort, and because of the virtual inability of the authority to prevent terrorist attacks no matter its efforts, terrorist attacks trigger deep insecurity, lasting paranoia, and a general societal malaise. Its objectives are both tactical or immediate and strategic or ultimate. Tactically, the attacks seek to generate publicity through terror in order to achieve a less apparent, legitimate or illegitimate, ultimate political goal. Immediate strategic objectives such as revenge, widespread terror and political provocation may also be sought.

Though terrorism as a tactic is, in fact, illegal, its strategic goal can be legitimate when it is provoked by despair in a struggle for national independence, or for liberation from a formidable oppressor. Among history's many examples, the most recent are those perpetrated in Northern Ireland and Israel/Palestine. Terrorism in such cases is often exploited by both sides; it provides justification to both the terrorist organization and its target state for the prosecution of a relentless, vicious cycle of reciprocal inhumanity. Its solution resides only in open communications that lead to a just solution of the grievances.

Clearly, therefore, while terrorism represents a real threat to international security, its propagandistic use—absent an international compromise on its definition— has assumed inflationary proportions, as have such terms as "communist" "anti-Semitic" and more recently, "liberal,"[20] or "big L" as Ronald Reagan sarcastically dubbed it. Bigots and intolerants customarily seize upon crises to spew their venom to silence opponents and critics and curtail liberty and freedom of expression. In totalitarian and undemocratic states, all dissent is violently repressed through passive or active terrorism.

During periods of political insecurity, democracies, unfortunately, feel compelled to abridge these freedoms. Indeed, even the United States, despite the towering symbol of the Statue of Liberty, has succumbed more than once to this unfortunate practice. Under the Bush–Cheney administration, individuals have been termed "unpatriotic" and have been intimidated, threatened, or reprimanded for dissenting from, or criticizing, unwise policies and aggression directly or tangentially concerned with the "War on Terrorism." This inhibits intelligent communication and erodes media and academic freedom. European allies—including France, the nation that contributed inspirationally and militarily to the American Revolution in its quest for independence—were castigated and derided by politicians and the media; they were vilified because of disagreements with Washington over the invasion of Iraq, and this inhibited a more constructive approach in the confrontation with global terrorism. Lesser countries that did not support the American effort were threatened with denial of economic assistance.

So while there is no disagreement that transnational terrorism exists and is a scourge, the definition of who is a terrorist will continue to evade the United Nations as long as imperialist and hegemonic design continue to animate powerful nations, while historically induced hypernationalism fuels the lesser ones. Thus the definition of terrorism and of terrorists will continue to be a reflection in the eye of the beholder, shaped at will by the political vagary of national strategy.

Terrorism is illegitimate, as well as illegal, when it is motivated by ideological, theopolitical, or apocalyptic considerations as in jehādist terrorism. Jehādism is a magnet to many ardently religious Muslims, who are seduced by, or who adhere to, extremist Islāmic schools of jurisprudence. Their strategic objective is to accelerate the establishment of the worldwide caliphate anticipated in the *Qur'ān*. Tactically, they opportunistically ride on available, deeply-felt, legitimate, popular and religious grievances and selectively pick Qur'ānic verses and examples from the *Hadīth* to assert the sanctity and claimed legitimacy of their mission and so justify their use of inhumane violence.

A solution to this type of terrorism is more elusive; it resides in the ability of the victimized parties to work through society and the mainstream religious establishment whence that terrorism finds its support. It also resides in their ability to encourage liberal and moderate Muslim leaders to discredit and defeat the mindless theories based on scriptural selectivity that stimulate it. This task is difficult. It requires a profound understanding of the culture, *weltanschauung* and religion of that society, as well as patience, perseverance, and an appreciation of the subtle distortions the ideologues weave from it to poison minds and lead them to insane crime. But this in itself will remain futile without a fundamental reappraisal of American foreign policy and institution of change based on justice toward the dispossessed Palestinians. Without this imperative, the ongoing heavy-handed attempt to "spread" democracy in the Middle East will not defeat islāmist rage against the West, and the brutal and mindless "war on terrorism," without addressing its causes, will further compound the existing chasm and fuel an interminable vicious cycle of reciprocal inhumanities.

The massacre in London's public transport system on July 7, 2005, perpetrated by young, first generation British and other naturalized subjects, complicates the problem of terrorism. These acts and perhaps some of those perpetrated in Paris during the 1980s and 1990s, were presumably carried out by nonassimilated children of Muslim refugees. These are young people reared in an alien culture and who are unable to achieve equal status with the prevailing local, traditional Euro-Christian one. Feeling rejected, some of these individuals perceive themselves as outcasts and seek solace and refuge in the most extreme expression of their Islāmic culture; they are seduced by the call to violence of charismatic *mullās* seeking to impose, by transposition, the nationality of the *umma*, or universal Islāmic nation, over that of the nation wherein they live, an unacceptable notion in any society.

Prime Minister Tony Blair's emphatic rejection of the Chatham House Reports criticizing Britain's alliance with American Foreign policy in the Middle East, dubbing her a "pillion passenger,"[21] is disingenuous. In fact, his invasion of Iraq, particularly in view of his own failure to bring about, as promised and hoped for, a *quid-pro-quo* modification of U.S. policy toward the Arab–Israeli conflict, has undoubtedly exacerbated resentment among the more vulnerable Muslim-British subjects adding to their feelings of alienation. Britain was wise to treat the massacres as criminal acts rather than acts of international or transnational terrorism, and to unleash judicial means against the perpetrators, instead of seizing the opportunity to war, say, against Pakistan. Yet one can only share Blair's statement that "there is no justification for suicide bombing whether in Palestine, Iraq, London, Egypt, Turkey, the United States or anywhere else." Nonetheless, this does nothing to mitigate the underlying factors that cause such crimes. Furthermore, one might add that there is no justification either for a state to dispossess a native people based on ancient historical consideration. This, in fact, represents a dangerous political precedent; one that is undoubtedly animating the islāmists in their violent quest for the caliphal restoration and expansion.

The vicious violence inherent in a terrorist attack per se—hijacking, suicide-bombing, booby-trapping vehicles, etc.—triggers in the victimized state an avalanche of interrelated, nefarious, long-lasting widespread consequences in all areas of national life. Its immediate effect is not only death and physical and material devastation but also stunning incomprehension and psychological trauma. Like an initial seismic shock, it is followed by a series of tremors that translate into a climate of exaggerated, generalized fear, insecurity, and psychological disorientation that gnaws away at society, clouding its perceptions, affecting its industry and élan and disrupting the cadence of ordinary life.

Civilians, in contrast, take the violence of war for granted even when they do not completely understand its causes; they generally support their soldiers even when disagreeing with their government's decision to go to war; and many seldom question the inhumane and terrorizing "collateral damage" inflicted upon the civilians of the enemy. Yet civilians account for a major part of a war's casualties.

And the states that bomb urban centers in war, sowing even more damage and terror than the occasional terrorist massacre, invariably rationalize their actions by saying it was unintentional, or by accusing the enemy of using civilians as human shields; and as long as they are the victors, they get away with it.

In fact, states do not really care about the civilian war casualties of their opponents as long as their military objective is achieved. Because war occurs after a series of tangible events, civilian casualties are expected; and so is the suffering of the innocents, however extreme. Terrorism, however, explodes randomly and unexpectedly in presumed peacetime, and the rage causing it is consciously manipulated and blurred by the authorities, thereby obscuring the ability of the average citizen to question the policies causing it.

A terrorist strike on a modern, complex, free and mostly urban society taxes all aspects of democratic life, as hasty measures are enacted to insure security. Urgent measures are promulgated, ostensibly to inhibit subsequent attacks—an impossibility—but actually, the measures' objectives are multiple; they seek to reassure and calm the public, restore its confidence in the government, facilitate the passage of restrictive laws and questionable budgetary spending, but also to inhibit criticism of the government and the questioning of its policies.

The mere enactment of restrictive measures and laws in a democracy is disquieting and unnerving. Damage from daring terrorist attacks on New York and Washington, D.C., of the magnitude of September 11, 2001; on Madrid on March 11, 2004; on London on July 7, 2005 and on Sharm-el-Sheikh on July 23, 2005, is infrastructurally, economically, psychologically, and socially devastating and its impact long-lasting. Thus the diabolically planned and perfectly executed 9/11 attack resulted in staggering human, economic, and political toll at a minimal cost to the al-Qā'ida planners. The following partial inventory provides a general idea of the attack's scope of impact, whose direct and indirect cost—both immediate and long-term—to the national economy was evaluated in 2002 at 639.3 billion dollars,[22] but is likely to triple once the consequent Afghan and Iraq wars are factored in. Above any material loss, of course, are not only the painful 2,948 deaths and their impact on family structure, society and cohesion, and the extra cost of medical and psychological therapies, but also the over 3,000 U.S. servicemen killed in action and the many thousands injured and maimed. To this must be added the huge destruction of real estate assets[23]; the reduced or crippled economic activity by virtue of the loss of human talents and the destruction of the Twin Towers and of nearby buildings; the related loss of businesses, documents, equipment, business; and financial plans, of jobs, careers, and professional relationships; the difficult and expensive clean-up of debris and hazardous material; the need to replace buildings and to repair the infrastructure; the high expense related to business and individual insurance indemnification ($38.1 billion, $15.8 billion of which came from Government programs),[24] and the loss of commercial and industrial revenues. Then there is the devastating economic impact on the price of fuel and on all else that is affected by it, such as air, road, and rail transportation; the crippling of the tourist industry and its financial impact on the maintenance and upkeep of historic sites, museums, restaurants, hotels, and parks, etc.—in addition to which, the billions that have been poured into buying and installing security equipment; on devising security measures; on training and deploying security personnel at airports and bus and ferry terminals; at railroad stations, harbors, bridges, tunnels, national borders, and other public places, not to mention the economic paralysis, bankruptcies; the cost of commissions of inquiry; the shattered public confidence in the political leadership; the deplorable assault on civil liberty and democracy; and the lack of free and normal access to public servants and political officials barricaded behind ugly, armored cement blocks, etc.

There are also, of course, other consequences, including an overreactive impulse by the attacked state to strike back disproportionately at the invisible but ubiquitous enemy, ostensibly to defeat it, but more accurately, to reassure a traumatized population and settle personal grudges. The overreaction, however, not only causes raised eyebrows, dissentions, and criticism from friendly countries, it fulfills another intermediate terrorist objective by compounding resentment among sympathizing sideliners and netting them new admirers and recruits. A vicious cycle ensues, producing on one hand, a general climate of sustained, unnerving legitimate fear and fanciful paranoia that further disrupts normal social, economic, and political life, and on the other hand, wounded pride and a need to avenge and punish, as well as unreasonable, undemocratic emotionalism.

Indeed, after a severe terrorist attack, any rational appreciation of terrorism's fundamental causes evaporates, and the more emotional concept that "evil" and wanton criminality are behind it, prevails, adding complexity to incomprehension and further affecting the possibility of rational communications and feasible solutions.

The unavoidable media frenzy that follows an attack then benefits the terrorists by providing the necessary dramatic exposure to transform insecurity into paranoia in the target country, and to elicit among the inevitably stunned fanatics and sympathizers alike, the necessary admiration to move them into becoming volunteers, two probable tactical objectives.

The question then arises as to what could be rationally devised to minimize and prevent such calamities without "giving in" to the terrorists. Clearly all preventive physical and technological security measures, supplemented by the best possible intelligence capabilities, will never be able to anticipate every well-planned or spontaneous surprise attack. The decades of Irish violence against Great Britain and of Palestinian violence against Israel are a clear confirmation of that theory. The enactment of draconian measures to insure national security only succeeds in curtailing the enjoyment of liberty and the pursuit of happiness so fundamental to democracy, a growing concern in the United States and in the United Kingdom.[25] Robbing the West of these basic rights may well be another objective of ideological terrorism. Security measures and self-defense must therefore be accompanied by a willingness to address the grievances that underlie terrorist violence. Claiming that terrorists have no grievances to be addressed, and that they are motivated only by the desire to kill, reflect arrogant self-righteousness and denial and is, in any case, counterproductive.

Indeed, in the age of globalization, a few local or foreign individuals ready to die for a cause can thus engender, at a ludicrously minimal cost, catastrophic damage to a powerful nation's modern urban society.

Without devaluing the criminal nature and barbaric aspect of terrorist violence, it behooves rational governments to accept the proposition that transnational terrorism is not, even when motivated by religiosity or ideology, simply perpetrated by evil persons for its own sake, out of hate for a way of life, freedom, and liberty. For as human beings, even the agents of terror possess a modicum of feelings and sensibility and must, therefore, be susceptible to rational discourse if treated accordingly. Historically, this has seldom been the case, as the powerful have a tendency to ignore the humanity of the weak and antagonize them with scorn and arrogance. Indeed, it may be said that hell hath no fury like a nation humiliated.

Economic and political domination is the unavoidable shadow cast by a towering power. The refusal by such a state to address the grievances it provokes beyond its shores, the overwhelming asymmetry of power and the prevailing disproportionality in offensive and defensive means between it and the powerless, lead some, among those who feel oppressed, to despair and collaboration, and others to truculence and vengeful crime.

Tyranny unconsciously sows the seeds of violent revolt in the minds of the weak. Once unleashed, it blazes inhumanely across borders fueled by the insensitivity of the oppressor and the ignorance or insouciance of its citizens. Without a realistic and rational approach to the tort the powerful state has created, its civilian population and material wealth become prey to the terrorizing vengefulness of those who feel oppressed. For by some perverse logic, partly inspired by the concept that democratic governments act on behalf of the governed, the civilian population of the oppressor is viewed as accessorily responsible for the misfortune of the oppressed and becomes, therefore, a target of opportunity—a kind of collateral damage—in their struggle.

Terrorism is often coupled with, or expressed by, incomprehensible inhumane truculence characterized in certain cultures by homicidal self-immolation. The "suicide bombers," in the terrorism of national liberation, often called "*kamikaze*," are undoubtedly fundamentally rational, proud, and sensitive individuals, but they are dehumanized and emotionally crippled by the humiliating subjugation their parents and society have been enduring in silence. They come to religiously believe that the "offensive" or murderous nature of their self-sacrifice "pro-actively" settles scores and restores their nation's collective dignity. Self-immolation to them may not always be an act of despair, it may be judged as a valiant act—a spiritually redemptive Calvary, a philosophical argument asserting the humanity they commonly share with their oppressor, but which is denied to them. It is, alternatively, a proclamation that life under the circumstances is not a gift, but an unbearable torture.

Unlike the terrorism of despair, massacre by suicide in ideological or theopolitical terror is carried out by zealots primarily convinced of their God-ordained mission; but they may also, of course, be motivated by nationalist or other temporal imperatives. Their action is not the result of an impulse or of despair, rather, it is akin to a heroic "suicidal" military mission carried out in war; it is reasoned, conscious, calculated and courageously executed under order, with deep conviction and irrational courage. Such combined suicides-cum-massacres are carried out with "serene piety" and in utter contempt for the hated "infidels." Redemption in these cases is strictly intellectual and eschatological.

Insane religiosity, hopelessness and despair, have a way of leading humans to violence as it overwhelms reason, dehumanizes ordinary people and rekindles in them, the primal barbaric instinct. This is true of individuals as well as of nations, powerful and weak.

Indeed, despair dehumanizes nations too, leading them to barbaric behavior and war. Wars lead them to wanton violation of International Law and Conventions. The Nazi's blitz on London and their unconscionable massacre of minorities under the Reich; Japan's inhumanities, such as the "Bataan death march" and its oppressive concentration camps; the United Kingdom's vengefully atrocious firebombing of German cities, all illustrate the annihilation of the civilized mind in war. Even the United States, historically a champion of international mediation and human rights, the progenitor of the League of Nations, the United Nations and the Nuremberg War Crimes Tribunal, has needlessly slaughtered, maimed, and morbidly irradiated well over a quarter million Japanese civilians in its needless nuking of Hiroshima and Nagasaki, massacred countless people in Vietnam and Cambodia, and indirectly caused the barbaric slaughter of innocents in Iraq as well.

The Second World War and its inhumanities have led the Atlantic Alliance to conceive the Untied Nations as an instrument for safeguarding peace and for mutual assistance and security. World War II's sequel, the cold war, institutionalized international paranoia as the United States and the Soviet Union consciously competed in building thermonuclear and chemical-biological deterrence capabilities—naively acronymed M.A.D. for Mutual Assured Destruction—based on the insane assumption that this "balance of terror" insured co-existence, however precariously. Yes, hopelessness and despair can indeed motivate states—even those conceived by the giants of the Enlightenment Age—to threaten their opponents with apocalyptic terror in their egotistical belief that it would protect their own security and particular way of life.

In the course of the many conflicts in Latin America, Asia, and Africa, as in the ongoing one between Israel and the Palestinians, terror is tactically used on both sides; on one side by ill-armed and defenseless insurgents and freedom fighters "heroically" transforming themselves into ambulatory terror weapons; on the other, by powerful hegemonic states stifling resistance with the constant, pervasive terror of occupation, dispossession, and collective punishment. Aggression and dispossession breed humiliation, grief and pain; these, in turn, coalesce to produce despair and the terrorist mind.

Terrorism is never one way; it uncompromisingly boomerangs in infernal reciprocity. One might, therefore, posit that terrorism is the hermaphroditic progeny of the coerced intercourse between power and powerlessness. It is a dance macabre that will continue its swirl unless legitimate grievances are acknowledged, addressed, and remedied. In the mushrooming village of ever shrinking planet earth, the problematic dichotomy between power and wealth, and powerlessness and misery, have brought the human species before the ultimate fork of destiny—a war of civilizations and chaos, or justice and universal concord.

Islām, Islāmism, and Apocalyptic Terrorism

"If one takes a life, it is as if one has taken the life of all humanity."—*Qur'ān: [5-32]*

Ideology-based terrorism, then, is not primarily driven by despair, oppression, humiliation, or any other tangible political factor; it is driven by intangible stimuli and inculcated concepts; but grievances, legitimate or otherwise, do enhance its appeal. As such, it may be as ephemeral as the socio-intellectual or spiritual climate that produced it; it is less amenable to a negotiated solution through rational dialogue, but some of the circumstances contributing to its vigor, if eliminated, can greatly curtail its appeal.

Islāmist terrorism is not simply the product of intellectual determination; it is inspired by metaphysical visions, driven by the lure of eschatological rewards and firmly anchored in the immutability of faith and in the belief that it is divinely ordained.

Religions have had a maturing and civilizing effect on society. They have contributed to providing peace of mind, succor, healing, compassion, serenity and often, intellectual stimuli. But they are malleable instruments in the hands of quasi magicians, and though they are opiates capable of soothing and healing, they are susceptible to irresistible misadministration and abuse leading impressionable individuals to servility, narrow-mindedness, intolerance and bigotry, to masochistic behavior, and to dehumanizing discord and war.

Islām, which stands for serene resignation to the will of God, does not escape this dichotomous, binary destiny. "Islāmism" is a label given in the West to any one of several particularistic fundamentalist interpretations of crucial elements of Islāmic teaching, especially the concepts of *'ibādāt*–religious observances and devotional acts ordained by divine law–and *jihād*–missionary ardor in proselytizing the "true" faith. Some of these deviant expressions of Islām are responsible for promoting what has come to be known as "jihādism." Jihādism advocates an implacable war, including terror, against "infidels" perceived as inimical to Islām—and therefore to the will of God—and against modernist Muslim statesmen and intellectuals considered "apostate."

Islāmism's ultimate goal is starkly precise and imperative. It seeks to impose a global, purified Muslim universe—*al-Umma'l Islāmiyyah*—under a narrow, immutable interpretation of Islāmic law. While this *umma* is anticipated in the various expressions of traditional Islām as the sacred will of God and therefore inevitable, mainstream Islām is resigned to the proposition that its realization is best obtained through missionary work, zeal, persuasion, and example. This is the authentic *jihād*, and it is, as such, not incompatible with modern civilized society.

The presumed God-ordained terrorist nature of islāmist eschatology, on the other hand, seems to preclude any possibility of compromise. The theological imperatives of islāmism have, over the past half century, fed on felt political grievances—Israeli occupation of Palestine, particularly Jerusalem, and its blind support by the United States; the related unending suffering and exile of the Palestinians; U.S. assistance to dictatorial regimes in Muslim lands and the implantation there of U.S. bases—adding a tangible, temporal dimension and enhancing its popular seductiveness.

Contemporary jihādism first expressed itself inwardly against the modernist leaders of Muslim states, notably in Egypt, whom it considered apostates. Its militancy was welcomed by xenophobic zealots, disabused youth, unemployed and underemployed intellectuals and by many from among the hopeless, poor, and uneducated masses.

But jihādism ultimately developed a transnational vocation as well, which was directed against the Western powers it held responsible for the people's misfortunes. This was due to the popularity of Western ways that insidiously accompany modernization in large cosmopolitan cities; to the subservience of government to foreign interests and ultimately to American support of often corrupt, self-perpetuating, autocratic, and ineffectual leaders in many Muslim states, a support dictated by economic interests, Cold War exigencies, geopolitics, and the obsession with Israel's security.

Contributing to jihādism's transnational bifurcation is the implacable repression of dissent in Muslim countries, driving a substantial emigration to the more liberal West. The substantial immigration of Muslims toward Europe, Australia and the Americas included countless honest and hard working people, as well as individuals who migrated simply for economic reasons but rejected assimilation; these antiassimilationists, by remaining strangers in a culture they are taught to reject, are of course, more susceptible to the pseudo-spiritual magnetism of al-Qā'ida. But quite a few inveterate islāmists, often accused of sedition in their country of origin, also emigrated carrying along their nefarious idealism and spreading their hateful and violent ideology.

Thus the reasons and circumstances energizing the appeal of "apocalyptic terrorism" are as eclectic as its inspiration is subliminal: awe, idealism, religious fanaticism, xenophobia, paranoia, resentment, intolerance, and totalitarian theocratic ambition. The mix is synergetic and even infects ordinarily sociable and kind individuals who have been reared within a traditional, usually quiet and serene Muslim culture. If George W. Bush believes, as he undoubtedly does, that Ms. Karen Hughes's public relations wizardry will succeed in containing and arresting this infection, he is making still another seriously mistaken assumption associated with his Middle East policy. Apocalyptic terrorism has become the *raison d' être* of many who stand in awe of al-Qā'ida's success in preoccupying the leaders of Earth's most powerful nation. Strangely though, the prominence of al-Qā'ida on the world scene is indeed the result of the publicity the United States, in pursuit of global power, has stupidly given it.

In Arabic, the word al-Qā'ida means "the base," as in foundation of a structure, ideology, or system of thought. In the present case, it is the foundation upon which extremist fundamentalist zealots have revived a theostrategic ideology that is anchored in their belief in a divine injunction that Islāmdom must be liberated from the "evil, decadent Western Civilization," and that the universe must be aggressively "cleansed of its satanic influence" through the spreading of the "true" message of Islām. The jihādists, therefore, profoundly believe they are fighting on Allah's behalf to realize his will as revealed to the Prophet Mohammed, to destroy evil and universalize his faith; in that sense they are very similar to our Evangelical political right. Thus motivated, jihādists are confident that it is their sacred duty to practice homicidal suicides, such as those which occurred in the events of 9/11, in the United States; July 7, in London; March 11, in Madrid; and in Beslan, Russia; in Sharm-el-Sheikh, Egypt; in Amman, Jordan; and in Indonesia, the Philippines, and elsewhere, as well as car bombings, beheadings, and other extreme forms of violence otherwise condemned by the *Qur'ān*.

Simplistic religious zealots and fanatics of all persuasions, not only those espousing Islām, blindly cling to convictions that peculiar and often phantasmagoric articles of faith are divinely ordained or revealed. Under the spell of charismatic and inspirational leaders, they stop at naught to realize what they are told is God's writ and gladly kill and give their lives for it. The faith-based murders of medical professionals involved in the legal practice of abortion; the Jonestown mass murder-suicide; the catastrophic outcome of the Waco, Texas, standoff; the belief in the divine ordination of white supremacy stemming from selective biblical citations; the conviction of certain Evangelical churches—some of them paradoxically anti-Semitic—and some Jewish fundamentalist congregations of the necessity to ethnically cleanse Palestine of non-Jews; their endorsement of the assassination of Yitzhak Rabin for his signing of the Oslo Accords; the threat by Jewish rabbis to kill Ariel Sharon for his decision to evacuate the overpopulated Gaza; indeed, Jerry Falwell's declaration of war against Islām and his declaration that Prime Minister Sharon's stroke was God's punishment for the Gaza evacuation, are but some examples of Christian and Jewish extremism. Just as unfortunate, is the claim by President George W. Bush that his irrational policies in the Middle East are the result of communications with "a higher father." Historically, theological and moral reasons have routinely been cited, as we know, in support of such violence as the Crusades, the Spanish Inquisition and the burning of the "witches of Salem."

Societies everywhere eagerly respond to what they believe are God's ordained wars against sinners and infidels. Indeed, which belligerent nation did never claim that God was on its side? The jihādists, like the crusaders before them, kill in good conscience for the same glory to the same God. In fact, the Arabic word *jihād* is philologically equivalent to crusade: a vigorous, concerted struggle on behalf of the faith. The earlier jihāds that spread Islām were not different from the crusades that terrorized and mercilessly slaughtered civilians—mostly Muslims.[1]

As was the case with the Crusades, jihādism, based as it is on divine writ, guarantees its martyrs the reward of eternal bliss in an anthropomorphized heavenly after-life, but arguably with the spices of profane delights. Some scholars posit that the Crusades might have inspired, in the thirteenth century, the elaboration by Ibn Hanbal and Ibn Taymiyya, of the rigidly uncompromising and violent Islām practiced today by *Salafi* sects in various parts of the Muslim world—*Wahhābism*, particularly in the Middle East, Maraboutism in West Africa, Deobandism in Central Asia, China, Southeast Asia, and the East Indies.[2]

A sententious, authoritative declaration, a legal injunction, a decree, or *Fatwa*, promulgated by a saintly or messianic figure, or by some other charismatic leader, is irresistibly stimulating to susceptible individuals, even educated and economically comfortable ones. They join the ranks of the would-be martyrs voluntarily, piously, and cheerfully. Once the movement's élan takes off, its replication becomes spontaneous, if not epidemic. Its adherents thrive on self-immolation and martyrdom, making them impervious to their powerful enemy's punishing retaliations.

Asymmetric retaliation, in fact, stimulates and fuels the spirit of martyrdom. In the case of al-Qā'ida, the basic message is that a satanic United States of America is leading an evil coalition of Christians, Jews, apostates, and atheists in a new crusade, the purpose of which is to deny God's will on earth, corrupt Islām's purity, adulterate its spiritual tradition and vocation, and physically violate the sanctity of its territorial integrity. The faithful are therefore duty-bound to strive (*ijtahad*) by all means to repel and defeat it. In so doing, they contribute to the realization of God's ultimate design, the Universal Peace of Islām in the anticipated universal *umma*.

The fact that contemporary transnational terrorism has primarily been carried under the banner of Islām and that it has targeted Western assets, has cast aspersions on that religion, which is the third of the great Abrahamic monotheistic tradition. Given, at some level, the theopolitical tenor of the conflict over Palestine and the ripples it causes beyond the confines of the Middle East—the involvement of pro-Zionist Jews and Evangelical Christians on one side, and anti-Zionist Muslims on the other—a new era of religious wars, if not a virtual clash of civilizations, stands on the bridge of the twentieth century's *fin de siècle* and the dawn of the twenty-first century, threatening the peace of the world with a new "dark age." The situation is reaching alarming proportions as modernist governments in Muslim states are threatened by theocratic forces and the United States' secular democracy witnesses the onslaught of a pernicious evangelicalist Christian influence.

All religions and cults stem from the mind's attempt to discover and understand the meaning and mysteries of being and existence, of life and destiny. Superstition prevailed as wise and thoughtful leaders emerged across time to assuage anxieties and provide explanations. Metaphysics and eschatology were elaborated with rich concepts and elucidations gleaned from meditative reflection and reinforced by presumptions of communication with the divine, along with manifestations, disclosures, and revelations. Thus supernatural worlds— inspired by the physical one and complete with their own hierarchies of spiritual personalities—were conceived. These spiritual personalities exhibited human-like intelligence, character, humor, needs, likes, and dislikes. The whole nobility of spirits had laws, concepts of good and evil, interdicts and sanctions. Magicians, intercessors, medicine men, weather men, and high priests also emerged, endowed with propitiating power and the ability to exercise control over nature, the spirits and the believers.

Imagining the unknown beyond the context of human experience is impossible. This suggests why all religions, with variations dictated by environment, culture and perceptions, explain the divine and its nature, the afterlife, its mysteries and laws anthropomorphically. Based in mystery, these ingenious subtleties are exploited and manipulated to differentiate, discriminate, and control. In the final analysis, it is all hypothesis, imagination, and rationalization, as there are no verifiable intrinsic truths beyond the physical and scientific world.

Religions and systems of beliefs are the result of choice, or of chance, geography, lineage, ethnicity, and family tradition and are, therefore, all co-equal. They have evolved values in the course of the spiritual explorations that led to the development of particular institutional *weltanschauungs*. These contribute to insuring order, cohesion, and harmony in a given cultural context. But the politics of faith have also historically led to human discord, divided minds and souls, inspired sectarianism and triggered wars between cultures, civilizations, and nationalities. Thus conflicting interpretations, philosophies, and theologies abound, not only among Christianity, Islām, Judaism, and all other systems of beliefs and ethics, but also within them.

With Judaism and Christianity, Islām constitutes the generic, monotheistic trilogy within the Abrahamic tradition. It shares the concept of the genesis, recognizes the same prophets, acknowledges the authenticity of their divinely revealed messages and, while disagreeing with some of their particularities, respects their religious values and rituals. Generically, Islām is an all-encompassing holistic civilization—a religion, a way of life and a jurisprudential system—with its own political theory, concept of government, worldview, human rights, and perception of international relations. In fact, its uncompromisingly absolute and impersonal monotheism is reminiscent of an earlier basic form of Judaism. It even follows almost identical dietary restrictions; the *hallāl* procedures and interdicts mirror *kosher* rules. This has led some scholars to argue that Islām is a veritable restatement of Judaism.

But Islām is more than that; it includes also in its message, important elements of pre-dogma Christianity and of the gospel. Its uncompromising monotheism, however, finds the concept of Christ's divinity blasphemous, and of the Holy Trinity offensively polytheistic; and while it holds the Virgin Mary in the highest esteem and veneration, it rejects the Virgin Mary's "motherhood of God" as unfathomable and sacrilegious. Anyway, Islām assigns a most privileged place to Jesus-Christ among the prophets, referring to him as "The Word."

To the faithful, the *Qur'ān* is coeval with God, and therefore eternal, and that it was first imparted to Adam, "the First of His prophets," upon his creation. Muslim scholars assert that during the passage of time, God's primordial message was ignored, forgotten, betrayed, abandoned and disfigured, prompting him to order it reissued. So it was imparted to man again through the biblical prophets, from Abraham through Jacob, Moses and Jesus and ultimately and "finally" through Mohammad (570–632), whom they regard as "the Seal of the True Prophets," the ultimate one—except, perhaps, for the "Twelvers" in Shī'ism, who have accepted subsequent prophets, and for other esoteric forms of Islām beyond the Arab world. To Islām, therefore, the *Qur'ān* is both God's very first and very last message to mankind.

Upon the death of the Prophet Muhammad, the issue of who should succeed him assumed a political tenor and led to open warfare between two pretenders, Abu Bakr and 'Ali, and to a lasting schism between their followers, the *sunni* and the *shī'i*, the orthodox and the disciples (of 'Ali), sometimes referred to as republicans and monarchists.

'Ali, the fourth Caliph of Islām, was the husband of Fātimah, Mohammad's favorite daughter. The *shī'i* claim that 'Ali was the true and natural heir to Mohammad's mantel, because, they claim, he was designated by him as his successor in a sermon delivered at Ghadir Khoms. For the *sunni*, Abu Bakr was freely elected by the leaders of the Community as Mohammad's successor.

Ali was assassinated in 661 A.D. in Kufa Adam, now in Irāq. The largest branch of the *shī'i* are the "twelvers," or *ithnā 'ashariyya;* they are the followers of the twelfth and "current *Imām*" known as the *Mahdi*, or redeemer. "Current" because he is believed to be still alive and in concealment. It is said that he will reemerge some day "to set things straight and restore order and unity within Islām." He remains their most venerated saint.

As a minority within the body of Islām, the *shī'i* have historically been considered heretics by the *sunni* and were subjected to persecution, repression, and worse. Consequently, as early as 700, the *shī'i*, inspired by the *mahdi* legend, have elaborated the doctrine of *ghayba*—invisibility or concealment—as a way to insure their survival. A corollary to this optimistic belief is the expedient and temporary practice of what has come to be referred to as political "quietism." This has not necessarily been universally practiced by the *shī'i*. In fact in Iran, Iraq, Pakistan, and other countries, followers of the sect have exhibited daring political activity.

Theoretically, Islām has but one dogma; it is concerned with the absolute unity of God and with the belief that Mohammad is his "Ultimate Prophet." Nonetheless, with the passage of time and in the course of the spread of Islām, *sunni* and *shī'i* sects developed divergently with distinct rituals and particularistic beliefs, which were adapted from their integration into various cultural traditions; hence the dogmatic accretions that color both *shī'i* and *sunni* traditions in different geographic areas. These include disparate esoteric practices, beliefs and Qur'ānic interpretations, some of which are deemed obligatory here and there in the different ethnic communities.

Extremism, intolerance, obscurantism, and jihādism are among the negative developments that have found their way into elements of the more austere sects and rites. However, beginning in the mid-nineteenth century, as a result of enlightened Qur'ānic interpretations, a liberal, reformist trend did take root among Muslim intellectuals. These "reformists" have helped governments in emerging Muslim states usher in progressive social and legislative measures, modernize education, and improve the quality of life. Unfortunately, the coincidental domination of Muslim nations by an implacably imperialist Europe stimulated, in reaction, pan-Islāmic ideologies tainted by intolerance, xenophobia, and fanaticism.

More recently, the rise of militant Zionism and the support it received in the West; the subsequent establishment of the ever-expanding State of Israel in Palestine, and its perception, by evangelicals in the United States and elsewhere, in theological terms; the concomitant mistreatment and ethnic cleansing of Palestinians, and the inability of corrupt Muslim states to prevent it, enhanced the popularity of reactionary and extremist religious fundamentalist organizations. These organizations provided a solid refuge and solace for the humiliated masses, refocusing a rage, heretofore expressed only against the European occupiers, toward their national modernist Muslim leaders, and later toward the United States and its allies.

In the final analysis, geography, ethnic and cultural diversity, inter-Islāmic and world politics have multiplied the face of a religion founded on the principle of absolute universal unity under the absolute oneness of God. Indeed, now, differences distinguish not only the two major branches of the religion, *sunni* and mahdist *shī'i*, from each other, but also from their many offshoots. Thus the *shī'i*, traditionally more inclined towards mysticism, have, unlike the majority of their *sunni* counterpart, spiritual intercessors in the guise of an established, structured hierarchical clergy, an institutional hagiocracy, a cult of saints with specific holy days honoring them and a traditional appreciation of iconographic art.

In many states where they existed as minorities, *shī'i*, after centuries of "quietism," are—as a result of the successful "*Mullah* Revolution" and the establishment in Iran of a *shī'a* theocracy, under the spiritual leadership of Ayatollah Ruhellah Khomeini—rising in protest, sometimes violently, abandoning the practice of *ghayba,* where it prevailed, and becoming generally more politically assertive. This new assertiveness is best exemplified by the armed and violent "*Mahdi* Army" militancy of Mortada al-Sadr, a minor *shī'i* cleric in Baghdad, who has been challenging the United States military occupation of Iraq.

The *sunni* religious structure is more diffuse, very much as the judaic is, and except for the authoritative 'ulemas—whose responsibility is the interpretation of the *Shāri'a* (Islāmic Law)—their clergy have no perceptible hierarchy, and the faithful communicate directly with God without a need for intercessors. This characteristic, however, does not negate the influence that imāms or such ad hoc religious leaders as Osama bin-Laden, or al-Zawāhiri can exert on the faithful.

Sunni Islām is strictly iconoclastic; it has no established hagiology, no pantheon and cult of saints, and its holy days honor only events associated with the Prophet Mohammad; nonetheless, mysticism is inherent in some sects, and among followers of certain schools of jurisprudence.

With the rapid spread of Islām, many *sunni* and *shī'i* communities around the globe have, as previously mentioned, retained substantial elements of their own pre-Islāmic culture, beliefs, and rituals. In the heart of the Arab world, and beyond it in Africa, Asia, and the East Indies, vibrant local cults of saints exist even among followers of the *sunni* way; in many instances, still-living mystics are perceived as holy, they are venerated as saints, and their miraculous intercession is prayerfully sought. The social and political influence these saintly persons exert, can be enormous.

A century of insensitive exploitation, cultural callousness, and political blunders by Western hegemonists have arguably triggered much resentment and humiliation among Muslims. More recently, the popular unhappiness was exacerbated by the continued subservience of nearly all modernist local politicos to their Western "mentors"; by the consequent loss of confidence in the Muslim reformers and modernists; and by the hopelessly corrupt and greedy ruling classes and their exploitation of the poor and underprivileged.

The failure of the modern political elite to boldly emulate the iron-fisted secularization of Turkey under Kemal Ataturk—at a time when it was possible—and to impose a firm separation of mosque and state, has hampered modernization and progress while providing the islāmist with the time and opportunity to exploit the engrained feudal and tribal mentalities and gain influence and prestige among the masses.

Indeed, this failure of leadership did not escape the theocrats who systematically and piously exploited the situation. They filled the pernicious vacuum of governmental leadership with assistance and goodwill, setting-up charitable organizations in every city and town, dispensing free, sorely needed medical and social services to the exploited poor, and free education to the young and old. They also provided work and therefore hope, and so gained popular gratitude as well as political stature and influence.

In oil-rich Sa'udi Arabia, the birthplace of the *Wahhābi* interpretation of the austere and fundamentalist *salafi* way, several crucial factors combined to create a time-ticking disaster. For about four generations, a traditionally frugal, self-reliant, nomadic, uneducated society was made dependent for its livelihood and security on the generosity of the royal tribe. This has created a welfare-dependent, jobless, aimless, sedentary, and religiously fanatical lower-middle class.

The enormous oil revenues at the basis of that nation's wealth, instead of being shared and used to create economic diversification and skills, have been usurped by the extensive ruling Sa'ūdi royal tribe, and much of it invested abroad for their personal enrichment and to propagate the *Wahhābi* faith.

An accelerated, massive development of the social and economic infrastructure and superstructure of the state was farmed out to foreign contractors using foreign labor, without concurrent real social modernization and training. A ubiquitous national religious police enforce socially and economically counterproductive traditional *Wahhābi* morality, hampering progress and promoting extremism and xenophobia; a *shāri'a* based judiciary dispenses inhumane dark ages punishment, and religious fundamentalist monitors in public schools and colleges inhibit the free flow of ideas. Thus scores of narrowly educated young people graduate, with few employment opportunities, and many of them, frustrated, turn to the salvation promised by religious extremism.

The Sa'ūdi royals have also poured vast amounts of monies into erecting mosques, religious elementary *madrasas*, and theological seminaries in Muslim and non-Muslim countries around the world, spreading the faith and creating what may be called "born-again Muslims," and potential *jihādists*.

Indeed, in many Muslim countries people feel crushed by economic stagnation; they resent being denied participation in the political process and are humiliated by the social insouciance of their government and by its failure to bring justice at home and in Palestine. Many, therefore, find refuge and solace in the strict austerity of *Wahhābism*, and some are swayed by the seduction of the eternal rewards of martyrdom in violent *jihād*.

Some of these young people have already made their mark in the *kamikaze* attacks of 9/11 on the World Trade Center and elsewhere, but also in challenging the very authority of the Sa'ūdi monarchy that nurtured them. Thus *Wahhabism*, far from leading to the universal peace of Islām called for in the *Qur'ān* and championed by the Sa'ūdi Monarchy, has unwittingly contributed to the diffusion of a deviant, hateful, and bigoted Islām that promotes terrorism and defames the very religion it seeks to honor.

By the turn of the twenty-first century, the Sa'ūdi Government's policy of reliance on religious charities in the matter of welfare had boomeranged. It spread terror and insecurity in the Kingdom and forced it to violently repress the enemy within that its own piety had created. The ibn al-Sa'ūd clan may have finally begun to understand the explosive danger that the blending of faith and state represents. One hopes that George W. Bush will be wise enough to learn from this friendly kingdom's experience and abandon his intent to transfer to "faith-based organizations," the Government's responsibility concerning the dismally minimal (for an industrialized country) social welfare system that America painfully developed in the course of the twentieth century.

The Sa'ūdi Government is trying to control the eschatological terrorism its religiosity has provoked, but it may be too late. Major upheaval is now not out of the question in this and other Muslim states where imported *salafi* Islām has gained hold, and where jihādist organizations are poised to take over the reins of government. The United States, with its injudicious double standard and unjust policies in the Middle East, will have to bear partial responsibility for this troubling prospect.

The ephemerality of ideology-based terrorism in the nineteenth and twentieth centuries may lead to the assumption that jihādism and also national liberation terrorisms are in various degrees transient phenomena. Theopolitical terrorism, however, be it Christian, Muslim, Hindu, or Jewish, anchored as it is in transcendental and eschatological motivations and objectives, is likely to be an enduring phenomenon. The Crusades and the earlier *Jihāds* still linger nostalgically in the memories of countless people.

Martyrdom, with its promise of eternal felicity, is magnetic. As a young catechist in a Jesuit school in Cairo, I remember prayerfully wishing for martyrdom while processing in the streets of that profoundly Muslim city, dressed as a crusader and braving jeers, insults, and even projectiles. Indubitably, a similar wish burns ardently in the souls of brainwashed pupils in the more extremist madrassas around the world. Indeed, islāmism has an infinite reservoir of self-righteous idealists and would-be volunteers itching to serve God and win eternal rewards.

But national liberation movements too, can motivate self-immolation and martyrdom, as exemplified by the history of anticolonialism, including the contemporary struggles of the Irish, Cypriots, Palestinians, Southern Sudanese, Tutsis, Hutus, Biafrans, Chechens, and so many others. Here too, the just resolution of nationalist problems can do more to eliminate terrorism than all the arsenals of the powerful. Furthermore, military force and the imposition of the Western-style democratic system in alien environments cannot succeed. Nor would they, in and of themself, be instrumental in defeating such inspired violence.

JIHĀDISM: CONTEMPORARY ISLĀMIC THEOPOLITICS

Contemporary islāmist theopolitics and its concomitant terrorist violence are fueled by a deep, emotional revulsion against foreign domination and against what fundamentalist Muslim scholars consider the corrupting influence of Western civilization. The earliest manifestation of such theopolitical insurgencies in modern times occurred in Egypt and were primarily directed by *Jamā'at al-Ikhwān-al-Muslimīn*—The Society of the Muslim Brotherhood—against its modernist government. The *ikhwān* movement sought to coerce the Egyptian Government into terminating what they referred to as the secular means, solutions, and institutions "imported" (*al-hulūl al-mustawrada*) from the democratic West to solve local social, economic, and political problems. Originally, therefore, islāmism was local and inwardly directed; it was only concerned with substituting a totally Islāmic government in Egypt, and reining in the influence of Christians, expatriates, and foreign institutions.[3]

The *Ikhwān Society* was founded in 1928 by Hassan al-Banna as a *sunni* fundamentalist cultural organization. But nationalist ferment against British over-lordship and later, U.S. policies in the Middle East, transformed it into a militantly pan-islāmist political and missionary (jihādist) organization.

Hassan al-Banna was born in 1906, in Ismā'iliyya, Egypt, into a family of *Hasafiyya sūfi* scholars who followed a very strict, *salafi* (*Wahhābism* is basically *salafi*) Islāmic way of life. During his university studies in Cairo, he grew increasingly disconcerted and appalled by the turn of events in Egypt, where the elites of Cairo, Alexandria, and Port Saïd emulated the lifestyles of London, Paris, and Rome, rather than that of Mecca and Jeddah. He was in admiration and awe of the austere, traditional purity and simplicity of the Islāmic life that he experienced, while in *Wahhābi* Sa'ūdi Arabia. Al-Banna organized a militant opposition to the timidly modernist and reformist tendencies of politicians and scholars who were inspired by Western secularism, which he deemed decadent, corrupting, and sinful. He held these leaders responsible for Egypt's dependence on, and subservience to, the British, and for the intolerable cosmopolitanism of its urban life and society.

In establishing the *Jamā'at al-Ikhwān al-Muslimīn*, Hassan al-Banna was seeking to lead an uprising against an Egyptian Government that, he felt, had abandoned Muslim norms (*nizam'ul-islāmi*) and social values. His ultimate goal, doubtless, was to have this Muslim revolution emulated everywhere in predominantly Muslim nations so that the vision of a universal Muslim nation (*al- umma-l-islāmiyya*), led by a caliph, could be closer at hand. To this end, and to counter the prevailing government's insouciance and neglect of the people's needs, and to discredit it while attracting followers, political power, and influence to his cause, he championed a reliance on the traditional Islāmic practice of pious public service as a religious obligation (*al-da'wa*).

During and following World War II, the massive humiliating presence of allied troops in Egypt, a reputedly depraved king and a quiescent Egyptian Government's impotence in preventing the establishment of a Jewish State in Palestine, gave rise to countless conspiracy theories implicating the Monarchy, many established politicians and generally also, the already resented Westernized Christian, Jewish, and foreign minorities—yet again appreciating the *ikhwān* in the eyes of the downtrodden masses.

In 1948, Hassan al-Banna contemptuously rejected a not too subtle British attempt to buy his allegiance and hence silence him. This rejection earned him a brief political exile, considered a badge of honor and heroism in colonized countries. A subsequent Government ban of the movement resulted in several assassinations of Egyptian political figures—including Ahmad Maher Pasha in 1945 and Prime Minister Mahmoud Fahmi al-Nokrashi Pasha in 1948—all allegedly carried out by the *ikhwān*. In reprisal, Government agents assassinated Hassan al-Banna in February 1949.

Islāmic nationalist unrest ensued, ultimately leading to the toppling (*al-inkilāb*) of the Egyptian monarchy in July 1952 by a military coup d'état.

The coup d'état was carried out by the "Free Officers" who, aside from their dissatisfaction with the corruption to which the Egyptian Army's defeat in Palestine had been attributed, sought to preclude a further political ascendance of the *ikhwān*, while shaking a stagnant Egypt into the twentieth century.

Among the Free Officers' strategies was a plan to substitute a modern, socialist pan-Arabism for the *ikhwān's* retrograde pan-islāmism. This resulted in a serious clash between the two ideologies, which turned violent. In 1954, the failed assassination of President Gamāl Abd'ul-Nāsser during an impassioned nationalist public speech in Alexandria, led to a massacre and a violent repression and banning of the Muslim Brotherhood.

President Nasser died of a massive heart attack in 1970. Vice-President Anwar al-Sadāt, a devout Muslim who had previously flirted with the *ikhwān*, supported the Axis powers against the British, and who was also implicated in a political assassination and incarcerated, succeeded him as president.

Confrontations between the Government and the Muslim brotherhood were interspersed with periods of truce; but following President Anwar el-Sadāt's daring November 1977 address to the Israeli *Knesset* and his signing of the peace treaty with Israel in November 1979, he was assassinated by the Muslim brotherhood on October 6, 1981.

The pressure to control the *ikhwān* continues under the Presidency of Hosni Mubārak. Today, a *modus vivendi* prevails between his Government and the brotherhood; but as its popularity spreads, the brotherhood is confident that given a free democratic national election, it can ascend to power legitimately and establish its vision of an Islāmic state. With Cairo as the seat of *al-Azhar*, the world's oldest standing university and the most prestigious among the Islāmic schools, the political repercussions in Muslim countries everywhere could be incalculable.

Following the decision by the *ikhwān* leadership to abandon violence and participate in mainstream Egyptian politics, the head of its most extreme jihādist faction, Dr. Aymān al-Zawāhiri, earlier implicated in the assassination of Anwar al-Sadāt and imprisoned, split from the main group, rejoined Osama bin-Lāden and became the brain and operational leader of al-Qā'ida.

The more extreme branch of the islāmists owe their unwavering militance to al-Zawāhiri's intellectual mentor, Sayyid al-Qutb. Sayyid was a scholar with some familiarity with Western culture and education. As a student of the nineteenth-century Islāmic reformers Jamāl-ul-Dīn al-Afghāni and Mohammad Abdu, who rejected the notion that Islām and modern science were incompatible, he was impressed by Western educational and scientific achievements and eagerly recommended incorporating them in Egyptian public education. As a devout Muslim, he was, nevertheless, shocked and offended by the liberal Western way of life, which he condemned. A 1948 educational sojourn in the United States confirmed in his mind what he referred to as the West's immoral social culture and practices.

Accordingly, he developed utter spiritual and political contempt for Muslim modernists and even went so far as to criticize the Muslim brotherhood for their narrow nationalist focus. Their interpretation of Islām, he complained, was contaminated by Western ideology and the concomitant alien conception of nationality and nationhood. His political philosophy was anchored in the *Shāri'a* and rested on the original concept of the single universal nation, al-*umma'l muhammadiyyah* (Mohammadan nation), an interpretation deemed anachronistic by reformist, liberal, and modernist Muslims. He rejected the notion that sovereignty resided in the people, finding it blasphemous, arrogant, and antithetical to the Islāmic concept of God's exclusive sovereignty over all matter in the universe. Sayyid al-Qutb and his disciples, therefore, initiated an Islāmic revolution against the government of modernist President Gamāl abd'ul-Nasser and against the "enemies of Islām," wherever they were, at home or abroad.[4]

Sayyid's *weltanschauung* was derived from the Qur'ānic concept of international relations, which views the world as a bipolar phenomenon characterized by an irreconcilable chasm between the nation of Islām and the other nations, between the believers (*al-mu'minīn*) and the infidels (*al-kuffār*). According to this view, a permanent and irrevocable, divinely ordained state of war exists between the nation of Islām and the heathen nations, respectively referred to in Muslim literature as the "abode of peace" (*dār-al-Islām*) and the "abode of war" (*dār al-harb*). This perpetual conflict shall only come to an end, and the peace of God restored on earth, when God's message, as transmitted to the Prophet Mohammed through Archangel Gabriel, finally prevails. This original Muslim concept of international relations, based as it is on what Wole Soyinka, in the BBC's Reith Lectures Series, called "the doctrine of submission," is not only arrogant and "contemptuous of humanity," it stands in contradiction to the other cardinal Qur'ānic concept of religious "tolerance," and it clashes with the universal, humane yearning for democracy and liberty.[5]

The *Qur'ān* is not any more immune from scriptural equivocation, vagueness and contradiction than its counterparts in other religions; it lends itself equally to all sorts of interpretation. In this context, fundamental interpretational divergences have developed between reformist and fundamentalist Muslims; an important one concerns *Qur'ān* verse [5:32] on the matter of when killing is permissible and when it is not and by extension, therefore, to lethal violence in terrorist acts:

> Whosoever killed a person—unless it be for that person to have killed, or for creating disorder in the land—it shall be as if he killed all mankind; and whoso saved a life, it shall be as if he had saved the life of all mankind.

Fundamentalist extremists, while acknowledging murder as a crime, seize upon the exception referring to those guilty of "creating disorder in the land" as a justification for wanton killing. This includes, by implication, individuals and entities such as invaders, colonialists, Western hegemonists and globalists who, arguably, create disorder in, and violate the sanctity of, the *umma*, and interfere in the traditional Muslim way of life. As for the Muslim agent of Westernization, he, or she, interferes with Islāmic purity and ways and consequently deserves death as an infidel (*qāfir*) or as a hypocrite (*munāfik*)—*Qur'ān*: [4.89–91]

> They desire that you should disbelieve as they have disbelieved . . . seize them and kill them wherever you find them. . . .

Muslim modernists do not espouse this interpretation and even differ as to what the term "Muslim" connotes in God's eyes. For if it means "whosoever" submits to his will, then it includes "all who believe in him and submit to his will"—basically, Christians, Jews, even Hindus; they are "muslims" with a small "m." This interpretation, however liberal and esoteric as it is, does not readily enjoy widespread recognition among mainstream Muslims, who are said to represent the overwhelming majority of the world's Muslims.

Indeed, the majority of Muslims—about 80 percent, according to the classification of Mohammad Habash, Director of the Islamic Studies Center of Damascus—may be considered mainstream conservatives, or, in his own terminology, "People of the Letter." Habash in his study posits that 20 percent of Muslims are reformers, or modernists—"People of Intellect"—and only about 1 percent are radicals or extremists.[6] This single percent is meaningless in terms of Islām as a whole, but it represents a considerable number of people, when one takes into account the billion and a half Muslims in the world. It goes without saying, however, that only a small minority of these is susceptible to actually commit murder in the name of God, and that terrorists are not necessarily recruited exclusively from among them.

Muslim reformists generally view the conflict between the "abode of peace" and the "abode of war" symbolically and subscribe to the notion that the will of God will ultimately be freely achieved through knowledge, rational discourse, and spiritual enlightenment. This is not ordinarily the case with the radical fundamentalists, many of whom trust that given man's inclination toward dissipation and vice, coercion and fear of God through violence is prescribed if the objective is the realization of the Divine design. Mainstream Muslim conservatives tergiversate on the issue.

Be that as it may, mainstreamers, reformists, and fundamentalists share the principle that divine revelation was imparted progressively beginning with Adam, that its last and definitive version is the one dictated by Archangel Gabriel to Mohammad, the "Seal of the Prophets" and that ultimately, it will prevail universally. Clearly, therefore, any subsequent pretense at divine revelation will be false and fraudulent: "There shall be none after the *Qur'ān*." One might surmise from this attitude that Islām assumes a fundamental spiritual dialectic, the last three stages of which, Judaism, Christianity, and Islām are, respectively, thesis, antithesis and synthesis.

The finality inherent in what I have called "dialectical spiritualism" is reminiscent of the clashing contradictions conceived in marxian "dialectical materialism."

In fact, both hold the hope for a rewarding final synthesis through the struggle of contradictions. But they are markedly dissimilar in that they are motivated by two different perspectives and objectives.

In the technically atheist, earthbound familiar Marxian system, the clash of contradictions is political, involving a struggle between socioeconomic classes; in theory its vocation is anchored in materialistic humanism, and its ultimate synthesis promises equality and social justice, with shared wealth and responsibility within a spontaneously self-regulated, virtuous society without government or need for coercion—a veritable nirvana on earth.

In the Islāmic system, the contradictions represent on one level, a clash of faiths between believers and nonbelievers and on the other, a clash within the community of believers based on scriptural selectivity and interpretations. The clash of contradictions necessarily takes place in the temporal world, but its ultimate vocation is eschatological and transcends temporality. Thus it has a fundamental holistic character involving both the body and the soul; its ineluctable, ultimate synthesis is binary, promising peace and serenity on earth and eternal felicity and joy in an anthropomorphized, sensualized heaven—a virtual garden of delight, according to the *Qur'ān*.

In Muslim scripture, *jihād* means exertion to propagate the faith. Historically, this exertion has been expressed both peaceably and martially, depending on sociopolitical circumstances. Today, the use of violence to propagate the faith is, as we have mentioned, generally dismissed by mainstream conservative Muslims. They do contemplate violent *jihād*, but only *in-extremis* where opposition to Islām threatens to violate or infringe upon the sanctity of its institutions, beliefs, and domain. Modernists and some reformist Muslims today have come to espouse a more enlightened and benevolent interpretation of *jihād*, one based on a spiritual and personal struggle against one's own evil inclinations.

In contradistinction, the extreme intolerant character of the fundamentalists and the religious impatience they express for the universal *umma*, under a single "theocrat," or *khalīfa*, suggest that a permanent, violent *jihād* is intrinsic to their worldview. In this indefinite conflict between the abode of peace and the abode of war, they admit to the necessity of what is referred to as *hudna*—peace, armistice, or truce.

Fundamentalists firmly believe that the United States, in association with Israel, seeks to destroy Islām. In support of their conviction, they refer to the Western assault on Afghanistan, where the regime of the *salafi* Tālibans was routed and replaced by a government promoting principles deemed antithetical to the faith; the invasion of Iraq and the perception that the United States is exacerbating and capitalizing on the latent enmities between the *shī'i* and *sunni* branches of Islām to further its own interests; and the conviction that Israel, America's touted "best ally," is indeed its imperialist proxy in the Middle East. Incidentally, this conviction is not limited to the extremists among the Muslims; it is generally accepted as fact, even by many non-Muslims around the world, and nothing but deeds can alter this.

Jihādism is an ideology based on the absolute submission to the *diktat* of Qur'ānic revelations. As any political endeavor seeking uniformity, and controlled by an organization claiming metaphysical knowledge and authority, it is based on the dehumanizing concept that Wole Soyinka discussed in his lecture: "I am Right, you are Dead."[7]

Jihād then is a malleable theopolitical concept, the character and vocation of which seem tailored to suit different mentalities and temperaments—peaceful, violent, strictly personal and spiritual, or somewhere in between. Because of the importance it holds in Islāmic theology, *jihād*, no matter its particular expression, emerges as a discrete "sixth" pillar to the proverbial "five pillars of Islām."

As already mentioned, the mainstream Islāmic perception of the world, with all its manifestations and complexities, is as absolutely unitary as the conception of the absolute unity of the Divine. Indeed God, his community, all his creation and his message, are absolutely indivisible—mere reflections of him.

Muslims, not unlike fundamentalist Christians and Jews, believe that victory of good over evil is preordained by God. And they are fatally confident that his will concerning the orderly, ultimate, universal submission of humanity to his immutable rule (*hākimat Allāh*) will be done, which means, in their case, the universal acceptance of Islām, his "true faith" (*al-dīn' ul hanīf*), its traditions (*al-sunnah*) and its law and jurisprudence (*al-shāri'a wa usûl' l fiqh*).[8] The anticipated "Universal Christian Peace" following the "Second Coming" of Christ is its equivalent.

It must, however, be emphasized that by referring to Jews and Christians as *ahl ul-Kitāb*, or "people of the Book," the *Qur'ān* philosophically includes these among the "believers." Indeed, their "books" are issued from the same revelatory source, and their faithful, therefore, have in their own way and in *various degrees* submitted to the will of God. But they are, as it were, *incomplete or lesser "muslims."* As such, they have, under Islāmic rule, traditionally enjoyed the legal status of *dhimmi*, or "protected" subjects. But because their protection varied in character and substance depending on the whims of Muslim rulers and on political circumstances, the extent and nature of the "protection" they enjoyed, and therefore of Islāmic "tolerance," has been a matter of conjecture. The tolerance of *dhimmi* has been favorably contrasted to Christian intolerance in Medieval times, or to the Judaic in biblical times. In the contemporary world, however, Islāmic tolerance is simply no match to the freedom of conscience and democracy evolved in the West, and has very much to learn from it.

In any case, Christians and Jews automatically become full-fledged "infidels" (*kāfirīn*) and lose their "protected" status should they reject, denounce, or somehow enter into conflict with Islām. Thus the Qur'ānic-prescribed tolerance and the historical protection, respect, and honor the Jews enjoyed in Muslim nations for centuries, was revoked upon the practical application of political Zionism in Palestine and the claim of Jerusalem as its "eternal capital." Indeed, the creation of the Jewish State and its promulgation of the so-called "Law of Return" that makes a virtual "nationality" of Jewishness, and Israel's negation of the United

Nations Resolution concerning the Palestinian refugees' "Right of Return," have unfortunately turned autochthonous Jews in Muslim lands, and their immigrant coreligionists, into undesirable foreign agents, or fifth columnists—a consequence that had long been feared by assimilationist Jews in the West, during the formative years of political Zionism. The original sympathy accorded the Jewish State by nations where Christian culture prevails, and the recent truculent statements in support of that country by American "Evangelicalists" have led to a concomitant serious alienation and persecution of Arab, Arabized, and immigrant Christian communities in Muslim states adjacent to Israel, and is irrevocably contributing to the de-Christianization of the very cradle of Christianity.

The imposition of the State of Israel in Palestine has thus given fuel to the growth of Muslim intolerance and strengthened the appeal of local islāmists. In time, unequivocal U.S. support of Israeli policies, and the inability of the Community of Western Nations to moderate America's bias, are giving islāmists the necessary ammunition to go global. Among the notable leaders of global islāmism are the Sa'ūdi-born Osāma bin-Lāden, and the Egyptian Aymān al-Zawāhiri.

Dr. Aymān al-Zawāhiri, a medical surgeon by profession, is the recognized jihādist strategist of the terrorist al-Qā'ida organization. Aymān was issued from a pious and prominent Egyptian family originally from the Nejd (today in Sa'ūdi Arabia), and brought up strictly in a devout *salafi* home. As a proud teenager, he, like his fellow countrymen, felt profoundly humiliated by Egypt's defeat in wars against Israel. At sixteen, he eagerly joined the Muslim Brotherhood; with them he shared the prevailing conspiratorial theory that Egypt's defeats were the result of an international, anti-Muslim conspiracy that used Israel as proxy. He was particularly traumatized when his mentor and hero, Sayyid al-Qutb, was arrested, summarily sentenced to death for political sedition and hanged, as hundreds of his fellow *ikhwān* were massacred by order of Egypt's then leader, Gamāl abd'ul-Nasser, who clearly perceived, and directly experienced, the danger inherent in the jihādists' extremist teachings. As a result, Aymān's theopolitics grew progressively more extreme, and in 1979, disenchanted with the narrow, national objective of the brotherhood, al-Zawāhiri, now an M.D., abandoned the organization for the more extremist one, the Egyptian *Jihād* that advocated the establishment of an islāmist fundamentalist theocracy. In one of his several books, *al-Hasīd al-Murr* (The Bitter Harvest), al-Zawāhiri lashed out at the brotherhood and other fundamentalist organizations that had agreed to abandon political violence in Egypt and participate in the political process, accusing them of betraying God's will by agreeing to transfer, to a human legislature, God's exclusive authority to make laws. Al-Zawāhiri rapidly assumed a position of leadership within the Egyptian *Jihād*, and his argument, that the "New Crusaders" could only be defeated through a universal islāmist *jihād*, was rapidly endorsed.

Dr. al-Zawāhiri and his followers and admirers consider Western culture, society, government, and way of life a satanic, blasphemous conspiracy bent on adulterating God's message and corrupting his community. They profoundly believe, given its policies in the Middle East, that America is the "Great Satan" leading a new crusade against Islām; that America manipulates Muslim leaders with its dollar subsidies and by wielding economic and military threats; that it has desecrated the territorial sanctity of Sa'ūdi Arabia—the land of Mecca and Medina, Islām's first and second holiest cities—with its corporate and military presence; that it has equally desecrated Palestine and Jerusalem, the seat of *"Harām'ul-Sharīf"* (The Noble Sanctuary) and the third holiest Muslim city, through its Israeli proxy. Furthermore, they accuse America of overtly and covertly promoting heathenish changes in the prescribed Islāmic way of life, norms, values and mores by its constant criticism of Muslim society and laws, and through its "intrusive and corrupting" television programs, movies, and publications. These are perceived as subtle psychological weapons that suffuse immorality, encourage foul language, exhibit nudity, and promote sexual promiscuity, pornography, prostitution, adultery, homosexuality, abuse [read liberation] of women, consumption of liquor, as well as untold other hell-bound sins.

Of course, even mainstream conservative Muslims share the fundamentalists' perception of Israel as America's imperialist surrogate and beachhead on "muslim soil." They cite as evidence, the huge financial grants, the sophisticated armaments and particularly, the exceptional diplomatic and political shield the United States provides that country. To Muslims everywhere, America's protection of Israel perpetuates Zionist occupation and desecration of Jerusalem, the dispossession of the Palestinians, and the violation of their religious, human, civil and political rights. Indeed, Arabs and Muslims, wherever they may live, even the educated and seemingly urbane ones who admire the United States for its brilliant Constitution, democratic values and ideals, personally share the humiliation of the Palestinian nation and profoundly resent it.[9]

The theological and emotional elements inherent in this perception may be fluid and difficult to understand and address, but justice and a fair and objective American policy toward the Palestine–Israel problem would go a long way toward assuaging feelings and enlisting the support of conservative mainstream and re-formist Muslims in the struggle to rein in the promoters of jehādist terrorism. It would certainly eliminate one of its two major stimuli, perhaps its most compelling one. Islāmist eschatological terrorism is, indeed, a by-product of what really is a transnational islāmist insurgency against the two pillars of American foreign policy in the Middle East—the inherent injustice of its anti-Palestinian bias and the arrogance of its cultural and geopolitical shadow over the region.

Be that as it may, al-Qā'ida and Egyptian *Jihād* formed a partnership sometime in 1998, thus combining Osāma bin-Lāden's financial resources and engineering knowledge with Aymān al Zawāhiri's analytical, psychological, and organizational talents.[10] Yet the name bin-Lāden remains more familiar than that of his associate. This is due to the publicity he received in the world's media following the devastating and well-coordinated September 11, 2001 terrorist attacks on U.S. soil. Yet while Osāma bin-Lāden may have given his blessing to the mission, subsidized it and provided the engineering analysis for it, its strategic diabolic planning must have been conceived by the brilliant and methodical Dr. Aymān al-Zawāhiri.

The strategic aim of the terrorist attack was twofold: to provoke the United States into unleashing military strikes—perhaps even war—against Afghanistan, a theocratic Islāmic state, thus dramatically confirming in the popular Muslims' psyche, that the "American-Zionist" alliance was indeed a new crusade that called for the Islāmic *levée-en-masse* required for the ultimate *Jihād*.

The titular leader of al-Qā'ida, Osāma bin-Lāden, was born in 1957, in Riyādh, Sa'ūdi Arabia. His father, a Yemeni, had amassed a fortune in construction during the country's massive infrastructure development in the early days of the oil boom. There is little that is distinguishable about Osāma's youth. After an eventless secondary education, he received a degree in civil engineering from King Abd'ul Aziz University in Jeddah.

Osāma was reared in a strict *Wahhābi* Muslim family. He was a frail, quiet, spiritual boy who exhibited pious devotion to his faith. He is said to have admired Western scientific genius and technological achievements, but was contemptuous and scornful of Western social mores, which offended his Muslim sensitivity. He is said to have consistently and openly complained about American political influence in Sa'ūdi Arabia, to have resented its economic and military implantations there, and to have been humiliated and angered by its blatant unfairness towards the Palestinians dispossession and the Israeli occupation of Jerusalem—sentiments widely shared by Muslims everywhere. He is also said to have sworn to punish the detractors of Palestinian rights and to strive to unite the Muslim world in a struggle to liberate Palestine.

Osāma was encouraged and heartened by the success of the Islāmic—albeit *shī'i* and therefore "heretic"—revolution in Iran, and by the demise of the secular regime of the Shāh. He was preoccupied and repulsed by the stranglehold of communist regimes over Muslim people in the now defunct Soviet Empire and resolved, in the early 1980s, to launch, in association with Dr. al-Zawāhiri, an armed *jihād* to defeat communism there, hoping to sow the kernel of a worldwide *salafi* society.

The contributions made by Muslim countries to the 1990 Gulf War alongside the United States, despite its active defense of Israel against Iraqi missiles, the "desecration" by Coalition Forces of Sa'ūdi territory—Islām's birthplace—and the subsequent long-term implantation of American bases there, profoundly shocked bin-Lāden and al-Zawāhiri and confirmed, beyond a shadow of a doubt, their conviction that the United States was hell-bound to desecrate Islām's holy patrimony and impose its "barbaric" ways on Muslims.

In 1995, after bin-Lāden claimed responsibility for several bombings of U.S. and Sa'ūdi installations in Riyādh and Dhahrān, the Sa'ūdi Government banished him from its territory and stripped him of its citizenship. Thereupon, he took up residency in Sudān, where he established construction and agricultural enterprises that provided employment to countless Sudanese and African Muslims. He also founded charitable organizations, health dispensaries, and *madrasas* (elementary Islāmic religious schools), thus earning himself respect and influence in the largest country in Africa. This easily gained him potential recruits for his *jihād*.

Bin-Lāden didn't waste time in setting up his jihādist operational headquarters in his new country of residence, and with Dr. al-Zawāhiri trained grateful recruits from all over the world, all the while quietly planning his next move, jihādist attacks on American interests. However, in 1996, the Sudanese Government was compelled to declare him *persona non-grata*, so he and the doctor packed their bags and left for Afghanistan.

Paradoxically, they had earlier liberated Talibāni Afghanistan from Communism and Soviet domination with weapons and intelligence contributed by the United States, and in association with its "Special Forces." Now, in 1998, from their haven in this country—their own created embryo of the universal *umma*—they proclaimed and launched the "World Islamic Front for the *Jihad* against Jews and Crusaders," a veritable declaration of war on the West. Under this banner, they financed and created terrorist training camps, and thousands of inspired, fanatical jihādist recruits from the four corners of the world came to Afghanistan and were rigorously prepared for anti-Western warfare. Their victory over Afghāni communist and Soviet forces had convinced them that they were God's earthly emissaries for waging *jihād* against the "zionist-crusaders" conspiracy and their allies, the apostates in Muslim states.

Islāmist fervor is not limited to Osāma bin-Lāden and Aymān al-Zawāhiri's al-Qā'ida organization and its members. Independent islāmist organizations, cells and ad hoc groups span the Muslim heartland and diaspora. Some are active in pursuit of terror tactics; some have as a sole objective, the installation of an islāmist government in their country; others hope to establish the global *umma*; and still others practice terror in pursuit of their own national liberation.

Most of those people who elect to kill and die for the islāmist cause, come from economically comfortable families and have a middle-class, bourgeois upbringing. They are often fairly well-educated young people, and some have graduate degrees in science and in engineering. This is even true of first generation Muslim children, whose parents emigrated to Western countries, and where they were constrained to lead lifestyles that are neither traditional nor western. As an uprooted and "deculturized" minority, these people sense and resent the inevitable differentiation and their estrangement in a country whose holidays and holy days are meaningless to them. For some of them, there eventually comes a time when spontaneously, or under the influence of a charismatic fundamentalist *imām*, they find comfort and solace in the anchor that fundamentalist religion provides and become islāmists, or "born-again Muslims." In resigned silence they reject the schizophrenic identity they inherited, rebel against their parents' quietism and docile respect for their adopted country and find their ultimate vocation and identity in jihādism. These otherwise fine young people exist in virtually most Western nations. Though the *Qur'ān* prohibits both killing and suicide, the jihādist relies on the following Qur'ānic [4:89–91] statement to justify such crimes:

They desire that you should believe as they have disbelieved, so that you might be alike; therefore take not from among them friends until they fly in Allah's way; but if they turn back, seize them and kill them wherever you find them . . . [but] if they withdraw from you and do not fight you and then Allah has not given you a way against them. . . . [but] if they do not withdraw from you and offer you peace . . . seize them and kill them wherever you find them. And against these We have given you a clear authority.[11]

The espousal of terror in nationalist causes is widespread in Africa, in Turkey, Iraq, Palestine, and the Caucasus; it has lasted a long time in Northern Ireland involving rival Christians, and in the former Yugoslavia where Christians and Muslims have exhibited a mutual lack of civilized respect; and it is equally evident in Chechnya, Myanmar, the Caribbean, and Central and South America.

In Muslim countries, many people, both young and old, despite different objectives and fuzzy philosophical concepts, share a deep disappointment in their national leaders' subservience to Western interests; in their dictatorial and corrupt rules, and in their timidity in countering the perceived Israeli-American geopolitical inroads into Muslim lands. They accuse them of betraying Islām and abandoning its ideals and mission.

As individuals, a majority of Muslims have historically been apolitical, and despite the excesses of their leaders, they have practiced "quietism" in accordance with Islāmic political theory that enjoins "obedience to the ruler" and resignation to his excesses, however outrageous, for "tyranny is better than anarchy." This political docility or passivity has historically inhibited widespread participation in the political process, in the elaboration of democracy, and in the separation of mosque and state. Nonetheless, it must be noted that Islām does not accept political submission to "foreign" rulers, infidels, and apostates; obedience is only mandated to a "true Muslim" ruler.

In the age of globalization, a sense of deep humiliation prevails among many Muslims concerning the growing dichotomy between tradition and modernity. The result is an almost universal feeling that their leaders have betrayed the Qur'ānic mission. This belief translates into anger and a profound resentment against the over-arching primacy of the West and the injustice in Palestine; these deep-seated feelings redound to the benefit of the theopolitical extremists. To be sure, many of them are secretly proud of *al-Qā'ida's* occasional violence, even if they are repulsed and confused by its inhumanity.

Insurgencies are brewing in practically all Muslim countries, from the former Soviet Republics in Central Asia, to the Asian subcontinent, the greater Middle East, Africa, and the Pacific and Indian Ocean island states. Some of the more important islāmist organizations involved in some kind of terrorism—including attacks on Western tourists to prevent governments from benefiting from the important revenue they bring—are the *abu Sayyāf* and the Moro Islamic Liberation Front in the Philippines, the G.I.A. (Armed Islamic Group) in Algeria, *al-Jamā' at ul-Islāmiyya* in Egypt, the *Deobandi Harkat ul-Mujāhidīn* in Pakistan,

Jayshi-Muhammad in Kashmir, *Jamā'at Islāmiyya* in Indonesia; the Moroccan Islamic Combatant Group, *Hamas* and the Islāmic *jihād* in occupied Palestine, I.B.D.A.C. (Great Eastern Islamic Raiders Front) in Turkey, S.P.I.R. (Special Chechen Islamic Regiment), *abu-Dzeit* and others in Chechnya, etc. From the numerous members of such primarily inward-looking islāmist terrorist groups, transnational terrorist organizations such as *al- Qā'ida* find eager recruits. About these would-be "martyrs," al-Zawāhiri wrote:

> They possess a quality that their enemies cannot hope to acquire. They are the people who most eloquently bear witness to their God's power, Who has given them a strength drawn from his own strength, until they have turned from a scattered few who possess little and know little, into a power that is feared and threatens the stability of the new world order.

Good and evil may be intrinsic, well-defined universal values, but their nature becomes blurred when perceived through the prism of politics, and more so through that of theopolitics. Extremists of all faiths are persuaded that their particular world view, way of life, conception of morality and of good and evil is the correct one; indeed, that only their religious establishment is graced with the authority to issue the symbolic, virtual visa that insures passage through the gates of the "Kingdom of Heaven." Religious exclusivism and totalitarianism find their twins in the political arena. Religious fanatics are prone to the belief that abusing and even killing miscreants, infidels, and sinners are permissible for the glory of God. Likewise, political extremists often share such violent intolerance toward their ideological dissenters and critics for the glory of the nation. Violent fanaticism is not the exclusive frailty of islāmists; it finds its counterparts in what may be referred to as *"christianists, catholicists, evangelicalists, judaists"* and all other wayward religious fundamentalists.

Recently, the *ad-hominem* use of the terms "good" and "evil" in international relations has added fuel to intercultural misunderstanding. The peace of the world is always at risk whenever theopolitics displaces humanism and contaminates the intent of politics and religion. Western democracies have separated church from state in full awareness of the pernicious threat of their confluence. Sadly, the Christian Right in the United States, not unlike other extreme religious fundamentalists, seems to find perversion and sin in this constitutional wisdom.

It is frightening, indeed, when a convergence of theopolitical figures from both the most and least advanced nations emerge simultaneously to compete cacophonically on the international scene for the prevalence of their own particular, narrow-minded *weltanschauung*. It is as though islāmists, christianists, and judaists, armed with cataclysmic weapons, have joined hands across a discordant ether to resurrect from the ashes of history, the sinister, bloodthirsty intolerance of a bygone medievalist mentality, to usher in, at the very dawn of the twenty-first century, a *"New Dark Age."*

Consequential or Reactive Nationalism-based Terrorism

"Forbid it, Almighty God! I know not what course others may take; but as for me, give me liberty or give me death!"—*Patrick Henry, March 23, 1775*

"Consequential," or "reactive" contemporary terrorism is, by contrast, not fundamentally ideological or religious in nature, though some of those who practice it may be motivated by extremist religious considerations. Its motivations are primarily nationalism and other sociopolitical factors. It is ordinarily expressed in the context of an insurgency when all other peaceful means of communication with a political overlord have been exhausted and despair has set in. In a way, this kind of terrorism, albeit illegal and criminal, is an offensive strategy of last resort. A judicious response to it must primarily include the honest acknowledgment of its essential causes and a readiness to address them justly.

Reactive terrorism ordinarily occurs within a geographical area controlled by the overlord and has a limited practical vocation; the geographic operating field of "ideological" or "theopolitical terrorism," on the other hand, is wider, sometimes even global and its vocation, as discussed in the previous chapter, idealistic and virtually unachievable. For the nations fighting the so-called "Global War on Terrorism" to refer to them as one and the same is not only confusing, it is unjustified, counterproductive, and even politically tendentious. It may provoke them into an unwanted alliance and add the tangible grievances of the former to the esoteric character of the latter, thus increasing their appeal and recruiting pool and needlessly creating a more formidable enemy.

Religion is not the fundamental motor of reactive terrorism, but it could be infused into it as sublimation, as in the Irish, Palestinian, Chechen, and other cases. A careful study of the emotions impelling otherwise normal individuals to engage in terrorist activities suggests the development of an idealized, selfless patriotism, including a sense of duty and honor not dissimilar from that which inspires and motivates the truculence of volunteers who undertake "suicidal" missions in conventional war. In either case, the acts of dying and killing in the service of one's nation are highly valued and rationalized as a badge of patriotic valor, honor, and heroism. In a developed, "patriotic" state of mind, the honor associated with one's selfless sacrifice is invariably commensurate with the awe provoked by the degree of the danger involved, by the tactical and strategic value of the damage inflicted on the enemy, and by the seriousness of injuries sustained by the hero, or by his death.

Reactive terrorism is usually caused by extreme, tangible, legitimate grievances, stifled national aspirations, and other abuses; it is based on the concept that the terror caused by violence will finally bring about a resolution of the persistent problem and ultimately, mutual respect. This rationale used by the "oppressed" is not any different from that used by an "oppressor" seeking to impose its will. Reactive terrorism, however, will exacerbate if stubbornly ignored or countered with draconian repression. Arguably, the prevailing U.S. policy of refusal to negotiate with terrorist organizations under any circumstance, regardless of existing legitimate grievances that could be remedied peacefully, can only prolong needless agony and violence. The death of innocents—both civilian and military— is not worth the vainglory of absolute victory; after all, politics is the art of the possible. Stateless people and those who stand in the margin of society, devoid of political rights or legal status—even if they happen to be one's enemies—have rights that deserve consideration by the mighty state.

The conceptual U.S. refusal to negotiate with terrorists seems predicated on the assumption that negotiating with "terrorists," or with so-called "rogue" states, encourages more terrorism or political recklessness. But one might also wonder whether it is not equally inspired by arrogance and contempt. Other nations' nonnegotiating stand with terrorism may be motivated by still other considerations; the Israelis, for instance, use this method as subterfuge to "create" what they call—and undoubtedly consider irrevocable—"facts on the ground."

Negotiations are as indispensable a process in democratic life and in judicial and criminal proceedings, as they are in diplomacy and international relations; they may seek a peaceful settlement of a dispute, a *modus vivendi*, or they may be a tool toward some other end; they need not be interpreted by one side or the other as an expression of weakness or of "loss of nerve." They will be counterproductive if they are used as a means to impose a solution rather than a freely arrived at mutual consensus.

On the other hand, the inflexibility inherent in the refusal of the powerful state to negotiate, suggests an inability to concede, or a fear that negotiating might imply the existence of contributory guilt in a conflict. In disputes involving reactive terrorism, the willingness of the powerful state to reappraise its policies vis-à-vis an insurgency and to engage in rational communications with the insurgents, are a surer and faster means—than the arrogant use of violence and repression—of insuring national security. The terrorizing violence of repression can only guarantee more resentment and despair and perpetuate reciprocal deadly violence; the fateful consequence of the Treaty of Versailles is a case in point.

Victims of hopelessness and suffocating oppression are not readily sensitive to the wisdom of "the end does not justify the means," particularly when the oppressor himself ignores it in his own attempt to perpetuate his domination and exploitation. The anger and humiliation born of the violence inherent in domination and neglect constitute the seeds of the savage reaction of the dominated. Thus a vicious cycle of infernal and mutually terrorizing violence develops with seemingly no end in sight. The powerful is seldom magnanimous and wise, and has the means to dissimulate its share of responsibility in disputes. As the source and enforcer of laws, its possesses a monopoly of means to impose and diffuse its version of the truth over that of the weak and defenseless. Furthermore, the powerful often ignores historical facts when these do not serve its needs, and when the willingness to negotiate implies a recognition that two rights do indeed exist and need to be reconciled. Here lies the cardinal reason why governments refuse to negotiate with insurgents-turned-terrorists.

So while reactive terrorism is an unacceptable crime against civil society and humanity, those, who by virtue of their power impose on the weak and innocent, the unshakable injustice that drives them to despair and violence, must bear contributory responsibility.

It is a fact that the powerful state always justifies its own violence, egregious as it may be, as necessary to insure national security, while referring to that of the insurgents' as "uncivilized"; and uncivilized it is, given the prevailing disparity in means. So it may be fairly concluded that when the powerful state refuses to address the legitimate grievances that cause terrorism, it becomes accessorial to it and must share responsibility for its savagery. This presumption was clearly voiced by London's Lord Mayor Ken Livingstone during an interview with *BBC News* following the July 7, 2005, terrorist attack that killed and maimed innocents and ravaged his city's transportation system. While emphasizing his lack of sympathy for the terrorists and firmly expressing his opposition to all kinds of violence, he denounced:

> Those governments which use indiscriminate slaughter to advance their foreign policy, as we have occasionally seen with the Israeli government bombing areas from which a terrorist group will have come, irrespective of the casualties it inflicts [on] women, children and men. . . . under foreign occupation and denied the right to vote, denied the right to run their own affairs, often denied the right to work for three generations, I suspect that if it had happened here, in England, we would have produced a lot of suicide bombers ourselves.[1]

Great nations should use power primarily to promote peace and security and to insure justice; using power otherwise is injudicious and contributes to the mindset that ultimately leads the oppressed to the terror of inhumane violence. The Irish precedent stands as a confirmation of this verity. So long as the British Government refused negotiations with the Irish Republican Army, fratricidal terrorism persisted relentlessly. It was only when, through the good offices of the Clinton administration and the able mediation of former Senator George Mitchell, Ten Downing Street finally consented to engage in constructive dialogue and negotiations that ended terrorism. This lesson must not escape those who assume military power is a match for a people's determination to regain their human and political rights. These people, ordinarily, are determined to "live free or die."

The inhumane character of all types of terrorism suggests that it is a transient mental illness sparked by political despondency, and recovery can only be obtained through reason, fairness, and justice. Studies abound demonstrating that it is crucial and more important to address the specific causes of mental and other illnesses, than to simply treat symptoms, or forcibly institutionalize an otherwise healthy subject and treat him improperly.

Correspondingly, reactive terrorism is a curable, politically induced and environmentally specific mental illness with intrinsic causes that are evident; attempts by governments to repress it senselessly through violent means are a legal and political dereliction of duty and a betrayal of their commitment to insure peace and security. Irrational states' violent counterviolence only stimulates more individuals to join the insurgency because it exacerbates the conditions that cause it in the first place. Furthermore, brutal repression by the authorities is often used by ill-intentioned parties as justification to undertake totally unrelated criminal aggressions. A case in point is the stimulus that the continued repression of Palestinians in the Occupied Territories gives to al-Qā'ida's recruitment efforts among otherwise physically unaffected Arabs and Muslims around the world.

In this context, the Palestinian tragedy provides a particularly pertinent laboratory for the analysis of the causes of contemporary islāmist anti-American terrorism. Above all, the disposition of the "Palestinian Question" are one of the most blatant injustices thoughtlessly and "legally" inflicted on a nation temporarily administered under the trusteeship of the Community of Nations in the twentieth century. Certainly the bare majority in the General Assembly of the United Nations that supported the division of Palestine into an Arab and a Jewish state, though generally well-intentioned, was obtained as a result of arm-twisting by the United States. Intended to make amends for the terrible suffering of European Jews under the Nazi regime, this decision has resulted in unending, extreme harm and misery for the hitherto serene life, not only of the Palestinian people, but also of the Middle Eastern Jews and of the region's autochthonous Christian minorities. It has set in motion seemingly interminable, pernicious, international discord; recurring sectarian violence; oppression; terror and counterterror; and it has regretfully led to anti-Arab racism as well as to anti-Semitism around the world. It has also contributed to the pernicious growth of Muslim, Christian, and Jewish fundamentalism; transformed local, petty, antimodernist islāmists into global transnational jihādists and sparked a needless, potential conflict of civilizations.

What is remarkable about the United Nations' vote on the creation of Israel is that there was no precedent or provision in International Law for the restoration of a state that existed in antiquity, on a land inhabited for centuries by a different society, and against the will of that society, to an ethnically and linguistically disparate people claiming cultural affinity with those who inhabited it in ancient times, and to converts to their faith. Should the restoration of Israel in Palestine after twenty centuries constitute a precedent, it would catapult the international political order into a vertiginous terminal centrifuge.

As a result of the clear rejection of colonialism by the drafters of the United Nations' Charter, colonial empires in the Third World came to a dramatic end in two major steps. The so-called "colonies of exploitation" acquired independence first with relative ease, while the relinquishing of power by the foreign colonial minorities in the "colonies of settlement"—Kenya, Algeria, "Rhodesia," and South Africa particularly— took longer and was more painful and difficult. Here, the settlers were finally compelled, by years and decades of violence and internationally imposed sanctions, to abandon or share power with the autochthonous. It was therefore an egregious decision that Palestine, a territory originally administered under mandate by the League of Nations and subsequently under its successor, the United Nations' Trusteeship Council, should have been exempted from the norm and divided between its recent colonizers and its local, native population.

To be sure, Palestine was raked by a bloody tripartite conflict involving the traditional, native Arab majority, the mostly European Zionist settlers and illegal immigrants, and the British Mandatory Authority. The question arises as to what pressure had the Great Powers exerted in the United Nations—an organization entrusted with the safeguarding of the inherent national rights of native populations—to marshal a vote in the General Assembly to "partition" Palestine, a territory under its trust and jurisdiction, tear away a chunk of it from its legitimate nationals and assign it to a largely foreign colonizing society?[2]

The injustice to the Palestinians is particularly egregious because despite the numerous Security Council resolutions seeking reasonable redress, their undoubtedly unintended total dispossession continues unabated. Indeed, while all the basic elements of the conflict—land, borders, right of return, compensation, Jerusalem and Palestinian statehood—have already been delineated in these resolutions, the Community of Nations remains incapable of implementing them because of American political subservience to the Zionist "lobby." Nevertheless, the initial intransigent refusal by Arab and other Islāmic states to accept the partition of Palestine has been particularly prejudicial to Palestinian interests; witness the several wars between them and Israel that have only resulted in Israel's occupation and control of all of mandatory Palestine.

In June 1967, capitalizing on truculent statements by President Gamal Abd'ul -Nasser, Israel surprised the world with a strategic[3] "preventive" attack against Egypt, which, because of treaty obligations, automatically involved Jordan and Syria. This attack netted Israel the remainder of territorial Palestine, plus the

Sinai Peninsula—later returned to Egypt and demilitarized—as well as the Golan Heights, that it illegally annexed, as it also did Jerusalem. The shock and brutality of the Israeli occupation drove the exiled Palestinian communities into further senseless, transnational terrorist activities; this brought umbrage on the Palestinian cause and elicited sympathy and support for Israel.

Thus, in a Kafkaesque turn of the tables, the Israeli aggressor became the pitied victim and was hailed as heroic defender of its national security, while the exiled and dispossessed Palestinians and those existing under oppressive living conditions under occupation, came to be equated with violence, culpabilized for the tragedy that befell them, demonized for their resistance to foreign domination and for daring to struggle to regain their national rights and identity. In fact, in the eyes of many observers, including Jews and Israelis—as the next chapter discusses—the establishment of the State of Israel in Palestine was, under the circumstances, only possible through willful genocidal ethnic cleansing. According to these analysts, Israeli genocidal practices in the territories were, and continue to be, carried out with the tacit acquiescence of the U.S. government. In fact, its shielding and unqualified support of Israel are the main reasons for the anti-Western Arab and Muslim people's terrorist rage. It has brought about a vindictive redirection of jihādism, from its original local-cum-national vocation, to a transnational, global anti-Western one.

In 1993, the Oslo Accords suggested that peace and mutual recognition could finally be at hand. But negotiations dragged until their collapse at Camp David on July 25, 2000, with each side blaming the other.[4] President Clinton did cast particular blame on the Palestinians for the failure, but he should have appreciated that the final offer he negotiated was woefully unfair to the Palestinians. But subsequent negotiations at Sharm-el-Sheikh produced a tentative accord. Sadly, on September 28 of that year, Ariel Sharon, surrounded by a swarm of Israeli security officers detailed by Israeli Internal Security Minister Shlomo Ben-Ami, marched on the *Harām-ul-Sharif* on Temple Mount, intentionally wrecking the implementation of any agreement under these accords. Palestinian Security Minister Jabril Rajoub warned Mr. Ben-Ami that given the provocative, symbolic nature of the visit and the recent collapse of Camp David talks, the Palestinian police would not be in a position to provide security for Sharon, nor would it attempt to.

The Likud Party leader's untimely visit was as much a provocative assertion of Israeli sovereignty over the Temple Mount [and *Harām-ul-Sharif*] as it was a clever ploy on behalf of his candidacy in the anticipated national Israeli elections. Thus was sparked the *al-Aksa*, or the *Second Intifāda* and insured the Likud Party's success in the Israeli national elections.

The beginning of a new, violent chapter in the mutually dehumanizing relationship between Israel and the Palestinians was at hand; terrorism and counterterrorism ensued, including Israeli assassinations and abduction (Israel prefers to use "apprehension") of Palestinian leaders, harsh military repression, collective punishment, and curfews on one side and Palestinian stone-throwing and suicide bombings on the other. Ultimately, the "house arrest" of Nobel Peace Laureate

Yasser Arafat and his sidelining by Israel and the United States, corresponded with the widest expansion of Israeli settlements in the Occupied Territories.

The so-called "Road Map" in 2005 was President George W. Bush's feeble, if not disingenuous, gesture to placate Islāmic ire by working toward the establishment of a Palestinian State in the Occupied Territories; it has so far, resulted only in Israel's strategic, theoretical withdrawal from Gaza, arguably Prime Minister Sharon's final conception of a Bantustan-type state for the Palestinians, and for more inhumane violence and misery.

In the eyes and minds of Arabs and Muslims everywhere, the evolving tragic events in occupied Palestine—Israel's admittedly draconian policies there[5] and its constant and progressive expropriation of Palestinian territories—could not be possible without American connivance. In large part, therefore, the "Washington-Tel-Aviv Axis" is interpreted as blatant confirmation of an ongoing American-led Judeo-Christian Crusade against Islām. It explains the growing influence of the prevailing virulent islāmist violent anti-Israeli and anti-Western mood in the Muslim world.

This perception was axiomatic, we repeat, in the decision by jihādist movements to suspend, or at least reduce, their once limited terrorist activities against modernist governments in Muslim countries and redirect them mostly against the United States and the West. The jihādist perception of the existence of an American-led anti-Muslim Crusade seemed further confirmed by George W. Bush's unwise Christian-centric statements in connection with his aggressive Middle Eastern foreign policy and particularly, his characterization of the "Global War on Terrorism" as a "Crusade." His inclusion of the Palestinians' violent struggle for self-determination in that war and the enthusiastic support his foreign policy enjoys among the Evangelical Christian and pro-Zionist electorate further appear to Muslims as additional confirmation of their perception.

American equanimity toward the illegal Israeli settlements in Palestine; Israel's annexation of Jerusalem, Lebanese and Syrian land; the implantation of U.S. military bases in Sa'ūdi Arabia; the American-led occupation of Afghanistan; the trumped-up reasons advanced for the war on Iraq; Washington's more recent aggressive diplomacy toward Syria and Iran, and its support of the 2006 Israeli overreaction in Lebanon to *Hizb'Allah's* kidnapping of two of its soldiers, combine to fuel in the Muslim mind, that a "conflict of civilizations" animated by a crusading America, has apocalyptically dawned on the world, threatening Islām's survival—therefore, "God's design on earth."

The violent establishment of the Jewish state in the Holy Land disturbed centuries of history in a region haunted by the specter of the "barbaric" crusaders and where, in a very medieval sense, religion overshadows culture, politics, and ethnicity, and determines one's social and political perceptions, "nationality," and orientations. While the early Zionists were basically secular and their ideology inspired by the colonial mentality in vogue in the nineteenth century, their dream had religious undertones as it was inspired by Biblical tradition as well as history. But it was equally influenced by the rampant racism in vogue then as well.

The forceful, violent establishment of the Jewish State in the Middle East took place during a period of agonizing Muslim theological and philosophical reappraisal, a period of social and intellectual ferment characterized by a deep crisis of identity and clashing nationalisms, one pan-Arabist looking forward, the other pan-Islāmic looking backward.

Thus the intentions behind the establishment of the Jewish State were extremely troubling, suspect, and inflammatory in the Muslim world and ominously consequential globally. Furthermore, Israel has since reinforced the perception that it may be an incompatible foreign transplant in the body of the Arab world by consciously projecting an extra-Middle-Eastern character, identifying with and stressing the East-European and North American cultural heritage of its people, while warning against the looming threat of their "levantinization."

Also, the implacable pro-Israel American bias reinforces, in the mind of the Muslim world, the concept that Israel is but the physical expression of American "satanic" or "crusading imperialism," its "creeping expansionist proxy." In this lie the seminal sources and rationale for the contemporary heightened Islāmic xenophobia and anti-Western jihādist violence. The blame for this dangerous situation must be squarely placed on the total subservience of Congress to the unparalleled influence of the U.S.-Zionist "lobbies," whose concern seems to be primarily motivated by Israel's strategic interests.[6]

For forty years—from Israel's declaration of independence to 1988, when the Palestinian National Council recognized and accepted Security Council Resolutions 242 and 338, and therefore the existence of Israel as a legitimate state—the Palestinians obstinately, but expectedly, rejected the "partition" of Palestine, in the fantasy that the neighboring "powerful" Arab armies would help them recover their country; this clearly played into the strategy of a Jewish state hungry for *lebensraum*. Indeed, by June of 1968, Israel had extended its control beyond Mandatory Palestine's frontiers, scattering multitudes of refugees into inhospitable neighboring countries and driving the remnants into subservient dependency and discrimination.

The untimely colonization of Palestine took place when a weakened, more liberal Europe—prodded by an emergent and victorious United States and an idealistic United Nations—was constrained to shed its colonial empires. The exuberant ideological and theocultural arguments in support of this anachronistic colonization clashed coincidentally with the equally intense nationalist and islāmist ferment in Arab and Muslim countries and sparked conflicting claims, triggered enmities, wars, and interference by the superpowers.

The religious undertone in the festering rivalries over Palestine and Middle East oil is responsible for the pernicious clash of civilizations characterized by conflicting claims that war is being waged to fulfill different versions of God's true will; it is responsible for the global insecurity inherent in the violence of transnational terrorism and international wars. For the Muslim, history is repeating itself some nine centuries later. Many are convinced that this modern "Crusade" must be countered by a countervailing *jihād*.

It may therefore be argued that the well-meaning, but unwise historic equanimity and support for the Zionist design on Palestine—in total disregard of the web of facts, circumstances, traditions, politics, and theologies woven in the course of twenty long centuries—may be considered as the most repercussive international political blunder the twenty-first century will be haunted by.

Controversial as this statement may be, it is incontrovertibly evident that all principles of international law and practice were violated when a bare majority in the General Assembly of the United Nations endorsed, in November 1947, the resuscitation of a state on a land, where in the intervening centuries, a different people had lived and developed a distinctive culture, and to which move, these people were distinctly opposed. This violation has now created an international political conundrum.

Undoubtedly, many among those who supported the creation of Israel in Palestine did so in good faith; they may have been in ignorance of the facts of Palestine and they may have felt guilt for the *Shoah* (Holocaust); others may have felt secure in creating this new state believing that because of the centuries of Jewish suffering in Europe, the Jewish State would treat the natives with kindness, compassion, and magnanimity; yet others may have been motivated by political, racist, or theological considerations, or by ethnocentric bias against the non-European Palestinians; and still others may have been moved, paradoxically, by anti-Semitism: "better these undesirable Jews in Palestine than here."

Having refused to accept the recommended "usurpation" of the most desirable areas of their land, the Palestinian people were later equally dispossessed of the areas reserved for them by the United Nations' General Assembly and, in a Kafkaesque twist, continue to be found culpable of villainy and stigmatized for the admittedly often barbaric methods extremists in their midst have used in defense of their national patrimony. And yet, as history witnesses, few countries, if any, have wrenched freedom from their foreign overlords without resorting to cruel violence, not India where terrible violence was perpetrated despite Gandhi's preference for civil disobedience and certainly not England's American Colonies.

As a nation that per-force used terrible violence, both in pursuit of its own independence from colonial domination, to wrest land from the native inhabitants and to preserve the integrity of its Union, one might have expected the United States to appreciate the plight of the dispossessed Palestinians. Doubtless, the double standard characteristic of American policies concerning the Israeli-Palestinian conflict and the indifference the United States Government expresses toward Israel's persistent suppression of the Palestinian people's rights and aspirations, constitute the fundamental factors at the base of anti-American, global islāmist violent bitterness; and they provide a needed tangibility and practical appeal to the otherwise ethereal goal of transnational, "apocalyptic" jihādism.

It is indeed one thing to defend the security of Israel within its recognized boundaries, but it is another to do so irrespective of its non-compliance and violation of Human Rights and of so many relevant Security Council resolutions.

For the United States to go to war against Iraq, ostensibly to enforce the implementation of United Nations Resolutions, while shielding Israel in its non-compliance with similar mandatory resolutions, is proving to be counterproductive. Indeed, such a double standard defeats the need to unite the world against the scourge of transnational terrorism and lays to waste all deaths, efforts, and appropriations designed to combat it.

By acting as an honest, unbiased broker and by exerting the appropriate zeal to enforce all Security Council resolutions, the United States would radically contribute to bringing about the peace so desperately needed in the Middle East and, at the same time, discretely starve the main engine that fuels al-Qā'ida's appeal and recruiting ability.

But it is, so far, politically incorrect in the United States, particularly after the hysteria and paranoia caused by the treacherous terrorist attacks of 9/11, to objectively discuss terrorism's underlying causes. Sensitivities toward those who lost kin in the criminal attacks and in the wars waged against Afghanistan and Iraq, party politics, jingoism, and a politically calculated misinterpretation of what patriotism really stands for, have further limited free and rational exchanges and the analysis of war and violence and their connection to Israel and the Palestinian issue.

As a result, the elaboration of judicious means of addressing the transnational terrorist scourge defensively and preventively, has sadly given way to dramatic but ineffective martial means to combat it. Propagandistically called the "War on Global Terrorism," it is a quixotic enterprise needlessly costly in human lives, in legal standing, in moral value, and in political, financial, and diplomatic capital. In fact, this fuzzy slogan, given the Bush administration's policies in the Middle East, has compounded popular hostility there toward the United States and complicated the effort to gain allies and control and defeat transnational terrorism.

As things stand, absent a distinction between the realities of what we have labeled reactive transnational terrorism seeking national liberation and of its opportunistic and theologically misguided cousin, islāmist apocalyptic terrorism, a peaceful solution to the first and the psycho-theological defeat of the second will continue to evade us.

Violence is one of the many natural means of human intercourse; a given nationality or ethnic group is not anymore predisposed to engage in it than any other; there are no inherently "evil" people; evil is an environmental and circumstantial hazard.

Indeed, members of any human society denied freedom and subjected to generalized vilification and demonization, will perhaps, after a period of stifling submission, ultimately succumb to hopelessness and despair; and these will eventually translate into antisocial and self-destructive behavior.

The causes of the prevailing stagnation in Muslim countries are many. Among them are a persistent obscurantism, a lack of generalized modern education free of traditional religious constraints, intolerance, fatalism, interconnection between mosque and state, and a related lack of self-esteem. Another cause is a corrupt leadership having more interest in political survival than in bridging the socio-economic disparity between the upper and lower classes.

Western strides over the past half millenary in culture, science, economics, politics and power, as well as its hegemonic expansion over the world; its influence on the cultural traditions of the Islāmic elite; and its support of an ever-expanding "alien colony" in the holiest of Islām's domains, contribute greatly to Arab and Muslim insecurity and humiliation.

Inevitably, this triggers the xenophobic resentment and animosity that fuel globalized jihādist terrorism. While xenophobia and resentment were not originally directed at the distant and admired United States of America, they became redirected toward it when it emerged as the uncontested power-broker in the Middle East and it failed to meet their hopes and expectations.

Because the circumstances in the Occupied Territories of Palestine are a constant social, cultural, and political irritant to Muslims globally, offending their sense of justice and violating their sense of self, they stand seminal in the globalization of islāmist transnational terrorism. They have triggered in Muslim societies, an agonizing introspection concerning the reasons for their apparent humiliating subordination to the alien, secular West and their deep disappointment in Western democratic principles.

This has led many Muslims to misguided theopolitical conclusions and unfortunate determinations. Given, then, the centrality of the Palestine problem and the bitterness it provokes in the Muslim world, an examination of the nature and character of the Israeli occupation is imperative; it will help better understand the fundamental causes of the hatred behind global transnational terrorism.[7]

The inhumanely abusive conditions under which many Christian and Muslim Palestinians have lived since November 1948 must be coolly and candidly considered in order to understand the factors that have shaped the minds of those who participate in the violence we have referred to as consequential terrorism and its corollary transnational apocalyptic or ideological cousin. These conditions remain largely unfamiliar to the average American, despite occasional perfunctory reportage and documentaries in the media. By and large, they were never dealt with candidly, sympathetically, or systematically, nor were they given the prominence that issues involving the violation of human rights and international law deserve. Some of the most egregious among these violations will be mentioned in this essay, not to provoke controversy and offend sensitivities, but to attempt to bring understanding to the depth of human indignities and degradation suffered that have led to the dehumanization behind terrorism—suicidal and homicidal—and because those who remain indifferent to human abuse, are, by omission, equally guilty of it.

Certainly, the interminable domination of the Palestinians—and the complex of violent measures its sustenance requires—tragically produce the insane state of mind that motivates suicidal bombers. Responsibility, therefore, for the inhumane and barbaric tactics of the Palestinian *kamikaze* rests not only with the perpetrators, but must be equally shared by Israel and its supporters, just as they must also share responsibility for the violence perpetrated by the islāmists in New York, Washington, DC, Madrid, Moscow, London, and elsewhere. In this context, the title chosen by André Cayatte for his celebrated film *"Nous sommes tous des Assassins"* is very fitting indeed.

Be that as it may, terrorism, no matter its causes, is not acceptable and we are not, in these pages, attempting to mitigate its criminality, nor to excuse it, but, realistically, *"noblesse oblige."*

Islām is a great civilization going through a crisis of identity in a rapidly changing world. Muslims today lament the passing of the brilliant Islāmic civilization that dominated the Middle Ages and helped spark the European Renaissance. They are loath to rationally analyze the causes of its supersedure, preferring instead to interpret it unscientifically as divine punishment for religious laxity.

Nonetheless, they also blame Western imperialism and the "corrupting" influence of Christianity and Judaism—the two pillars upon which their own faith was built—for the diminished status to which they have been relegated.

The inevitable cultural hybridism of the new Muslim elite has further threatened the traditionalists' peace of mind and their societal comfort and authority. It has profoundly jolted their spiritual serenity and offended their sensibility. This traditional majority vehemently rejects the intrusion of Western ways and sees in them nothing but moral decay; and it resents the seductive affects of foreign mores on malleable Muslim youth who attend Western schools and universities.

But the tendency to shift blame and hold the West responsible for all the problems affecting the nations of Islām is not altogether warranted, the humiliating military defeats suffered in wars with an Israel armed and diplomatically shielded by the United States and our expedient association and support of corrupt dictators and monarchs notwithstanding.

Most of the lack of fundamental progress in Muslim countries is basically inherent in their cultural traditions and corrupt leadership, and is related to the unshakable stranglehold that religion, intolerance, narrow-mindedness, and ignorance have over national life; it is anchored in their historical inability to dissociate religion from law, society, education, government, and politics.

Nevertheless, resentment of foreign power-meddling and fear of foreign domination have a way of taking precedence over dissatisfaction with one's government. In the mind of the Muslim traditionalist, therefore, America's support of Israeli aggression in Palestine, the aggressiveness that characterizes its foreign activities and the support it extends to self-serving dictators, while paying lip service to democracy, reinforce the notion that the United States is fundamentally responsible for their misfortune.

Terrorism and the Palestine Problem

"Should the creation of the Jewish State result in maltreatment and abuse of the Palestinian populations, the Jewish people will have strictly failed to learn anything from two thousand years of suffering."—*Albert Einstein, 1929*

In pre-Israel, the Palestinians—the Muslim majority, as well as the Christian and Jewish minorities—have historically interacted with remarkable mutual tolerance and constituted urbane, politically passive traditional communities; thanks to British reassurances, this harmony persisted generally for a while after the announcement of the November 2, 1917, Balfour Declaration, which viewed:

with favour the establishment in Palestine of a national home for the Jewish People, and will use their best endeavours to facilitate the achievement of this object, it being clearly understood that nothing shall be done which may prejudice the civil and religious rights of existing non-Jewish communities in Palestine.[1]

Indeed, the earlier flow of mostly religious East-European Jewish immigrants, such as members of *Hovevei Zion* (or *Hibbat Tziyyon*), had been welcomed with characteristic Palestinian hospitality. Palestinian suspicion of Zionist intentions emerged only when Jewish immigration became heavy in the later twenties and beyond, and the intention to create a Jewish State became obvious. It culminated in the so-called 1930s "Arab Revolt." Ahad Ha'am (Asher Ginsburg), the eminent leader of the Cultural Zionism Movement, had in fact anticipated, in his 1881 essay *Truth from Eretz Israel*, the coming of a conflict between the indigenous Palestinians and the Zionist immigrants:

> From abroad we are accustomed to believing that the Arabs are all desert savages, like donkeys, who neither see nor understand what goes on around them. But this is a big mistake ... The Arabs, and especially those in the cities, understand our deeds and our desires in Eretz Israel, but they keep quiet and pretend not to understand, since they do not see our present activities as a threat to their future ... However, if the time comes when the life of our people in Eretz Israel develops to the point of encroaching upon the native population, they will not easily yield their place.[2]

Indeed, the traditional civility of native Palestinians has been noted by many Jewish notables, and particularly by Martin Buber and Judah Magnes, two eminent Jewish scholars, humanists, and philosophers.[3]

Civility and hospitality are inherent in Middle Eastern culture; in Palestine this trend was reinforced by the geographic situation of the country at the crossroads of world history and civilizations, where the indigenous intermingled interminably with invaders, scholars, piety seekers, and pilgrims.

These cultural traits, however, were often misconstrued by the Zionist new-comers as indicative of a lack of distinctive sense of nationhood; this confirmed in their minds, the fiction then prevalent among colonizers everywhere, that Palestine was not a nation, and that its native inhabitants were squatters and tribesmen devoid of political identity separate from other Arabs. Palestine therefore was up for grabs. Theodor Herzl, the celebrated author of *Der Judenstaat* (The Jews' State), the visionary book that promoted the establishment of a "State for Jews," person-ified this biased mentality; without having ever set foot in Palestine, he noted in his book that a Jewish State there would neither be legitimately challenged nor prejudice anybody, as it was a "land without a people, for a people [the Jews] without a land."

Later, roughly up to the "Oslo Accords" of August-September 1993, that fiction was restated by many Israeli leaders, and most notably by Prime Minister Golda Meier who, following the 1967 war and Israel's occupation of the West Bank, Gaza, the Sinai peninsula, and the Syrian Golan, dismissingly proclaimed during a press conference: "there is no such thing as Palestinians."

Thus Zionist propaganda quite brilliantly succeeded in virtually vaporizing Palestine and Palestinians, substituting Israel and Israelis for them, while project-ing the notion that the various Arab states were in fact nothing but an artificial division of a huge single homeland and Palestine the eternal Jewish State. It con-veyed the notion that the so-called Palestinians were mere Arab squatters there, who should move back to that huge "Arabistan."

Thus the blame for the plight of the Palestinian refugees quite successfully shifted to the Arab states that refused to integrate them. Indeed, in most of these states, refugees have been practically held hostage, in filthy camps, as undesirables. The Palestinian refugees themselves had rejected all United Nations' attempts to settle them in permanent habitations, for fear of losing their right to their homeland. Nevertheless, Israel gained international sympathy by projecting itself through the biblical prism of a small but determined David valiantly standing up and defending its own refugees against the formidable, greedy and cruel Arab Goliath.

Basically, the Palestine problem bears much constitutional similarities to the now resolved South African one—a dispute over control of a land between a local people and European colonizers claiming rights by way of selective biblical references.

Thus a historically persecuted, mostly immigrant people of diverse national origins—some ethnically Semitic, others converts to Judaism—imbued with dreams inspired by the Bible and by memories gleaned from ancient history, resolved to abandon their native homelands and "restore" by imposition, their sovereignty over a divinely "promised land."

But admixed originals, immigrants, and invaders had continuously settled Palestine, where Judaic states had prevailed between 1491 B.C. and 70 A.D. These too, had ancient historical memories and cultural traditions anchored in "revelations" and the scriptures—the Bible, its supplements and complements. They, therefore, harbored equally deep feelings, emotions, and attachment to the land of Palestine, but with a difference; they had kept a continuous physical presence on it, going back in some cases to periods even pre-dating the very first Israelite invasion.

Undeniably, the Palestinians are the descendents of ancestors dating back to ancient Palestine—with admixture of Sumerian, Phoenician, Canaanite, Hebrew, Philistine, Assyrian, Persian, Hellen, Roman, Egyptian, Arab, Mongol, Ottoman European, and others. With the advent of Islām, beginning in the seventh century, the people of Palestine, like their contiguous neighbors, became Arabized. Some however still cling to their ancient cultures and tongues, such as Aramaic. In 1882, before the First *Aliya*, the total Palestinian population stood at slightly less than 550,000, including 15,000 mostly native Jews.[4]

To claim that the Jews of the Diaspora—whether descendent from the original Hebrew tribes, from Kazars, or from European and other converts to Judaism— have a greater legitimacy over Palestine than the native Arabized Palestinian Muslims, Christians and Jews is disingenuous. And so is the argument that these natives have lost their legal claim because for centuries they were dominated by foreign suzerains; for in fact real sovereignty resides in the native resident people, even when arrogated or temporarily "exorcised" by a foreign legal entity. Furthermore, the presumption that the land was promised by God to Abraham's descendents is just that, a religious presumption with no international legal validity. For us in the United States, where the separation of Church and State is engraved constitutionally, this presumption should be doubly unacceptable.

Ever since the birth of Political Zionism—with the publication in 1862 of Moses Hess's *Rome and Jerusalem: The Last Nationalist Question* and particularly since 1947—geopolitics, wars, illegal settlements, annexations, terrorism, diplomatic meddling, and theological pretensions have catapulted a simple colonial problem concerning a piece of real estate dear to all branches of the Abrahamic tradition, into a multifaceted and multidimensional international imbroglio.

Indeed, the entrenched spiritual and cultural marrow of Palestine's destiny, and the emotions it raises among Jews, Christians, and Muslims around the world, make the conflict over Palestine an intractable, festering political cancer. Exacerbated by the rise of religious fundamentalism, be it Muslim, Christian, or Jewish, the Palestine problem is paramount among the seminal causes of Palestinian and islāmist transnational terrorism and axiomatic in the threatening clash of civilizations.

The emotional and symbolic identification of Judaism, Christianity, and Islām with the "Holy Land," the eschatology associated with it and the significance that the shrines gracing its landscape hold for the faithful, have resurrected the dormant, poisonous intolerance and hatred of a darker age, disrupting progress toward international humanism, and threatening the fragile security of the world.

It goes without saying that imposing an alien state over a piece of real estate by way of a massive immigration and against the expressed will of its native population, invites reciprocating extraordinary violence; history stands witness to this verity whether in the Americas, in Australasia, or wherever colonies of settlements were erected. Buttressed by their superior power and exclusivist claims to civilization, the settlers' arrogant overlordship, and their appropriation of the best of the native's land and resources, have often ultimately translated into attempts at mutual ethnic cleansings.

The colonization of the "Promised Land" has, sadly, not transcended this tendency. In occupied Palestine, inhumane and illegal reciprocal terrorism unfolds unchecked—in the glare of the information age—by a politicized United Nations and is inspiring equally terrorizing transnational jihādist activities. Indeed, terrorism, however abhorrent, does not incubate in a vacuum; its placenta is humiliation, anger, and despair. Understanding its causes, both fundamental and ancillary, and addressing them with justice and humanity should provide a more potent weapon than any technologically superior arsenal that can be fielded by a "Coalition of the Willing." Terrorism between Israelis and Palestinians and its concomitant transnational and international jihādist echo will persist as long as injustice continues to prevail.

Given the circumstances, violent Palestinian reaction to dispossession should not come as a surprise. But its terrorist expression, no matter its rationalization, is just as illegal and violative of Human Rights as that of the occupation. But should one assign different values to the terrorism of the occupier and to that of the dispossessed, considering that the former is the cause of the latter?

Israeli violence of illegal occupation against a population under its jurisdiction, is committed by an established state whose membership in the United Nations was conditioned on a pledge to respect that Organization's Charter. Palestinian extremists' crimes, on the other hand, are committed by stateless, nationalist organizations necessarily outlawed by the occupier, or by individual desperados, mostly against innocent Jewish civilians, in a struggle for national liberation. In the first case, the military power and violence used have regularly been deemed by the international community to be disproportionate, and as collective punishment, a violation of International Law. In the second, the indiscriminate, senseless violence is equally inhumane and criminal, though perforce sporadic and usually involving ad hoc terrorizing acts of self-immolation, mostly to avenge the occupier's heavy-handed punishment.

The *Likud* and other extremist right wing political parties in Israel are often singularly blamed for any and all excesses against Palestinians; history, however, demonstrates that mainstream Labor, under any of its celebrated statesmen, including Nobel Peace Laureates Yitzhak Rabin and Shimon Peres,[5] has been just as guilty of Human Rights violations, including blatant ethnic cleansing, which the left wing of the Labor Party, the *Gush Shalom*, and other Israeli peace and Human Rights organizations deplore.

Here in the United States, the term "genocide" evokes gruesome flashbacks of the Nazi Holocaust. Consequently, the word is routinely used with great circumspection. Indeed, it carries in the American psyche a particularistic significance, one that has unfortunately constrained its scope only to targeted massive killing, leaving out other crippling forms of mass psychological, emotional, and cultural crimes. This narrow conception evolved in the context of the diabolical Nazi intent to annihilate Jewish presence in Europe.

In consideration of the contemporary prevalence of massive crimes against defenseless people around the world, the term genocide objectively deserves a wider applicability. With this in mind, it is fitting to recall that in March 1975, Richard Rubenstein, the author of *After Auschwitz*,[6] had already hinted at that necessity when, at a lecture delivered before the New York City Conference on the Holocaust, he sadly mused that, "perhaps we are at the beginning, not the end of the Age of Genocide."

Israel, AIPAC (American Israel Public Affairs Committee) and its other "lobbies" and supporters in the United States vehemently reject accusations of racism and of ethnic cleansing in Palestine, let alone genocide, aggressively terming them and any other criticisms of Israel as "anti-Semitic slurs." Even the many Jews and Israelis, who often proffer such criticism, are swiftly labeled "Jew-hating-Jews."[7] "Such a holier-than-thou attitude is not only disingenuous, it is designed to inhibit open and frank discussion of Israeli occupation policies and laws.[8] Academics are blacklisted and harassed by such extremist, pro-Zionist publicists as Daniel Pipes, who encourages Jewish students to report to his organization, the names of professors whose lectures may include criticism of Israeli policies. These names are then published on a specially designed Web site, www.campus-watch.org, in order for students to avoid them—a virtual Zionist quarantine.[9]

Israel has, undeniably, consciously practiced ethnic cleansing in Palestine. How otherwise, one might wonder, could the territory that now constitutes Israel, have been cleared of most of its original Palestinian inhabitants, with many forced into refugee camps and many others scattered around the world and barred from returning? Does not this dispersion remind one of the Roman-engineered Babylonian exile?

Israel continues to claim that these were refugees of choice. But a whole nation does not, en masse, leave abode and possessions for the leisure of exile. The Palestinians were dispossessed, chased, and herded into the hopelessness of refugee camps, and they have been hounded generation after generation.

Zionism's objective was and remains the creation and preservation of as pure a Jewish state as possible. This is confirmed in its absolute rejection, today more than ever, of the U.N. Security Council Resolution concerning the "Right of Return" of Palestinian refugees. The rejection is based on the fear that this would alter the state's "Jewishness," transforming Israel into a bi-national one. Can one imagine the outcry in the United States if our Government rejoined the white supremacists' objective to expel all whom they term "undesirable," Catholics, Jews, and people of color, to restore an America with a strict Anglo-Saxon character? Why, then, has the United States Congress been adamant in supporting Israel in what amounts to a similar endeavor?

Statements by extremist Zionist leaders before and after the establishment of the Jewish State abound, unmistakably pointing to the need and intent of ethnic cleansing. Palestine's autochthonous population has to be "spirited away," wrote Theodor Herzl, the titular father and architect of the Jewish State, to make room for Jewish immigrants.[10] Herzl's statement has been echoed and reinforced by many other great Zionists, among them Joseph Weitz, the former head of the Jewish Agency's Colonizing Department, who wrote in his *Diaries*:

> between ourselves, it must be clear that there is no room for both people together in this country ... the only solution is Palestine ... without Arabs and there is no way but to transfer the Arabs from here to neighboring countries, to transfer all of them, not one village, not one tribe should be left.[11]

Indeed, the Jewish State had to become "as Jewish as England is English," asserted Chaim Weizmann, Israel's first President in, *Trial and Error*, his fascinating memoirs.[12] More recently, the original preexpurgated memoirs of General Yitzhak Rabin candidly reported that David Ben Gurion, Israel's celebrated first Prime Minister, "ordered, silently in a telling gesture," during the 1948 "War of Independence," the implementation of the "secret" policy of ethnic cleansing in Galilee. This and other passages, censored in the published version of the book were reported in the October 23, 1979, *New York Times* article[13] :

> ... We walked outside, Ben Gurion accompanying us. Allon repeated his question, 'What is to be done with the Palestinian population?' Ben Gurion waved his hand in a gesture which suggested, 'drive them out!'

Rabin also reported in the virgin version of his book that Ben Gurion called on him to rid Galilee of its Palestinian inhabitants. And Professor Benny Morris, the imminent Ben Gurion University historian, detailed the stratagem used by General Allon to cleanse Galilee of its non-Jewish inhabitants.[14]

Authoritative statements such as these and so many others continue to be uttered by settlers, right-wing politicians, and military officers; they are bravely reported by peace-loving Israeli organizations such as *Gush Shalom*, and occasionally, but uncritically, by the American media. This continued Israeli preoccupation with the preservation of a de-Arabized, expanding Jewish state—be it for security concerns, or for ideological or theopolitical ones—is perturbing indeed.

Nevertheless, many early Zionist leaders such as Ahad Ha'am, Moshe Smilansky, Ernst Simon, philosopher Martin Buber and Judah Magnes rejected that notion, as do many contemporary humanist Israelis and Jews around the world.[15] These people openly deplore that the dream to find a haven where Jews would be spared intolerance and bigotry has turned into a nightmare in which some Israeli leaders are following, as it were, in the footsteps of their historical tormentors. Albert Einstein worried about that eventuality and in a November 25, 1929 letter to Chaim Weizmann, warned against it in these words:

> Should we prove incapable of finding a way to cohabitate, or to reaching honest agreements with the Arabs, then we have absolutely learned nothing from 2000 years of suffering and will deserve the consequences.[16]

Uri Avneri, Meron Benvenisti, Avraham Burg, Nehama Ronen, Amos Oz, Felicia Langer, Michail Warschawski, and so many other liberal-minded individuals, Israeli social and human rights organizations, and left of center political parties, continue to speak loudly against ethnic cleansing.[17] Despite them, however, subliminally at least, an ethnically cleansed Jewish Israel continues to drive the nation's politics.[18] This objective is evident in the countless Israeli demographic and sociological studies. These studies emphasize the fear that the more rapid the growth of the Palestinian population, the greater the threat to Israel's Jewishness.[19] Furthermore, the state's discriminatory policies toward the non-Jewish Israeli population and the draconian ones devised to control, humiliate, and dispossess the Palestinians in the Occupied Territories, have been cited, given their alleged intent to stimulate emigration through despair, as consistent with the notion of ethnic cleansing.

One might wonder, given the remarkable inclination of Jews in Western countries to support liberal causes, particularly the notion of diversity, if the anachronistic Israeli fear of "bi-nationalism," indeed the desire for Jewish ethnic exclusivity, is not part of the residual antiassimilationist mentality of the *shtetl*. It is certainly a central ideological imperative of the powerful political right wing dominated by the East European, mostly Russian immigrants, such as Avigdor Lieberman and Natan Sharansky, and of zealots and religious fundamentalists, who insist on continuing to expand exclusive Jewish settlements in the occupied territories. But one might also muse poetically whether an Israel cleansed of Palestinians is not also subconsciously born of the dispossessor's need to escape the memory of his crime; indeed, might not the presence of the Palestinians—a people consciously dispossessed in order to make room for Israel—be the subliminal equivalent to the ubiquitous "eye" that obsessively haunted Cain down to his sealed grave, in "La Conscience," Victor Hugo's unforgettable poem?

> *Lorsque avec ses enfants vêtus de peaux de bêtes,*
> *Echevelé, livide au milieu des tempêtes*
> *. . .*
> *Rien ne me verra plus, je ne verrai plus rien.*
> *On fit donc une fosse et Caïn dit: C'est bien.*
> *Puis il descendit seul dans cette voute sombre.*
> *Et quand il se fut assis sur sa chaise dans l'ombre*
> *Et qu'on eu sur son front fermé le souterrain,*
> *L'œil était dans la tombe et regardait Caïn.*

There are really two Israels: the legal Israel, whose borders already extend beyond the ones originally drawn by the United Nations and include the territories behind the 1949 Armistice lines; and the other Israel that stretches beyond these borders and include the occupied territories of biblical Judea and Samaria, the Gaza strip, and "annexed" East Jerusalem, the Sha'aba enclave and the Syrian Golan Heights.

This illegal Israel resulted when, in June 1967, Israel launched its long-planned "Six Days War" against Egypt, drawing its contiguous Arab neighbors into battle, defeating them, and seizing land.[20] Unlike the occupation resulting from the 1956 war, this occupation remains without serious opposition from successive American Administrations, as does "Susannah," the treacherous terrorist attacks, also known as the "Lavon Affair." These attacks were launched by Mossad in 1954 against U.S. installations in Egypt, in order to disrupt the evolving Egyptian-American rapprochement. The 1967—ostensibly "mistaken"—Israeli bombing of the clearly-identified *U.S.N. Liberty* at the beginning of the "Six Days War," also remains without official American opposition. The occupation continues to date, relentlessly brutal and in violation of United Nations Security Council Resolutions 242 of November 22, 1967, and 338 of October 22, 1973.[21,22]

Resolution 242, drafted by British Ambassador Lord Caradon[23] and unanimously endorsed by the Security Council, remains the legal basis for the settlement of the "Palestinian Question." Though restated and made once more mandatory in Security Council Resolution 338, its implementation has been frozen by quibbling over whether the ordered Israeli withdrawal refers to all (French and Russian language versions of the Resolution), or to some (English language version) of the occupied territory. The United States, virtually alone and in deference to Israeli sensitivity, supports the second interpretation despite the intent imbedded in its preamble, that emphasizes unequivocally "the inadmissibility of the acquisition of territory by war." In fact, Lord Caradon personally confirmed that intent to this author when he visited the University of Bridgeport to receive a doctorate, *honoris causa.*

The United States position on the matter has contributed to the Muslim world's bitter resentment of American policies. Angered and filled with hopelessness, factions under the umbrella of the Palestine Liberation Organization in exile reacted to the situation with repeated, indiscriminate terrorist attacks that were both senseless, criminal, and counterproductive.

Throughout most of the history of the Israeli occupation, Ariel Sharon's political strategy has been consistent—the settling of all of historic Palestine by creating "facts on the ground."[24] As prime minister, his decision to evacuate the jihādist-infested, densely populated, and uncontrollable Gaza strip[25] suggests a pragmatic modification seeking to divert the world's attention from the actively progressing expansion of Israeli settlements in Judea and Samaria, thus blatantly maximizing the West Bank's "Judaization."[26] The massive stroke that incapacitated him will, in all likelihood, bring no significant diversion from his territorial vision. In fact, *Kadima*, the center right party he splintered out of *Likud*, endorses his vision.

Just as in South Africa's Apartheid regime, two distinct legal systems prevail in Israel-Palestine; one system for the Israelis and the other for the Palestinians. The first system applies to all Israelis, including, theoretically, its "Arab citizens," who, nevertheless, are commonly perceived as "fifth columnists" and are regularly discriminated against; Jewish settlers in the Occupied Territories, fall under this system and enjoy generous financial, fiscal, and political privileges, incentives devised to promote the further expansion of settlements in the territories.

The second system is one of highly restrictive and coercively draconian military laws, some resurrected from the Ottoman era and others retained or adapted from the turbulent British Mandatory period. These laws are supplemented by ordinances promulgated by the Military Occupation Authority and apply only to the Palestinians of the occupied territories, never to the Israeli settlers there.

In light of what Israel calls the "Arab demographic threat," its absolute rejection of the Palestinian refugees' "Right of Return," its "Absentee Property Law," its establishment of "facts on the ground," and the draconian policies and laws some have determined to be designed to stimulate the permanent emigration of Palestinians, one is inclined to believe that there is, indeed, substance to the argument that ethnic cleansing continues to be Israeli policy.

The brutal aspect of the occupation, the corresponding equanimity and the lack of evenhandedness and objectivity on the part of successive U.S. administrations, and the blind and assertive diplomatic, economic and military support lavished on Israel are fundamental stimuli in the ongoing—"reactive" and "eschatological"—terrorism against Israel and the West.[27]

Israel identifies with Euro-American culture and boasts a highly educated, inventive and productive population; it enjoys a standard of living similar to that of Western Europe. Despite this "advanced" status, and quite apart from periodic special requests for additional funding, Israel has been receiving—beginning in the 1960s—nearly 4 billion dollars a year in economic and military aid, grants, and loans that are routinely forgiven by an especially benevolent, one might even say "maternal" U.S. Congress.

This unprecedented American profligacy with the taxpayers' money, if used as leverage to bring about Israeli compliance with Security Council resolutions, could be pivotal in accelerating the two states' solution and thus in cutting off the lifeblood of terrorism; it would, indeed, achieve the long sought security for Israel and assuage the Muslim sense of abuse.

Israel's nuclear activities are shielded from the scrutiny of the International Atomic Energy Agency, and its stockpile of nuclear and biochemical weapons, as well as its means of delivering them, are said to surpass in number the arsenal of major European countries; yet Israel remains unchallenged, threatening a terrifying nuclear arms race in the region.

Given these facts, Israel's neighbors and Muslims around the world have become convinced that the United States is directly implicated in Israeli political objectives at the expense of Islām. In fact, the crisis between the world community and Iran on the matter of that country's determination to develop its own nuclear industry must be partly viewed in the context of the perceived threat of Israel's nuclear arsenal in the Middle East. A nuclear-free Islāmic Middle East cannot be rationally avoided without a denuclearization of Israel.

American laymen and scholars, Jews and gentiles alike, have been expressing their loyal dissent with the Government's Middle East policy, but always in vain. Government officials, military brass, and particularly retired statesmen, diplomats, and intelligence officers have also done so, but privately and in a more muted way. Their deep frustration with, and resentment of, the Government's political subservience to the Israeli lobby is exemplified in the following acerbic statement by Admiral Thomas H. Moorer, former Chairman of the Joint Chiefs of Staff:

> I've never seen a President—I don't care who he is—stand up to [Israel] ... They always get what they want. The Israelis know what is going on all the time. I got to the point where I wouldn't write anything down. If the American people understood what a grip these people have got on our government, they would rise up in arms.[28]

As for the average American voters, they remain uninterested, ignorant of the facts, or at least quiescent as if conditioned by a corporate-owned media that is motivated more by profit than by duty. Likewise, our congressmen and congresswomen are cowed into unintelligent parroting of pro-Israeli clichés, in willing subservience to the powerful pro-Israeli lobby and to its neoconservative and evangelical allies.[29] Even the better informed, politically savvy citizens prefer to be largely circumspect on the issue out of sensitivity for the feelings of Jewish friends and neighbors, or to avoid misinterpretations and accusations of anti-Semitism.[30] Simply expressed, the pro-Israel "lobby" has succeeded in rendering the Palestinian tragedy—a crucial factor in world security—taboo to the average American.

Pro-Zionist apologists and supporters in the United States bristle at the mere mention of the influence of the pro-Israeli lobby, the existence of which is routinely denied by some. Professor Israel Shahak, however, a Holocaust survivor and Chairman of the Israeli League of Human and Civil Rights, openly acknowledges the powerful influence of the organized Jewish community in the United States:

The politically prodigious and financially unprecedented support which Israel has received from the United States since the early 1960s can be attributed to two factors. On the one hand, Israeli policies serve American interests, not only in the Middle East but all over the world. Whenever the United States finds it inconvenient to get directly involved in something particularly unsavory, for example in supporting a regime or an organization whose reputation is particularly opprobrious, Israel comes in handy to do the job on the U.S. behalf. On the other hand, however, Israel wields tremendous influence within the United States, in my view, regardless of whether Israeli policies match U.S. interests or not. Although to some extent this fact can be attributed to the support Israel receives from many strains of Christian fundamentalism, there is no doubt in my mind that its primary reason is the role performed by the organized Jewish community in the United States in backing Israel and its policies unconditionally.[31]

If nothing else, the 9/11 tragedy should have stimulated Americans to question the motives behind the resentment that led to that atrocity. But the Bush administration seized upon Iraq's noncompliance with several Security Council resolutions, implicated it in the terrorist attack, and further confused and frightened the public with allegations that it possessed "weapons of mass destruction" (W.M.Ds.) that posed a "grave and gathering threat" to the United States and the world.[32] Thus brainwashed, the nation "patriotically" endorsed the needless and illegal war against that third party.

If Iraq were guilty of unreasonable noncompliance with several Security Council resolutions, Israel too is guilty of noncompliance with at least as many Security Council resolutions; also, it *does* possess weapons of mass destruction that Iraq did not. Yet it remains shielded from consequences thanks to over forty United States vetoes in the Security Council. This double standard does not escape the Muslim world; undoubtedly, it is contributorily axiomatic in the rage that fuels anti-American terrorism.

The United States could do so much to enforce the Security Council resolutions on the Palestinian issue. Justice to the Palestinians would surely be a better bet in insuring Israel's security than the costly American military assistance to that country; it would also surely mollify the rock-base appeal of transnational jihādism. In our shrunken planet, injustice is universally consequential indeed!

The physical and psychic toll of a half century of misery in refugee camps, in exile, or under occupation, can, and does, ultimately lead to dehumanization, and dehumanization leads to indiscriminate violence, whether in Palestine or anywhere else. In a fascinating article in *The New York Times Magazine*, "Are We Driving Elephants Crazy?" Charles Siebert wrote that researchers who studied emerging violent tendencies of these ordinarily placid and serene pachyderms in the wild, have determined that "our encroachment on their way of life is to blame.[33]

Ravaged by feelings of worthlessness, humiliated by the nakedness of their impotence and alienation, and deprived of food and medicine, and of life, liberty and the pursuit of happiness, many innocent young persons look hopelessly at their truncated tomorrows and opt for the perceived dignifying cloak of nationalist truculence and martyrdom. Thus irrational patriotism—this inexplicable wish for self-immolation—overtakes their futureless wasting and shackled life, and offers them a kind of "liberating redemption" that is readily exploited by the professional nationalist. And so the decision to die mixing one's innocent flesh and blood with the flesh and blood of the dispossessor's equally innocent and anonymous "kin," may seem to the dispossessed, perhaps not simply as a just retribution, but paradoxically, also as a prayer to "live free or die"—but to die in communion with one's oppressor and "estranged cousin."

Symbolically, therefore, the terrorizing suicide-cum-homicide can be viewed as the ultimate expression of the mutually denied humanity of both dispossessor and dispossessed, oppressor and oppressed—the senseless assertion of their cousinly right to the ground they deny each other. The decision to volunteer in this virtual hecatomb is, arguably, sparked in the solitude of meditation by a mind ossified by the seeming unending denial of the natural joy of life, in the limbo of no-bodyness, where death is perceived as redemptive and equalizing. Mass killing in self-immolation is a macabre, philosophical symbolization of the supreme power of the powerless.

There is no such thing as humane military occupation. Superior power and its twin, domination, are inherently oppressive; the colonial experience stands witness to that verity. Invariably, the colonized ultimately rise in pitiless rage against the usurper of their serenity. Likewise, there is no humane insurgency. Even Mahatma Gandhi, the reputed prince of nonviolence, could not prevent his people's vengeful violence and terror during the anti-British nationalist uprising; nor could David Ben-Gurion, Jomo Kenyata, Martin Luther King, Nelson Mandela, and yes, since the Oslo Accords, Yasser Arafat.

Counter-insurrectionary brutality is naturally more consequential than that of the insurrectionists, not only because of the inherent disproportionate ratio of forces, organization, and weaponry, but also because it is pervasive, impersonal, generalized, and relentless, not stealthy, random, and sporadic. But it is often the underdog who is castigated for wrenching his freedom from his masters. In the long run, however, the occupier is less resilient than the occupied, because internally, he knows he is a usurper. Yet general political perceptions on violence between oppressor and oppressed depend less on merit, justice, and rights, than on geopolitical, philosophical, cultural, and ideological affinities and considerations. Consider that evidence in America's profound indignation against repression in Tibet, and compare it to its quasi equanimity toward repression in occupied Palestine.

Occupation, once it is imposed, is intrinsically a terror-producing phenomenon. While it may initially assume a benign character, as popular resentment mounts and opposition turns violent, a destructive spiraling and ever-increasing vicious *pas-de-deux* is triggered in which a mutual denial of guilt rides in tandem with mutual hatred, murder, and paranoia. Once it sets in, this *quid-pro-quo* will persist until its original cause—oppression—is removed. In the course of an insurgency, however, reason progressively gives way to stubborn false pride and to a concomitant crescendo of preconditions to negotiations, usually by the more powerful belligerent seeking unacceptable, unconditional surrender.

The characteristic lack of immediate, locally organized, reactive violence to the imposed splitting of Palestine into two states, the subsequent invasions and occupation of the area preserved by the U.N. for the Palestinians, and the incompetent military involvement of contiguous Arab states in the conflict, helped Israel to promote the fiction of an alleged absence of a distinct Palestinian nationality or identity. The native inhabitants of Palestine were "Arab squatters" whose home was elsewhere in the Arab states. The conception that Arab people, irrespective of nationality and citizenship, were generically a single nation, corresponds to the strategic assumption exploited by the Zionists that the Jewish nationals of the world's states constitute a distinct nationality—whence their "Right of Return."

In the mind of the innocent laymen across the world, the massive tree-planting and the world-financed infrastructural and superstructural development in the new state, compared with the somnolence of traditional economic conditions in Palestine, served to justify Israel's progressive land grab, its illegal annexation of territories and its settlement expansions, muting criticism and reducing the Palestinians to the status of primitives unworthy of any national rights. That Israel was able to absorb the large, successive flows of Jewish immigrants, contributed to the shifting of blame for the Palestinian refugee problem onto the Arab states with accompanying accusations—indeed with some justification—of inhospitality and abuse. In its confrontation with the Arab and Muslim world, Israel also successfully resurrected the biblical imagery of David versus Goliath and gained widespread sympathy.[34]

In retrospect, the absence of organized local resistance during the first years of the occupation was arguably due to several factors. Among them, the bewilderment born of the successful result of young Israel's superior strategic military planning and execution and the ironclad control they exercised over a stunned and disoriented preindustrial people, who believed in their imminent rescue by their neighboring, presumed mighty states and by the United Nations.

But a Palestinian reaction did slowly develop and has, like the occupation, grown inordinately inhumane and violent. It was first carried out by members of the exiled Palestinian community from the relative security of their squalid refugee camps. Israeli nationals, including diplomats, spies, tourists, and Israeli interests wherever vulnerable were targeted, but on occasion, they also attacked American interests and citizens, as well as innocent Europeans and non-Israeli Jews. Likewise, Israel's secret service pursued, kidnapped, or killed Palestinians abroad.

Palestinian Transnational Terrorism finds its origin in the earlier terrorist activities of Zionist settlers in Palestine. During the British mandate, the *Irgun Zvai Le'umi, the Lohamei Herut Israel, the Avraham Stern Gang*,[35] and other Zionist terrorist organizations, headed by such future statesmen as Menachem Begin and Yizthak Shamir, bombed British installations and interests, assassinated British and United Nations officials and terrorized Palestinian civilians.

Since the onset of the Second *Intifada*, Israel has been using terror tactics, not only against Palestinians, but, in order to intimidate them, also on the foreign press corps, on members of the Israeli *Peace Now* organization and on young international visitors to the Occupied Territories, who support the Palestinian cause. In 2003, Rachel Corrie,[36] a vibrant young American, who had joined other members of the *International Solidarity Movement* in a peaceful demonstration against collective punishment in Palestine, was viciously crushed by an Israeli "Caterpillar" bulldozer while attempting to halt the destruction of a Palestinian home. As usual, the driver was not found guilty.

Israel's state-sponsored terrorism manifests itself in bombings, the shooting of unarmed civilians, curfews, water rationing, expropriations, assassinations, kidnappings, and the like. In fact, one could justifiably say that Palestinian terrorism has been inspired by Israeli terrorism and by Israel's worldwide undercover operations against hiding former German Nazi officials and exiled Palestinians.

During the exile of its leadership, Palestinian terrorism was randomly carried out around the Mediterranean basin and adjacent countries. Later, it was mainly expressed in the course of two main armed insurgencies or *intifada*, and carried out deep in Israel proper, mostly by volunteers. More recently, the simmering Palestinian tragedy was theologized, contributing to a general feeling in the Muslim world that the West, primarily the United States and Israel, are waging a new anti-Islāmic crusade that must be combated. Crossnational apocalyptic jihādism was thus born, poisoning relations between civilizations and creating a global aura of insecurity.

Wars and popular uprisings are caused by any number of factors; but a need for independence, oppressive policies, nationalism, ideology, geopolitics and economics are more often than not, involved. Uprisings are usually triggered by an event that may or may not be significant. As outlaws, the insurgents' *modus operandi* is necessarily unregulated and often shockingly brutal. Violence in uprisings and insurrections is often related to, and commensurate with, the character, intensity and longevity of the grievances that provoke it. It also reflects the sociocultural milieu where it occurs. Its target is not limited to the immediate "oppressor," but includes any entity or person associated with the perceived enemy.

In this case, the resentment and violence against the United States is primarily related to its close relationship with, and generous support of, an aggressively unjust Israel. This resentment results from a deep disappointment in the failure of the United States to deliver justice in Palestine. For if these vindictive people remain largely unfamiliar with democracy as practiced in the West, and if they only appreciate personal freedom in the context of Muslim Divine Law and, or, customary decency, they nevertheless believe in the ideals of America and its promise of fairness.

In traditional societies, justice however interpreted, is a principle that supersedes freedom; indeed, there is an unspoken assumption that freedom is not a gift to be expected of the powerful, but justice is. In the eyes of Islām, therefore, the

Palestinian tragedy does not only represent an alien encroachment on the land of Islām, it is, fundamentally, a gathering and intolerable injustice.

This injustice looms monumental and threatening to Muslims everywhere. It is expressed in the tyranny of dispossession and exile with no right of return; in the unchallenged collective punishments; in the indiscriminate shooting of youngsters fighting with stones; in an oppression imposed by military might; in the unending kidnapping and assassination of resistance leaders; in the mass arrests and deportations; in the terrorizing nocturnal intrusion of foreign soldiers into homes; in imprisonment without charge; in torture; in dehumanizing treatment meted out to parents before their offspring; in the heartless disregard of pregnant women forced, on their way to a hospital, to wait indefinitely at check-points; in the bombing of densely populated refugee camps; in the routine destruction of homes of parents and relatives of terror suspects (over 30,000 houses have been demolished since 1967); in the expropriation of land[37]; in the confiscation of farmland and turned into settlements for the occupier[38]; in the destruction of crops and cherished century-old olive groves; in the indefinite curfews that truncate civil life; in the bribes that buy "collaborators," pitting family against family, and friend against friend; in the indefinite closures of schools and universities; in the interventions in the work of charitable and humanitarian agencies; in the illegal exploitation of Palestinian aquifers, and the rationing of water to Palestinian households and farms while its free flow is permitted to Israeli settlers (settlers consume nearly 80% of the Occupied Territories renewable water resources); in the equanimity shown toward the criminal behavior of armed settlers and soldiers against Palestinian civilians; in the erection of the illegal and socially and economically destructive separation wall on Palestinian land, etc., etc.

Indubitably, the fundamentally generous, liberal, and humane international Jewish community is not responsible for, nor supportive of these barbarisms; however, the Zionist establishment and fanatics seem to view it as a necessity, despite Albert Einstein's warning in 1929 to Chaim Weizman, the respected scientist who later became Israel's first President, that the Jewish people "will have strictly failed to learn anything from two thousand years of suffering" should the creation of the Jewish State result in the maltreatment and abuse of the Palestinian population. A brilliant man, Einstein seemed to have feared the eventual coming of the mutual carnage in Palestine, realizing that those who suffer stand at the fork of compassion and tyranny, some embracing their neighbors in pain, while others assume a right gained from their own misfortune to inflict tyranny on those who stand in the way of their deliverance.

Clearly, Israel feels, as other colonizers did, that its needs for security dictate such draconian measures, claiming that "Arabs only understand force." The Community of Nations respects Israel's right to live behind secure borders, but it also expects Israel to comply with all its obligations under the Security Council Resolutions and International Conventions and Law.

The establishment of the State of Israel in Palestine was legitimized in 1947 by United Nations General Assembly Resolution 181, upon the recommendation of the United Nations Special Commission On Palestine. The resolution called for the partition of Palestine into two states—a Jewish one and an Arab one—as a solution to a bloody tripartite conflict that involved non-Jewish Palestinians, the mostly immigrant European Jews, and the British.

Despite the expressed objection of Palestine's native inhabitants, Resolution 181 was approved with 33 votes for, 13 against and 10 abstentions, including that of Great Britain, the power to whom the Palestinian Mandate was temporarily assigned on July 24, 1922, by the League of Nations.[39]

The successful passage of Resolution 181 resulted from the intense diplomatic pressure brought to bear on member states by America. With gubernatorial elections on the horizon, President Truman's decision to support the partition of Palestine was, as he wrote in his memoirs,[40] dictated by local political imperatives and unbearable "arm-twisting" by the pro-Zionist lobby; it was reached despite the objections of State Department "Arabists," the National Military Establishment, and by James V. Forrestal, the First U.S. Secretary of Defense.

Should peace finally dawn on Palestine and Israel, these quarrelling twins will have been forged by the hammer and anvil of dispossession and terrorism. In this and similar colonial and territorial disputes, the terrorism of the occupying power and that of the dispossessed has often emerged as a method of last resort. Israel was molded from the coagulated blood of the victimized lambs of anti-Semitism; and so is the incubating Palestinian state; for like their *Sephardim* cousins, the Palestinian people are an original, indigenous Semitic people.

But the strange parallelism does not end here; the "fathers" of both nations, David Ben Gurion and Yasser Arafat exhibited the same diabolical cunning concerning the terrorist activities carried out by their own freedom fighters. Indeed, they both feigned to oppose it, they both condemned it officially, but did or could do little to stop it; for they knew that attempting to do so would have spelled the chaos of civil war and their own demise. Undoubtedly, they secretly admired the boldness and determination of their particular agents of terror, positing perhaps, that given the circumstances, the use of illegal violence was unavoidable in reaching their objective—statehood. In fact, sober analysts know all too well that Yasser Arafat patterned his political deviousness on that of his nemesis twin, David Ben Gurion, but certainly with less skill, less capital, and less support and international sympathy.

Articles 22 and 23 of the Covenant of the League of Nations, the Universal Declaration of Human Rights, the 1948 Convention on the Prevention and Punishment of the Crime of Genocide, the four basic Geneva Conventions of 1949, and the 1977 Geneva Protocols on Victims of Armed Conflicts have brought the world a long way since Customary International Law was minimally and tangentially concerned with Human Rights. The two world wars have sparked in humanity's consciousness, the appreciation of the universal, intrinsic capacity of nations for both kindness and brutality and for justice and injustice. Yet violations of Human Rights persist unabated in many parts of our planet; they are consciously perpetrated and, depending on geopolitical considerations, tolerated by one great power or another. Indeed, even the United States has, in reaction to the 9/11 attacks, fallen prey to the seduction of inhumanity for the sake of national security; the critical reports of several American and foreign Human Rights organizations, including Amnesty International U.S.A., sadly uphold this shameful fact.[41]

In the Middle East, where abuse and violence are synonymous with life, religion, and politics, the leaders of the Holocaust survivors' children too seem to ignore the responsibility of power, setting aside justice in the name of national security. The Department of State's Annual Report on Human Rights Violations often mentions Israel among the violators, but a slavish Congress picks and chooses whom it should impose sanctions on, adding to the perception that Judeo-Christians have anti-Islāmic intentions. In fact, ethnic cleansing and genocide continue to afflict minorities in Africa and Central America as well, evoking little reaction from Washington.

True success in what the George W. Bush administration calls "the War on Global Terrorism," will continue to evade us, and transnational jihādism will continue to plague the world, no matter how much military power we field against it, as long as American politicians continue to choose political expediency over justice. For what is the Muslim world to think, when from our lofty tribune we differentiate between the evil perpetrated in despair by victims of inhumane occupation and dispossession and the evil perpetrated by their tormentor, upon whom we lavish admiration, praise, and half of our total precious foreign financial and military assistance?

The creation of Israel in Palestine, as a segregated state for the Jews, was conceived as a palliative to anti-Semitism; as such it was well intentioned.[42] Nevertheless this does not negate the basic fact that because of its expansionism and the concomitant Palestinian tragedy, it constitutes a problem of colonialism and imperialism.[43] As a Euro-American colony of settlement in the midst of the United Nations' de-colonization strategy, the circumstances surrounding the creation of the State of Israel constitute a historical anachronism.[44] Given this anomaly, and because of the religious and theological factors involved, is it a wonder that the festering tragedy of Palestine remains a major fuel energizing al-Qā'ida, its cells, and its multiplying clones? Indeed, the solution to mutual Israeli and Palestinian terrorism and to the concomitant anti-Western jihādism lies in the fair implementation of Security Council Resolutions 242 and 338, and greater compassion, justice, and understanding among cultures and between the powerful and the powerless.

While the more extreme among the Palestinian factions cling vainly to the impossible dream of regaining sovereignty over all of former Palestine, and the more extreme elements of Israeli society assert their divine or historic right to all of Palestine, the signing by Yasser Arafat and Yitzhak Rabin, on the White House lawn, of "The Declaration of Principles on Interim Self-Government Arrangements," in September 1993—now commonly referred to as the Oslo

Accords—ushered in a fair basis for a final peace based on the 1949 Armistice line.[45] Yet progress beyond these accords continues to elude the world, as "facts on the ground," and treachery and quibbling over details continue under the sponsorship of a politically conflicted and dysfunctional Washington. Thus, the agony of occupation, dispossession, insecurity, mutual and transnational terrorism, alas, continues relentless.

Human Rights and Israel's National Security

"Our lives begin to end the day we become silent about things that matter."—*Martin Luther King, Jr.*

Humanity continues to be plagued by genocides carried out by rogue governments. Genocide can be explicit or implicit. It is explicit when a conscious policy aiming at eliminating an ethnic group expresses itself through open massacres; but the intention to rid one's country of people ethnically undesirable need not involve physical death; it can be carried out more subtly through material and psychological attrition, or through mental or cultural death. While these means are ordinarily referred to as "ethnic cleansing," their ultimate intention is equally devastating, the elimination of a people. Some advocates of Human Rights do perceive genocide in Israeli policies in the Occupied Territories, precisely because of the explicit objective to Judaize all of Palestine. The United States' close alliance with Israel and the ongoing islāmist reliance on Palestinian suffering to legitimize their anti-Western terrorism, impel a review of Israeli intention and deeds in light of available evidence and in the context of the letter and spirit of the Genocide Convention.

According to these advocates, the assertion by Israel that its harsh policies in the Occupied Territories are defensive in nature and needed to counteract the Palestinian determination to destroy the Jewish State, is disingenuous. They point out that maximalists on both the Palestinian and Israeli sides share a mutual determination to destroy each other, and that Israel has already gone much further in this regard. For their part, Palestinian extremists seek to reverse history and restore Palestine within its original mandatory borders, but without its "illegal" Jewish immigrants. In this deadly tug-of-war, the voices of moderates on both sides perceive peace in two neighboring and complementary states, while a minority of utopians find a binational state to be more consonant with democratic principles. So Israeli repressive policies and laws enacted in response to Palestinian extremists' activities and objectives, and generally applicable to all Palestinians in the Occupied Territories, have been regarded as a subterfuge seeking to politically exploit Palestinian resistance, and as an excuse to justify a repression that encourages de-Arabization through despair and emigration. Furthermore, the critics of Israeli policies have cited historic documents and statements expressed by Zionist pioneers about the need to "spirit away" the native inhabitants and Judaize all of Palestine.

Israel's unchallenged superiority, the support it gets from the United States and the world's consensus that it deserves to exist within safe and secure borders, obviously render the objectives of Palestine's maximalists mute. A resolution of the conflict, based on Security Council Resolutions 242 and 338, and endorsed by Israeli and Palestinian moderates, as well as by the League of Arab States, and known as the Geneva Accords, would go a long way toward resolving the scourge of transnational terrorism. But Israel's ideological imperative to exist as a Jewish State, its claim that Judea and Samaria (the Occupied Territories) constitute an integral part of *Eretz Yisrael*, and its large and exclusive Jewish settlements spreading on Palestinian land, buttress the perception of an ongoing conscious Israeli ethnic cleansing policy.

Israeli articles and studies abound emphasizing the concern that an expanding Arab population would ultimately denature the "jewishness" of the State and result in a binational one; some of these, however, argue that keeping the Palestinians confined and ruled under restrictive occupation laws would confirm accusations of apartheidism and therefore, racism.

Since neither of these alternatives is acceptable, what then would the remaining option reasonably be? It is this question that leads critics to determine that the draconian rules are indeed designed to silently coerce emigration. They find the difficulties Palestinians experience in returning to their homeland, Israel's adamant rejection of the Palestinian refugees' "Right of Return" as sanctioned in International Law, compelling, particularly in light of the automatic exclusivist Israeli legislation that grants the "Right of Return" to Israel of any Jew, of any nationality.

Furthermore, these "returning" Jews are encouraged, through preferential financing and subsidies, to purchase land expropriated from the Palestinians in the expanding West Bank settlements to create "facts on the ground." International protestations do not seem to have much effect, absent United States support.

Israeli Governments have actively and systematically encroached upon Palestinian territories, sowing, as it were, "naturally" growing seeds of Israel in such a way as to ultimately render normal social, economic, and national life progressively impossible for the local population; the Palestinians are scattered by expropriations; family ties are severed; properties, factories, and farmland disconnected from owners and workers; and access to health care and schooling made extremely difficult and time consuming, if not virtually impossible.

The created settlements are veritable embryos of exclusive Jewish life; some are termed "legal" by the Israeli Government, because they are officially implanted, though in contravention of the Fourth Geneva Convention and others are termed "illegal," in that they are not. They are ultimately and methodically gathered into townships, thus establishing immutable "facts on the ground" or, as some say, potential "bargainable" chips. They are intimately conjugated with Israel's long-range expansionist patrimonial plan.

A special 300-page "Report on Illegal Outposts" by Israel's Housing Minister Talia Sasson, complained, in March 2005, of government's surreptitious support and financing of "illegal" settlements in the Occupied Territories.[1] The Sasson inquiry, long resisted by the Sharon Government, reported, despite "insurmountable bureaucratic obstacles," that more than 105 "illegal settlements," complete with all necessary infrastructure, had been recently established, or expanded, with the connivance of the Israeli Government. The complaint does not seem to have slowed down the erection of new settlements.

The World Zionist Organization, in association with the Government of Israel, according to the Sasson Report, provided "hundreds of mobile homes to [these] outposts and channeled millions of dollars to them" under the benevolent eye of the Military Administration [and] that fifty-four of these were constructed on Palestinian private land."

Dror Etkes of the Peace Now organization reported in a related interview with *The Christian Science Monitor*, that fifty such outposts were erected after March 2001, despite Sharon's claim of adhering to the U.S.-backed "Road Map to Peace."[2]

The constant hardship these related dispossessions exact on helpless Palestinian communities are doubtless provocative; and the senseless suicidal terrorism that often result in desperate reaction is then conveniently seized upon by the Israeli Government to justify the harsh and repressive laws stimulating the land's de-Palestinization. Thus, critics of Israeli policies argue that without justice, and without determined American pressure on Israel to respect its obligations under Security Council Resolutions and International Law, the vicious cycle of violence and dispossession will proceed relentlessly, defeating any peace process and augmenting Western vulnerability to jihādist violence.

The Middle East sits at the crossroads of the world; it is a region endowed with some of the world's richest oil deposits. Geopolitically and strategically, therefore, its alliance and destiny should be of primordial importance to the United States. Given these considerations, one might assume that American policies would pay particular attention to preserving and enhancing good relations with Muslim countries, while preserving its fundamental philosophical principles and values.

It seems, though, that the influence of pro-Israel organizations—including elements of both extremist Evangelical and pro-Zionist Jewish constituencies—has overshadowed all other determinants of United States foreign policy, obscuring friendly relations with the Muslim world and galvanizing anti-American jihādist tendencies. Thus, the need to control the sources of Middle East oil, and the compulsion to insure Israel's military superiority and preserve its exclusive nuclear capability, seem to have played a major role in the decision to invade Iraq as a precursor to possible action against the Syrian and Iranian regimes.

Indeed, it seems that the evangelical extremists, the "neocons," and their Israeli counterparts had strategized to invade Iraq with the ultimate clear objective of toppling the other two main enemies of the Jewish State, even before the installation of George W. Bush in the Oval Office.

Their strategy held that the direct military involvement of the United States in the Middle East, with its consequent physical implantation there, would further confirm in the Muslim mind, its confusion of Israel with the United States. This would contribute to cementing the notion of their imperialist and crusading symbiosis and of the inseparability of their strategy and security. The binary objective is obvious—insuring, on its own terms, Israel's survival, while hastening the evangelical advent of The Rapture. Indeed, a conflict of civilization with Islām serves both the zionist and the evangelical extremists. In that eventuality, Israel's long-standing, ultimate strategic objective to insure its hegemony over the Middle East will have been achieved. This, incidentally, is part and parcel of what has been referred to as the "Samson Option" or the "Armageddon." [3]

The 2004 decision by Prime Minister Ariel Sharon—the architect of the judaization of the West Bank—to evacuate the densely populated and unruly Gaza strip, while holding on to what he considers as "legal" settlements in Judea and Samaria, is far from deserving of the accolades bestowed upon it; in fact, it appears as a ruse consistent with Israel's ethnic cleansing strategy. Indeed, his feigned generosity calmed the critics of Israeli expansionism, accommodated American diplomatic requirements and weakened Abu Mazen and the Palestinian Authority. The stinging defeat of *Fatah* in the parliamentary elections of January 2006—that startled the Bush Administration—was in no small measure, a direct consequence of the systematic debilitation of the moderate Palestinian Authority, for the P.L.O. and Fatah's prestige and standing among Palestinians have been systematically sapped by U.S.-Israeli obfuscation and short-shifting of justice. Meanwhile, the settlement of Judea and Samaria proceeds,[4] creating still more "facts on the ground" and eroding the chance of a foreseeable Islāmo-Western cultural peace. From the Israeli right of center, all the way to its extreme fascist wing, the wish, if not intent, is to confine an eventual Palestine to the surpopulated and arid Gaza Strip and to a few other scattered Bantustan-like "reservations."

Because ethnic cleansing is considered by some as a form of genocide, and given the deep emotion the term genocide provokes, it is important to closely scrutinize the essential elements of the December 9, 1948 United Nations General Assembly Resolution 260 (III) A, Convention on the Prevention and Punishment of the Crime of Genocide, and its interpretation by its principal progenitor, the Polish scholar, Dr. Raphael Lemkin.[5]

The Genocide Convention, which entered into force on January 12, 1951, now incontestably forms an integral part of the customary phase of the Law of Nations.[6] It declares, *inter-alia*, that "Genocide, whether committed in time of peace or in time of war, is a crime under International Law which [adherent member states undertake] to prevent and punish."[7] It defines genocide as "any of the following acts committed with the intent to destroy, in whole or in part, a national, ethnic, racial or religious group as such."[8] It goes on, in Art. II, to list the acts that fall under the term genocide:

(a) Killing members of the group
(b) Causing serious bodily or mental harm to members of the group
(c) Deliberately inflicting on the group conditions of life calculated to bring about its physical destruction in whole or in part
(d) Imposing measures intended to prevent births within the group
(e) Forcibly transferring children of the group to another group.[9]

In Art. III, the following genocidal acts are punishable:

(a) Genocide
(b) Conspiracy to commit genocide
(c) Direct and public incitement to commit genocide
(d) Attempt to commit genocide
(e) Complicity in genocide.[10]

With Articles II and III of the Convention on Genocide exposed, a consideration of Dr. Lemkin's own interpretation seems imperative; for there is in it a clear implication that an occupier's strategic and coordinated attempt to inhibit productive and normal social and political life of a people under occupation, with the intention of driving its inhabitants into exile, and then settling the occupied territory exclusively with its own citizens, is genocidal in character. "Generally speaking," Lemkin commented,

> Genocide does not necessarily mean the immediate destruction of a nation. . . . It is intended, rather, to signify a coordinated plan of different actions aiming at the destruction of essential foundations of the life of national groups, with the aim of annihilating the groups themselves. . . . Genocide has two phases: one, destruction of the national pattern of the oppressed group; the other, the imposition of the national pattern of the oppressor. This imposition, in turn, may be made upon the oppressed population which is allowed to remain, or upon the territory alone, after removal of the population and the colonization of the area by the oppressor's own nationals.[11]

According to Richard Aren, late Professor of International Human Rights Law, eminent jurist, former colleague, friend, past President of Survival International USA, and, coincidentally, brother of the Israeli industrialist, diplomat, and former Foreign Minister, Moshe Aren:

> genocide can take the form of what anthropologists have called deculturation, and it can involve the disintegration of some or all of the following: political and social institutions, culture, language, national feelings, religion, economic stability, personal [and group] security, liberty, health [mental and physical], and dignity.[12]

Professor Aren was convinced that except for Deir Yassin, Tantura, Ain-el-Hilwa, Jenin, and Sabra and Shatila particularly, the Israeli leadership did not directly or intentionally order or officially condone massacres; but during Israel's War of Independence, in order to make room for Jewish immigrants, Israel did, through terror, impel the massive one-way flight of about 90 percent of the Palestinian inhabitants from Galilee and elsewhere, areas that are now Israel.[13]

Professor Richard Aren felt that the sum total of the special Israeli laws, behavior, practices, and military ordinances applicable exclusively to Palestinians in the Occupied Territories, such as the permanent closure of the Palestine Cultural Institute of Jerusalem in 1982, that marked the beginning of a policy aiming to undermine the city as the hub of Palestinian civic, cultural, and economic existence; the practice of collective punishments; the leniency expressed toward Jewish zealots who forcibly occupied and "judaized" Palestinian dwellings in the city's Arab sector; the development of the massive and continuing urban plan to completely isolate the city from the rest of the West Bank; the expropriations of Palestinian land; the exclusively Jewish settlements that constantly expand on Palestinian land; the road blocks and check-points that spell physical and psychological hardship and often caused the death of sick people en route to hospitals; the severe water rationing exclusively imposed on Palestinians; the absurd prohibition of the cultivation of certain legumes; the destruction of venerable olive and orange groves that were so much a part of the traditional, emotional and economic life and folklore of the Palestinian; the constant practice of humiliating elderly men in front of their families; the imposition of inordinately lengthy curfews; the closure of schools and universities; the targeting for assassination of political leaders, ad infinitum—were all designed to make life for the Palestinians unbearable in order to induce the necessary "generalized despair" that would stimulate their emigration. He argued that in the aggregate, these impositions dehumanize individuals, lead them down the path of moral and cultural disintegration, such as often engendered by genocide, and ultimately culminate in the insanity of suicide bombing.

The foregoing depredations substantially correspond to what Dr. Lemkin considered, in his interpretive comments, as genocidal in character.[14]

The Psychiatrist Dr. Chaim Shatan, a scholar of the Paraguayan Amerindian genocide, also touched upon the relevance and possible applicability of the term genocide in cases other than those involving organized, systematic physical killings; he observed that:

> there is suggestive evidence that pervasive and persistent despair kills through a complex psychic and hormonal process which exhausts the cortex of the adrenal glands and ... destroys the ability to adapt to stress.... This 'psychic death' is real ... it kills more surely than malnutrition.[15]

This observation was deemed to be particularly relevant in the Palestinian case by his coauthor, Professor Aren. Other scholars have also established causal relationships between the mental stress in despair and serious mental disorientation and other psycho-pathological consequences.[16] Fantasy, confusion, pathological religiosity, loss of touch with reality, and suicidal tendencies are symptomatic. The social dislocation and the "deculturation" resulting from decades of direct and indirect oppression, and the mental stress resulting from the humiliation of helplessness, lack of privacy, and arbitrary social and political restrictions, are at least as devastating in psychological terms as bodily harm and physical torture.[17] Indeed, according to Aren and Shatan:

> ... the term broken heart ... ceases to be a deeply felt metaphor and becomes the product of a compelling and predictable interaction between a familiar environment that has become hostile and the cortical responses of people within the victimized group.[18]

No nation, people, ethnic or cultural group is inherently cruel; but no society, no matter its level of culture, civilization, and refinement, is immune from cruelty and inhumanity. And it is virtually impossible to compare relatively, the crimes perpetrated by one nation with those perpetrated by another. So it is understandably horrifying and particularly baffling, even insulting, for victims of a monstrous political crime such as the *Holocaust* (*Shoah*) to have their suffering compared to the suffering of a people victimized by their kin. The mere idea seems blasphemous and abusive, betraying the memory of their own victimization and violating its singularity.

It is no wonder, therefore, that the mere consideration of the possible genocidal nature of Israeli policies toward Palestinians should offend and raise indignation amongst many innocent and decent Israelis and Jews around the world; and to be in denial is a natural human frailty. Nobody knows better than those who survived the Holocaust, as well as their relatives and descendents, what toll years of silence in the face of tyranny can exact from the victims of atrocities. Thus, neither this essay nor the scholars it cites in the context of the argumentation concerning genocide, means to belittle the intolerable inhumanities suffered by the victims of the Nazi Holocaust, or to be disrespectful to the memory of their agony; the main concern here is to raise consciousness to the fact that the half century of inhumanities relentlessly endured by five million Palestinians cannot be dissociated from the dehumanization inherent in anti-Israeli terrorism, its related anti-Western, transnational jihādism and to the looming danger of a global "conflict of civilizations." Justice, not further incomprehension and repression, is the fundamental prescription to crossnational peace and harmony.

Gregory H. Stanton of Genocide Watch,[19] in a paper deserving wide dissemination and originally written in 1996 at the Department of State, posits that genocide does not just happen in a vacuum; that "eight stages" characterize the evolution of most genocides, and that "preventive measures" taken at any one of the stages "can stop it."[20] Stanton's "eight stages" are per force generic and must be flexibly and cautiously applied to particular cases, with history, environment, causality, circumstantialities, intentionality, intensity, politics, and ideology taken into consideration.

His paper defines the "eight stages of genocide" as "classification, symbolization, dehumanization, organization, polarization, preparation, extermination, and denial." His proposed stages may have relevance in the context of the issues raised by the interpreters of the Genocide Convention and the applicability of the crime in the Palestinian case. They might also indicate whether an awareness of the developmental nature and stages of genocide could have led to international preventive intervention.

Stanton suggests that determining the nature of a society under scrutiny may give a clue as to whether characteristics exist that can lead to genocide. In this context, he posits that societies that "lack mixed categories, such as Rwanda" and "Burundi" (which he terms as "bi-polar"), are the most likely candidates for that crime, and that developing "universalistic institutions that transcend ethnic and racial divisions . . . [can] inhibit an eventual progression toward the tragedy."

Technically, according to Stanton's study, the largest ethnic/cultural group is usually the one with the power to impose its yoke and perpetrate such a crime; but this was not the case in 1948 Palestine, where the immigrant Jews were vastly outnumbered by the non-Jewish Palestinians; they benefited, however, from their greater sophistication and motivation and from their better organization and experience in the art of modern warfare. Another case in point is Iraq: Before the U.S. intervention, the Sunni minority held the reins of power, and under Saddam Hussein perpetrated crimes that have been deemed genocidal. "Bi-polarity" obviously existed in pre-Israel Palestine; it reemerged in the Occupied Territories with the Israeli invasion of 1967 and the related, exclusive claims over the land.

The Nazi imposition of the "yellow star" insignia on Jews, symbolized their perceived differentiality and undesirability. It is not unusual human behavior to distinguish social and cultural differences and values, and to classify communities based on ethnicity, color, dress or religion; but according to Stanton, this can also be a prefatory basis for genocide, if the collecting of information is motivated by hatred and discrimination, and is based on racism, or is motivated by other ethnic or sectarian malevolence. In the relationship between Jews and non-Jews in the Palestine-Israel situation, the problem of "symbolization" through differentiation is ubiquitous; it is expressed at all levels: in the different license plates issued to Jewish and non-Jewish vehicles in the Occupied Territories; in the chain of checkpoints and road blocks that control, restrict, and harass only non-Jewish traffic; in the different treatment accorded to the Palestinians and to the Israelis who live in the Occupied Territories; in the democratic laws that apply only to Jewish settlers, and the draconian laws and restrictions that are imposed only upon the Palestinians who live in neighboring villages; in the financial support available to the Jews for illegally erected buildings, purchasing homes in new, exclusive settlements and in the seizure of Palestinian land and property and in the prompt bulldozing of their buildings erected without proper permits; in the judicial laxity shown toward Jewish settlers' violence and the violent intolerance of Palestinian protests, even by children and women; in the severe water rationing of Palestinians, in comparison with the free flow of water to the settlers; and certainly, in the Jews' right to carry and use arms, while the Palestinians are incarcerated for the same.

"Dehumanization" may also be a prelude to genocide; it occurs in many ways through humiliating and oppressive practices, and when a whole people are equated with vile animals, insects, or diseases, or when they are referred to as oversexed, thieves and murderers. Reciprocal dehumanization is, of course, extant in most conflicts; however, when it becomes habitual within a "bi-polar" society and is buttressed by selective biblical underpinnings, it too, can be a contributing factor that leads to genocide. Mutual dehumanization is common between Palestinians and Israelis—the former call the latter pigs, dogs, infidels, and bloodsucking vampires, while the latter refer to the former as savage animals, primitives, and uncivilized or repugnant critters, as noted in the recent comment of General Raphael Eitan, the retired Chief of Staff of Israel's armed forces: "when we have settled the land, all [that] the Arabs will be able to do will be to scurry around like drugged roaches in a bottle."[21]

According to Stanton, "Genocide is always organized, usually by the state, or by ... terrorist groups." Again, here it can be said that both the Israeli power structure and the Palestinian extremist organizations have factions seeking to rid the land of each other; statements, literature, and policies attest to that fact. Thus *Hamas* and Islāmic *jihād* do not hide their intent to end the existence of the Jewish State in Palestine, while systematic planning, blunt statements by *Ysrael Beytenu*, and historic literature confirm the clear Zionists' intent to de-arabize and judaize all of Palestine. It is in fact evident that, if this goal has not been achieved, Palestine as a juridical entity has already been eliminated by Israel.

"Polarization" occurs when policies, broadcasts, speeches, and other proclamations are used to foment hate and separation, as evident in Palestinian teaching material and in Israeli laws forbidding "social interaction," or cohabitation in case of marriage between Israelis and Palestinians. The historic Zionist aim of metamorphosing Palestine into a "Jewish State" has resulted in the polarization propitious to reciprocal massacres. United Nations General Assembly Resolution 181 (II), of November 29, 1947, which recommended the "Solomonic" splitting of Mandatory Palestine into "Jewish" and "Arab" States, exacerbated polarization, as has the creeping colonization that has blatantly ensued on the land reserved for the Palestinians, in contradiction of the ongoing global decolonization process.

Destitute and subjugated, the Palestinians have since lived in constant friction with their dispossessors and with resentment toward those who are allowing and helping finance their dispossession; in reaction, they have diligently promoted hatred, violence, and hostility toward Israel, in schools and at home. In that, they are not different from other people in a similar situation. Their hostility is a means to affirm their battered identity and their denied nationality and humanity.

Likewise, the Israelis are not any different from previous colonial or imperialist powers, trusting in the inherent rights of their superiority and denying any sense of guilt for the violence of their usurpation. As heirs to the victims of inexcusable inhumanities, they have walled themselves behind a culture of paranoia, and feel utter contempt vis-à-vis their hostile victims, reviling them, demeaning them, and disparaging them scornfully; thus to the Israelis, the "Arab" is congenitally lazy, incompetent, subservient, perfidiously obsequious, violent, and indeed, servile and mendacious—an ungrateful, contemptuous, subhuman, and vicious creature.

Domination and dispossession generate hate, and hate has a way of replicating itself in reflection; it lays the eggs of malignant polarization and predisposes to wishing for "final solutions."

In Stanton's "preparation" phase:

> Victims are identified and separated out because of their ethnic or religious identity. Death lists are drawn up. Members of victim groups are forced to wear identifying symbols. They are often segregated into ghettoes, forced into concentration camps, or confined to a famine-stricken region and starved.... At this stage a Genocide Alert must be called ... armed international intervention should be prepared, or heavy assistance [given] to the victim group in preparing for its self defense ...

In the Occupied Territories, segregation, on the basis of religion and culture, is a fact; prisons are chock-full of detainees including women and teenagers, mostly without specific charges; the best land and most of the water is reserved for the settlers. But this is not all; individuals on a list of suspects are targeted for kidnapping and assassination, and their families are given only a few minutes to evacuate before their homes are bulldozed. Indeed, while this brutal "collective punishment" avoids physical death per se, it constitutes the "psychic death" referred to by Shatan and Aren—it kills souls and hearts, promoting murderous suicidal vengeance.[22]

In the penultimate stage, "extermination begins" with the conviction by those who carry it out that their victims are not "fully human.... [and] genocide results in revenge killings by groups against each other, creating a downward whirlpool-like cycle or bi-lateral genocide." This is the tragic destiny of Palestine; Palestinians are "terminated" by aerial bombings and "smart" rockets on the basis of their affiliation and leadership position in militant organizations—*Hamas*, *Islāmic Jihād, al-Aksa Brigade*, etc.—along with relatives, kin, and innocent bystanders; these deaths are heartlessly dismissed as "collateral damage." In *quid pro quo*, criminal *kamikaze* attacks, in turn, violate the serenity of Israeli innocent life and, like an infernal merry-go-round, the reciprocal massacre of innocents continues its macabre cycles.

But the massacres that took place in many towns in Galilee, in Deir-Yassīn and elsewhere[23] during Israel's War of Independence, those of Sabra and Shatila carried out by Lebanese Maronite extremists, with the assistance of the Israel Defense Forces, and the more recent killings in Jenin and other towns during the *al-Aksa Intifāda*, did not require specific death lists; they were random. In a vicious cycle, these massacres have always resulted in retaliatory suicide bombings— inhumane yet celebrated by Palestinians— that kill and mutilate equally innocent Israeli civilians; this is indeed the morbid expression of what Stanton has called "bi-lateral genocide." Finally,

> Denial is the eighth stage of genocide; it accompanies or follows it. It is among [its] surest indicators ... [as] the perpetrators ... try to cover up the evidence and intimidate the witnesses. They deny that they committed any crimes, and often blame what happened on the victims ...[24]

For example, the murder of United Nations Special Peace Mediator, Count Folk Bernadotte, by the Zionist terrorist *L.E.H.I.* organization, on September 17, 1948; the rebuke of Ambassador Terje Roed-Larsen, the United Nation's Special Envoy to the West Bank and facilitator of the Oslo Accords, following his protestations of Israeli massacre in Jenin; the accusation of bias and of anti-Semitism leveled against critical European Union and Human Rights organizations' representatives; the occasional "accidental" shooting of clearly identified "unfriendly" foreign correspondents; the boycott of critical media, as in the case of the *Los Angeles Times,* and in the temporary barring of the British Broadcasting Corporation from interviewing Israeli officials.[25]

Indubitably, some will consider our use and interpretive adaptation of Stanton's "Eight Stages" as being tendentious and far-fetched; our aim, nevertheless, is to enlighten and reduce the causes of transnational terrorism, bring some sanity to East–West relations, and ultimately peace between Israelis and Palestinians, and across cultures.

Article II of the Convention on the Prevention and Punishment of Genocide supports Drs. Lemkin, Shatan and Aren's interpretation that actually killing or causing the physical death of members of a group, is not the only way to determine genocide; "causing serious bodily or mental harm ... when committed as part of a policy to destroy a group's existence" constitutes genocide as well.[26] It further states:

> The crime of Genocide has two elements: intent and action. 'Intentional' means purposeful. Intent can be proven directly from statements or orders.[27] But more often, it must be inferred from a systematic pattern of coordinated acts. "Intent is different from motive," it continues, "Whatever may be the motive for the crime (land expropriation,

national security, territorial integrity, etc.) if the perpetrators commit acts intended to destroy a group, even part of a group, it is genocide.[28]

Critics of Israeli policies in Palestine, including the respected Israeli historian, Benny Morris, Human Rights attorney, Felicia Langer, *Peace Now* leader, Michail Warschauski, and the former Knesset member, Uri Avneri, have indeed complained about Israel's systematic de-Palestinization and of judaization in Palestine/Israel. Genocidal intent, of course, is not limited to the Israeli Government; islāmist organizations are guilty of it as well, and so are many governments. *Genocide Watch* has published lists of crimes against humanity, including genocide committed around the world; its last report, published in 2004, is alarming; it confirms Richard Rubenstein's observation, in the speech he gave in March, 1975, that "perhaps we are at the beginning, not the end of the age of genocide."

Let it be noted, however, that *Genocide Watch* has, rather diplomatically, and perhaps timidly, been labeling Israeli inhumane practices as "politicide," and Palestinian violence as "massacre." A rather odd characterization, given that the ratio of killed is more than ten Palestinians to one Israeli.[29]

Aren and Shatan's interpretation of Israeli activities in the Occupied Territories may be dismissed by some as hyperbole; the fact remains, however, that the activities are unquestionably incompatible with International Law, with established principles of Human Rights and particularly with the Fourth Geneva Convention as it applies to occupied territories and to their inhabitants.

Sadly, the United States' uncritical defense and support of Israel, given these violations, make us, at least in the minds of Arabs and Muslims generally, complicit with Israel and consequently, enemies of Islām. This defeats all efforts to win the "war on global terrorism." It fuels transnational terrorism and provides a rationale to the promoters of suicidal jihādism.

The Neocons and the Dishonoring of America

"Great nations do not have small wars." —*Duke of Wellington*

George W. Bush acceded to the Presidency of the United States in the Presidential Election of the year 2000, as a result of the historic "miracle" of Florida's hanging "chads." The legitimacy of his Presidency seemed doomed and his mandate to govern, truncated and challenged. As the leader of the most influential nation, his ignorance of the world beyond Texas, its baseball Rangers and oil, combined with his religiosity and the awkwardness of his oral expression, provoked consternation and elicited ridicule at home and around the world. September 11 turned all this topsy-turvy . . . for a while.

"*Aujourd' hui, nous sommes tous Americains.*" In this declarative statement— concise for Jacques Chirac—France's President expressed the world's empathy with, and support of, America following the murderous and devastating terrorist attacks on New York City and Washington, DC. Universal indignation and revulsion over the terrorist attacks provided the President's "neocon" handlers with the opportunity to recast him as the resolute and valiant Commander-in-Chief of a threatened and beleaguered America; indeed, "*la Patrie est en danger!*" as the French might have said. Understandably, the American public, stunned and shaken by the infamy, rallied blindly in support of their not-so-legitimate leader.

The ensuing, initially successful *blitzkrieg* on the Taliban regime in Afghanistan, where al-Qā'ida had been granted sanctuary and support, was greeted with widespread international empathy and cooperation. Capitalizing upon this reaction, the Bush Administration arrogantly, but vainly, endeavored to corral the United Nations and coerce friends and allies into a premeditated, hasty, and ill-planned invasion of Iraq. A conflagration of competitive patriotic fervor overtook the nation. The neocons cleverly manipulated the terrorism factor to legitimize their implementation of the aggressive foreign policy they had been keeping in abeyance. Uncritically, the American media too succumbed to the seduction of frenzied jingoism and eagerly regurgitated the hysterical propaganda emanating from the Pentagon and the White House, contributing significantly to the brain-washing of a suddenly vulnerable and paranoid American society.

A mostly clueless Congress was also cowed into quiescent, sheepish support, as the President, heretofore diminished by allegations of electoral fraud and in-competence, found himself catapulted, as if by a providential *pétard*, as a heroic leader. Thus by default, he had finally gained the legitimacy his stolen presidency painfully lacked.

Thus President Bush, like a veritable cheerleading automaton, turned com-fortably bellicose. He asserted and reasserted, with absolute gravitas, to be in possession of intelligence establishing an intimate connection between the 9/11 attacks and the regime of Saddam Hussein declared "War on Global Terrorism"; arrogantly proclaimed a new American foreign policy strategy based on the inter-nationally proscribed Doctrine of Preemptive Strike and issued an ultimatum for the Iraqi leader to step down or face a military showdown.

To an incredulous world, the invasion of Iraq was painted as part and parcel of a "war to save civilization," the ultimate war of "good against evil." In so doing, George W. Bush and his team were betraying the crucial, elementary military principle of concentration of forces. Thus the needed concentration of military might to defeat al-Qā'ida and to pacify Afghanistan was wasted, as tens of thousands of U.S. and Iraqi lives were unnecessarily lost or maimed, and billions in materiel and financial resources pilfered in a vain attempt to build on a faulty strategy.

Furthermore, Washington failed to give priority to addressing the rapid progress in nuclear technology development of Iran and North Korea; it ignored crucial pleas by the Community of Nations not to invade Iraq; and then brushed aside Egyptian President Mubarak's warning that the invasion of Muslim Irāq would confirm islāmist propaganda that a crusade was in progress, and therefore contribute to increasing the popularity of islāmism and to intensifying transna-tional terrorism.

The administration then opted to follow the belligerent counsel of Vice Pres-ident Cheney's entourage that the United States, as the sole world superpower, could defeat any combination of countries, alone and without international support or approbation.

Indeed, to the neocons, the United Nations was an irrelevant nuisance, and France, the midwife at America's independence, a worthless and ungrateful ally. The United State's oldest ally became the butt of vulgar insult, and it was demo-nized for its judicious disagreement with the decision to rush to war. Forgotten was Chirac's emotional declaration of solidarity with the American people on the day of the 9/11 attacks. In fact, customary French-bashing turned undiplomati-cally ugly, as a wide, front-page headline in *The New York Post* branded France's

President a "weasel"; the cafeteria of the U.S. Congress revoked, at a Congress-man's childish instigation, the traditional, illegitimate "French" nationality of fried potatoes, and T.V. news reporters gleefully videotaped "patriotic" restaurateurs as they foolishly, but nonetheless "patriotically," poured bottles of French wine into gutters.

Thus diplomacy gave way to thunderous hubris from Vice President Cheney, Paul Wolfowitz, and Richard Pearl; An exhilarated Defense Secretary, Donald Rumsfeld, delighted an intimidated and awed Press Corps with impish clowning during his vainglorious daily news conferences; he particularly relished gloat-ing about the military victories of the "Coalition of the Willing," without ever conceding that the enemy we had easily crushed was the incompetent, poorly trained and poorly equipped military of a debilitated underdeveloped country. He never failed to denigrate France and Germany, two crucial NATO allies, whom he contemptuously dismissed as "Old Europe," for their refusal to participate in the egregious aggression. More scandalous, was his dismissal of the prevailing chaos in Iraq and the looting of some of Western Civilization's inestimable and most precious archeological vestigial treasures; and he glibly termed the ongoing murderous mayhem and rampage that accompanied the "liberation" of Baghdad, as the joyful celebratory expression of freedom and democracy. The conned Press Corps loved it, and like addicts could not get enough of "Rummy!"

For its part, Israel seized upon Bush's declaration of war on global terror-ism to justify its repression of occupied Palestine and intensify its blockade of Yasser Arafat in his Ramallah Headquarters. The humiliation of the leader of the Palestine Liberation Organization, not only raised the prestige of the more militant Palestinian factions, but also insured the subsequent electoral victory of the radical *Hamas* party. Many right-wing Israelis felt that having an extremist regime in Palestine would give Israel a free hand in imposing its own solution and unilaterally drawing its own borders, irrespective of previous Security Council Resolutions and other accords.

The concern with the security of Israel and the influence of that country on U.S policies in the Middle East should not be underestimated in the context of the invasion of Iraq. Nor should the discreet advisory role played by the aging patron of American *realpolitik*, former Secretary of State, Henry Kissinger. According to reliable observers,[1] the preordained invasion of that nation—a staunch supporter of Palestinian nationalism—was predicated on the assumption that a government designed by the United States and a long-term American military presence in Iraq, would have a domino effect in neighboring Iran and Syria, Israel's other two implacable enemies, and perhaps elsewhere as well, and thus insure a U.S.–Israeli condominium over the Middle East and its oil resources for an indefinite period.[2]

Thus Washington turned its military might against Iraq—a previous ally against Iran, even when it was using proscribed Weapons of Mass Destruction against that country and carrying out genocide against the Kurds, *Shi'i*, and "swamp Arabs" for its noncompliance with Security Council Resolutions and for its detestable human rights record. Its wrath contrasted with its equanimity toward, and support for, countless other dictators and tyrants with at least equal sanguinary records.

The widely publicized notes purportedly taken by Britain's National Security Aide, Matthew Rycrift, during a July 2002 meeting of Britain's Prime Minister, Tony Blair, with MI-6 Head, Richard Dearlove, and other advisors, add credence to the allegation that Saddam Hussein's reaction to the U.S. ultimatum, was irrelevant to the decision to invade Iraq—it was, as it were, *maktub* (fate).

The justification for the invasion was to be obtained, according to these notes, through "the conjunction of terrorism and W.M.D . . . even if the timing was not yet decided.[3]" There is also evidence, according to London's *Sunday Times*,[4] that the U.K. and U.S. bombing raids, weeks before the invasion, doubled the rate at which they were dropping bombs on Iraq in 2002, "to goad Saddam into war."[5]

Questions arise, then, as to whether George W. Bush's memoirs, now undoubtedly being drafted by literate ghostwriters, will admit that the intelligence and facts against Saddam had been fixed around that preordained determination. Questions also arise as to the genuineness of the contempt expressed by candidate George W. Bush for a nation-building component to American foreign policy. Indeed, one might be inclined to believe that President George W. Bush was not the architect of U.S. foreign policy, and that his ideological associates of the Project for the New American Century—including, primarily, his Vice-President and *éminence grise*, Dick Cheney—may very well be the true framers of that policy.[6]

Though patently more than awkward diplomatically and less than knowledgeable in international affairs, George W. Bush is a skillful politician with folksy charm, a knack in manipulation and expertise in brainwashing technique. Furthermore, like an adolescent, he relishes putting the leverage of U.S. might at the service of his mostly unrealistic ideology. While not always successful, he at least gained the unwavering support of Prime Minister Tony Blair, a better educated and more refined politician, albeit one too eager to play the U.S. card against the European Union. Undeniably, the bedrock of this "Coalition of the Willing" is a reflection of the Roman adage—*asinus asinum fricat*.[7] Both of them, gingerly conjugated the decision to invade Iraq with the necessity to wage the war on terrorism. In so doing, they ignored the history of the defeat of the Soviet forces by the Taliban and its allies.

Indeed, instead of judiciously using the capital gained from his providential new status and cooperating with the United Nations to devise a wise response to the Iraqi leader's stubbornness and concentrating on pursuing the more important war in Afghanistan, George W. Bush opted, as history will show, for a brazenly hegemonic foreign policy in the Middle East, based on the illegal concept of military preemption. He was apparently inspired by Kissinger and the Israeli model. By ignoring the warnings of his father's seasoned foreign policy and national security advisers, George W. charted for the United States, a dangerous imperialist strategy not unlike the one that contributed to the ultimate collapse of the Soviet Union.

The recent vaporization of the Soviet pole had, in fact, created for a United States accustomed to operating in a bipolar environment, a national security vacuum that presented a challenge to its continued need for the lucrative military-industrial complex and its enormously wasteful pork. Islāmist jihādism and the terrorist attacks on the United States seem to have provided a suitable alternative pole and the opportunity to implement the strategic imperialist vision charted in the blueprint of the Twenty-First Century Project.[8]

To many in the situational, culturally paranoid Islāmic World, if the military campaign against Talibani Afghanistan was deemed justified, the Administration's bellicosity toward three other implacable pro-Palestinian Muslim states, Iraq, Iran and Syria, added substance to the claim by al-Qā'ida that a gathering clash of civilizations, triggered by a renascent anti-Islāmic crusade, was unfolding under Washington's leadership, and that only a global *jihād* would prevent it. The United States blatant support of Israel's near obliteration of Lebanon, in response to *Hizbollah's* incursion across the Lebanese-Israeli border, on July 12, 2006, and its abduction of two Israeli soldiers confirmed that perception across the Muslim world.

Sole superpowers have existed throughout history. Invariably, they failed to use the privilege of their preeminent power and prestige to promote social progress and humanity's good, using them ineptly instead, to exploit the weak and to further their own wealth. Swollen with arrogant omnipotence, today, as in yesteryears, they ponderously assume omniscience and infallibility, fall prey to the infection of preen and greed, and challenged by insurrections, they become intellectually crippled by paranoia, and ultimately disintegrate. Emasculated and their grandeur vaporized, they vegetate in the bin of the has-been, their glory reduced to memories lingering only in textbooks and their economic survival hinging only on their ability to woo tourists with the archeology of their glorious yesteryears. Such has been the fate of the grandest of empires; it is engraved on the eternal granite of history, and there it remains for all blind statesmen to palpate. Such is the ruthless vengeance of the oppressed.

Long before George W. Bush became a candidate for the presidency of the United States, the radical Republican right was hard at work drafting a strategy for the twenty-first century in anticipation of an eventual electoral victory. Rather than tackling the fundamental causes of the outstanding international problems and charting means to resolve them, their blueprint called on the United States to exercise its "imperial calling" and assert its political worldview and ideology on the hapless planet. On the whole, their blueprint underscores a geopolitical preoccupation with the Middle East and betrays an obsession with the need to secure and control the sources of oil "for a long time to come."

In the spring of 1997, the "Project for the New American Century" was cofounded by William Kristol, the editor of *The Weekly Standard*, and Robert Kagan, a leading neoconservative protagonist and publicist.[9] The organization included Gary Schmitt, John R. Bolton, Devon G. Cross, and Bruce Jackson. Other prominent intellectual neocons and proponents of right-wing Zionist objectives in the Middle East also contributed crucial input to the theoretical framework for a more aggressive American foreign policy in that region. Among these, Norman Podhoretz, Richard Perle, Lewis Libby, Elliott Abrams, Michael Ledeen, Frank Gafney, Jr., Paul Wolfowitz and their intellectual mentor, William Kristol's father, Irving Kristol, are worthy of mention.

In September 2000, the fateful blueprint was drafted under the principal authorship of Thomas Donnelly, by a think tank working from an original manuscript purportedly drafted by Dick Cheney and I. Lewis Libby. The blueprint "*Rebuilding America's Defenses—Strategy, Forces and Resources For a New Century*" was finalized in cooperation with Donald Rumsfeld and Paul Wolfowitz before George W. Bush's accession to the Presidency.[10]

The blueprint brings substantive alterations to two earlier congressionally mandated studies, and to the *Defense Policy Guidance*, which was drafted when Cheney served as Secretary of Defense. It bears all the earmarks of a grand strategy and reflects an aggressive interventionist political mentality reminiscent of the heyday of the Roman Empire.[11] This blueprint was axiomatic in the determination of the ill-advised and counterproductive Republican administration's foreign policy under George W. Bush. The tragedy of 9/11 provided the necessary political circumstance for its implementation and the propitious psychological environment for its positive public embrace.

The stated ultimate strategic objective of the blueprint's aggressive policy is, a priori, positive enough to promote "Western Civilization and Democracy." In fact, it masks, in its genericity, a similar objective enunciated by previous imperial powers. Did not the European Mercantile Powers, during the great Age of Explorations assert, as objective, the duty to "civilize the world and spread the Gospel and Christianity?" And was not the justification advanced by nineteenth century Western colonialists, to spread European culture and civilization among the natives? Did not France claim a "*Mission Civilisatrice?*"

The United States, the authors of the blueprint assert in their introduction, having emerged as the sole and unrivalled world superpower, combines

> preeminent military power, global technological leadership, and [enjoys] the world's largest economy . . . [it] stands at the head of a system of alliances which includes the world's other leading democratic powers . . . . [Consequently, its] grand strategy should aim to preserve and extend this advantageous position as far into the future as possible.

To prevent the emergence of eventual, competing, challenging rival states, the blueprint further states: "The challenge for the coming century is to preserve and enhance this American Peace by reserving the right to engage in unilateral international initiatives, including preemptive military actions, regardless of the will of the International community." Thus the need for "a military that is strong and ready to meet both present and future challenges; a foreign policy that boldly and purposefully promotes American principles abroad; and national leadership that accepts the United States global responsibilities . . . "

The authors also recommend, among other things, the creation of a new U.S. military: "Space Forces with the mission of space control. . . . " They conclude with this sentence, " . . . the failure to prepare for tomorrow's challenges will ensure that the current [Pax Americana] comes to an early end."[12]

Are there not, also in this document, eerie reminders of the hubristic, hegemonic objectives once held by the collapsed Soviet empire, whose stated objective was a *Pax Sovietica,* a world shaped after its own conception of a socialist nirvana? Does not one also perceive in the neocons' grand world design, a narrow missionary zeal similar to that of al-Qā'ida, whose grand strategy is a *Pax Islamica*?

Of particular relevance to the issue of Muslim sensitivities, and to anti-Western resentment, in the context of policies giving rise to what we have termed "reactionary terrorism," is the authors' imperative determination to dominate the Persian Gulf region.

They argued that the region was "of vital importance," demanding "the long-term commitment of the United States," the establishment there of "a substantial American force presence " and the need to deal with " the issue of the regime of Saddam Hussein."[13] One finds in this determination, the obvious reference to premeditation in the invasion of Iraq, irrespective of Saddam Hussein's compliance or noncompliance with United Nations Resolutions.

To the neocons, therefore, the 9/11 terrorist attacks were indeed a God-sent tragic opportunity, justifying the forceful implantation of an American military presence in the Persian/Arabian Gulf, a *sine qua non* to a desire for joint American-Israeli regional condominium.

Afghanistan itself had, of course, long been a theater of not-so-clandestine U.S. intervention, as aid and support were provided to the islāmist Taliban and al-Qā'ida during their struggle against Communist rule and the Soviet presence. In the past several decades, the world has witnessed a senseless, lethal, international game of politically revolving chairs, with changing alliances involving Western powers and nations of the greater Middle East. This opportunism has rendered us, as it were, coarchitects of the transnational islāmist power structure, an unwitting midwife in the birth of transnational terrorism and the ongoing clash of cultures.

In the final analysis, the emergence of international islāmist jihādism may prove to be, despite its lack of technological sophistication, a political pole to be counterbalanced, and a more pernicious threat to humanity than the "balance of terror" that characterized the Cold War; for if the seductive nature of Communism resided in its promise of an earthbound, materialistic nirvana, the eschatology inherent in islāmist jihādism transcends, in its promise, the physical ephemerality of that nirvana and provides anthropomorphized eternal felicity and joy, an infinitely more seductive bargain.

The unavoidable, unintended consequence of American political opportunism in the Greater Middle East, coupled with equivocations and lack of fairness in the eternalized conflict between Israel and Palestine, and Lebanon and Syria, have exacerbated Muslim resentment of Western power; this has mutated the focal point of the original rage they harbored against the modernist, political leadership of their respective countries into a pernicious rage against the United States, the perceived threat to their faith and way of life. This is stimulating the ascendancy of transnational islāmist sentiments throughout the Muslim world, particularly in Iran, Pakistan, Egypt, Iraq, Palestine, the Philippines, Indonesia, in all the former Soviet Muslim Republics, and even among discontented Muslim immigrants in Western countries.

Sadly, "Democracy in America" is progressively disfigured; the ever-growing national concern over security is eroding personal freedoms; the constitutional ideal of "life, liberty and the pursuit of happiness" is equated, today, more with unbridled capitalism than with the enlightened democracy envisaged by the Founding Fathers. Democracy, consequently, has virtually become amorphous, devoid of checks and balances, and increasingly defined by the privilege of voting for candidates configured by lobbyists. Politicians are more interested in promoting the objectives of those who finance their reelection, than in serving the best interests of the nation. The obsession with reelection has turned them into puppets in the hands of multinational conglomerates and domestic, foreign, and quasi-international lobbies. Indeed, democracy in America today is shackled by self-serving plutocrats; the United States of America has become a virtual "lobbycracy." Circles of wealthy individuals and lobbies compete to control the nation's destiny, and personal wealth, or the ability to raise millions determines a politician's suitability for endorsement as candidate by a political party.

Given these circumstances, the ultimate determination of domestic policies depends more on leaders favoring business interests, than on those more favorable to the middle class, labor, health, education, and social welfare. In international politics—of particular interest to this essay—the important issues of national interest, justice, democracy, and human rights are approached subjectively, and their determination equally shaped by lobbying interests.

Thus the U.S. military force, dispatched to Sa'ūdi Arabia to liberate Kuwait in 1990, should have been withdrawn soon after its objective was attained. Instead, it was meant to remain there permanently, to control the oil-rich Middle East and to enhance Israel's security, as envisaged in the Twenty-First Century Project's blueprint, "Rebuilding America's Defenses: Strategies, Forces and Resources for a New Century."[14]

Unwittingly perhaps, the unwelcome, lasting presence of "infidel troops" in the most sacred land of Islām, confirmed in the minds of countless xenophobic Muslims around the world, the jihādist claim that a new crusade, led by the United States, was in progress; hence the islāmist imperative to combat it by all means. A crucial religious dimension was thereby added to the hypernationalism—born of the colonial memory—and to the sensitive issue of justice to the Palestinians.

A more suitable strategy to fight the "Global War on Terror," is for the United States to urge the United Nations to assist Muslim intellectuals and Qur'ānic scholars of all persuasions and inclinations to plan, organize, and institutionalize world Islamic symposia to study and chart strategies consistent with twenty-first century conditions and exigencies.

The deliberations should be televised, and they should have an interactive component to allow for the widest possible intellectual participation; the rehumanization of the marginalized individuals and sects, and their reintegration into civil society might very well prove to be more effective in securing peace than the use of military might. The United Nations should also urge the institution of global ecumenical dialogues to foster interfaith, intercultural, and intersocietal tolerance and harmony, and minimize the fundamental social, political, and economic disparity that sows resentment and hatred among haves and have-nots and often leads to terrorist violence.

In Lebanon and in Palestine, Israeli occupation—tolerated by successive United States governments—has provoked the emergence of angry nationalist militias seeking freedom and independence at any cost. Some of these have limited themselves to civil national liberation activities, while others have become infected with the virus of misguided religious eschatology. Responsibility, therefore, for the emergence of anti-Western transnational jihādism must be shared by those who have provided the Petri dish for the incubation of this virus. They are the alchemists of the dehumanizing behemoth, injustice, the primogeniture of power.

One indeed wonders how much longer we are going to let our shortsighted and self-serving politicians bounce our nation from the embrace of Scylla into that of Charybdis.

In the global war against terrorism, the United States Government, by diverting its effort from Afghanistan to Iraq and by opting for a global imperialist agenda, has neglected the needed concentration of financial and military means to keep al-Qā'ida in check and swiftly pacify, unite, rebuild, and develop Afghanistan into an expression of America's goodwill toward its enemies. This scuttled opportunity is leading to a dangerous resurgence of Talibanism in Afghanistan, threatening the survival of the new regime in Kabul and laying waste the noble sacrifices of our brave soldiers.

Additionally, this egregious error, by lengthening the war in Afghanistan and involving tribes sympathetic to the Talibans, in autonomous Waziristan, is damaging our alliance with Pakistan and threatening the very existence of President Musharraf's regime. This error, furthermore, is also likely to set back the modernization of the Muslim world generally, by emboldening islāmists everywhere. The electoral landslide of Hamas in the Palestinian elections is a direct consequence of this and earlier administrations' blunders. The neocons' fantasy of imposing democracies in the Arab World to insure the security of Israel, is backfiring; democratic elections in the Arab Muslim states can only help the islāmists. Democracy is an evolutionary phenomenon; it has to develop from within.

Obsessed with imperial dreams, convinced of its moral superiority, lured by the scent of "black gold," inspired by evangelical fundamentalist theopolitical concepts, and guided by key Zionist mentors and lobbies, the George W. Bush Administration has pilfered the nation's prestige, warped its reputation around the world, and needlessly wasted assets and that most precious of resources, human lives, both American and Iraqi—*Ubi solitudinem faciunt, pacem appellant.*[15]

Appendix

UNITED NATIONS SECURITY COUNCIL RESOLUTION 242

November 22, 1967

The Security Council,

Expressing its continuing concern with the grave situation in the Middle East,

Emphasizing the inadmissibility of the acquisition of territory by war and the need to work for a just and lasting peace in which every State in the area can live in security,

Emphasizing further that all Member States in their acceptance of the Charter of the United Nations have undertaken a commitment to act in accordance with Article 2 of the Charter,

1. *Affirms* that the fulfilment of Charter principles requires the establishment of a just and lasting peace in the Middle East which should include the application of both the following principles:
   (i) Withdrawal of Israel armed forces from territories occupied in the recent conflict;
   (ii) Termination of all claims or states of belligerency and respect for and acknowledgment of the sovereignty, territorial integrity and political

independence of every State in the area and their right to live in peace within secure and recognized boundaries free from threats or acts of force;

2. *Affirms further* the necessity
   (a) For guaranteeing freedom of navigation through international waterways in the area;
   (b) For achieving a just settlement of the refugee problem;
   (c) For guaranteeing the territorial inviolability and political independence of every State in the area, through measures including the establishment of demilitarized zones;
3. *Requests* the Secretary-General to designate a Special Representative to proceed to the Middle East to establish and maintain contacts with the States concerned in order to promote agreement and assist efforts to achieve a peaceful and accepted settlement in accordance with the provisions and principles in this resolution;
4. *Requests* the Secretary-General to report to the Security Council on the progress of the efforts of the Special Representative as soon as possible.

telaviv.usembassy.gov/.

II

U.N. SECURITY COUNCIL RESOLUTION 338

October 22, 1973

In the later stages of the Yom Kippur War—after Israel repulsed the Syrian attack on the Golan Heights and established a bridgehead on the Egyptian side of the Suez Canal—international efforts to stop the fighting were intensified. US Secretary of State, Kissinger flew to Moscow on October 20, and, together with the Soviet Government, the US proposed a cease-fire resolution in the UN Security Council. The Council met on October 21 at the urgent request of both the US and the USSR, and by fourteen votes to none, adopted the following resolution:

The Security Council,

1. Calls upon all parties to present fighting to cease all firing and terminate all military activity immediately, no later than 12 hours after the moment of the adoption of this decision, in the positions after the moment of the adoption of this decision, in the positions they now occupy;
2. Calls upon all parties concerned to start immediately after the cease-fire the implementation of Security Council Resolution 242 (1967) in all of its parts;

3. Decides that, immediately and concurrently with the cease-fire, negotiations start between the parties concerned under appropriate auspices aimed at establishing a just and durable peace in the Middle East.

telaviv.usembassy.gov/

III

THE GENEVA ACCORD

Preamble

The State of Israel (hereinafter "Israel") and the Palestine Liberation Organization (hereinafter "PLO"), the representative of the Palestinian people (hereinafter the "Parties"):

Reaffirming their determination to put an end to decades of confrontation and conflict, and to live in peaceful coexistence, mutual dignity and security based on a just, lasting, and comprehensive peace and achieving historic reconciliation;

Recognizing that peace requires the transition from the logic of war and confrontation to the logic of peace and cooperation, and that acts and words characteristic of the state of war are neither appropriate nor acceptable in the era of peace;

Affirming their deep belief that the logic of peace requires compromise, and that the only viable solution is a two-state solution based on UNSC Resolution 242 and 338;

Affirming that this agreement marks the recognition of the right of the Jewish people to statehood and the recognition of the right of the Palestinian people to statehood, without prejudice to the equal rights of the Parties' respective citizens;

Recognizing that after years of living in mutual fear and insecurity, both peoples need to enter an era of peace, security and stability, entailing all necessary actions by the parties to guarantee the realization of this era;

Recognizing each other's right to peaceful and secure existence within secure and recognized boundaries free from threats or acts of force;

Determined to establish relations based on cooperation and the commitment to live side by side as good neighbors aiming both separately and jointly to contribute to the well-being of their peoples;

Reaffirming their obligation to conduct themselves in conformity with the norms of international law and the Charter of the United Nations;

Confirming that this Agreement is concluded within the framework of the Middle East peace process initiated in Madrid in October 1991, the Declaration of

Principles of September 13, 1993, the subsequent agreements including the Interim Agreement of September 1995, the Wye River Memorandum of October 1998 and the Sharm El-Sheikh Memorandum of September 4, 1999, and the permanent status negotiations including the Camp David Summit of July 2000, the Clinton Ideas of December 2000, and the Taba Negotiations of January 2001;

Reiterating their commitment to United Nations Security Council Resolutions 242, 338 and 1397 and confirming their understanding that this Agreement is based on, will lead to, and—by its fulfillment—will constitute the full implementation of these resolutions and to the settlement of the Israeli-Palestinian conflict in all its aspects;

Declaring that this Agreement constitutes the realization of the permanent status peace component envisaged in President Bush's speech of June 24, 2002 and in the Quartet Roadmap process;

Declaring that this Agreement marks the historic reconciliation between the Palestinians and Israelis, and paves the way to reconciliation between the Arab World and Israel and the establishment of normal, peaceful relations between the Arab states and Israel in accordance with the relevant clauses of the Beirut Arab League Resolution of March 28, 2002; and

Resolved to pursue the goal of attaining a comprehensive regional peace, thus contributing to stability, security, development and prosperity throughout the region;

Have agreed on the following:

Article 1—Purpose of the Permanent Status Agreement

1. The Permanent Status Agreement (hereinafter "this Agreement") ends the era of conflict and ushers in a new era based on peace, cooperation, and good neighborly relations between the Parties.
2. The implementation of this Agreement will settle all the claims of the Parties arising from events occurring prior to its signature. No further claims related to events prior to this Agreement may be raised by either Party.

Article 2—Relations between the Parties

1. The state of Israel shall recognize the state of Palestine (hereinafter "Palestine") upon its establishment. The state of Palestine shall immediately recognize the state of Israel.
2. The state of Palestine shall be the successor to the PLO with all its rights and obligations.
3. Israel and Palestine shall immediately establish full diplomatic and consular relations with each other and will exchange resident Ambassadors, within one month of their mutual recognition.

4. The Parties recognize Palestine and Israel as the homelands of their respective peoples. The Parties are committed not to interfere in each other's internal affairs.
5. This Agreement supercedes all prior agreements between the Parties.
6. Without prejudice to the commitments undertaken by them in this Agreement, relations between Israel and Palestine shall be based upon the provisions of the Charter of the United Nations.
7. With a view to the advancement of the relations between the two States and peoples, Palestine and Israel shall cooperate in areas of common interest. These shall include, but are not limited to, dialogue between their legislatures and state institutions, cooperation between their appropriate local authorities, promotion of non-governmental civil society cooperation, and joint programs and exchange in the areas of culture, media, youth, science, education, environment, health, agriculture, tourism, and crime prevention. The Israeli-Palestinian Cooperation Committee will oversee this cooperation in accordance with Article 8.
8. The Parties shall cooperate in areas of joint economic interest, to best realize the human potential of their respective peoples. In this regard, they will work bilaterally, regionally, and with the international community to maximize the benefit of peace to the broadest cross-section of their respective populations. Relevant standing bodies shall be established by the Parties to this effect.
9. The Parties shall establish robust modalities for security cooperation, and engage in a comprehensive and uninterrupted effort to end terrorism and violence directed against each others persons, property, institutions or territory. This effort shall continue at all times, and shall be insulated from any possible crises and other aspects of the Parties' relations.
10. Israel and Palestine shall work together and separately with other parties in the region to enhance and promote regional cooperation and coordination in spheres of common interest.
11. The Parties shall establish a ministerial-level Palestinian-Israeli High Steering Committee to guide, monitor, and facilitate the process of implementation of this Agreement, both bilaterally and in accordance with the mechanisms in Article 3 hereunder.

Article 3—Implementation and Verification Group

1. Establishment and Composition
   i. An Implementation and Verification Group (IVG) shall hereby be established to facilitate, assist in, guarantee, monitor, and resolve disputes relating to the implementation of this Agreement.
   ii. The IVG shall include the US, the Russian Federation, the EU, the UN, and other parties, both regional and international, to be agreed on by the Parties.

    iii. The IVG shall work in coordination with the Palestinian-Israeli High Steering Committee established in Article 2/11 above and subsequent to that with the Israeli-Palestinian Cooperation Committee (IPCC) established in Article 8 hereunder.

    iv. The structure, procedures, and modalities of the IVG are set forth below and detailed in Annex X.

2. Structure

    i. A senior political-level contact group (Contact Group), composed of all the IVG members, shall be the highest authority in the IVG.

    ii. The Contact Group shall appoint, in consultation with the Parties, a Special Representative who will be the principal executive of the IVG on the ground. The Special Representative shall manage the work of the IVG and maintain constant contact with the Parties, the Palestinian-Israeli High Steering Committee, and the Contact Group.

    iii. The IVG permanent headquarters and secretariat shall be based in an agreed upon location in Jerusalem.

    iv. The IVG shall establish its bodies referred to in this Agreement and additional bodies as it deems necessary. These bodies shall be an integral part of and under the authority of the IVG.

    v. The Multinational Force (MF) established under Article 5 shall be an integral part of the IVG. The Special Representative shall, subject to the approval of the Parties, appoint the Commander of the MF who shall be responsible for the daily command of the MF. Details relating to the Special Representative and MF Force Commander are set forth in Annex X.

    vi. The IVG shall establish a dispute settlement mechanism, in accordance with Article 16.

3. Coordination with the Parties

A Trilateral Committee composed of the Special Representative and the Palestinian-Israeli High Steering Committee shall be established and shall meet on at least a monthly basis to review the implementation of this Agreement. The Trilateral Committee will convene within 48 hours upon the request of any of the three parties represented.

4. Functions

In addition to the functions specified elsewhere in this Agreement, the IVG shall:

    i. Take appropriate measures based on the reports it receives from the MF,

    ii. Assist the Parties in implementing the Agreement and preempt and promptly mediate disputes on the ground.

5. Termination

In accordance with the progress in the implementation of this Agreement, and with the fulfillment of the specific mandated functions, the IVG shall terminate its activities in the said spheres. The IVG shall continue to exist unless otherwise agreed by the Parties.

Article 4—Territory

1. The International Borders between the States of Palestine and Israel
   i. In accordance with UNSC Resolution 242 and 338, the border between the states of Palestine and Israel shall be based on the June 4th 1967 lines with reciprocal modifications on a 1:1 basis as set forth in attached Map 1.
   ii. The Parties recognize the border, as set out in attached Map 1, as the permanent, secure and recognized international boundary between them.
2. Sovereignty and Inviolability
   i. The Parties recognize and respect each other's sovereignty, territorial integrity, and political independence, as well as the inviolability of each others territory, including territorial waters, and airspace. They shall respect this inviolability in accordance with this Agreement, the UN Charter, and other rules of international law.
   ii. The Parties recognize each other's rights in their exclusive economic zones in accordance with international law.
3. Israeli Withdrawal
   i. Israel shall withdraw in accordance with Article 5.
   ii. Palestine shall assume responsibility for the areas from which Israel withdraws.
   iii. The transfer of authority from Israel to Palestine shall be in accordance with Annex X.
   iv. The IVG shall monitor, verify, and facilitate the implementation of this Article.
4. Demarcation
   i. A Joint Technical Border Commission (Commission) composed of the two Parties shall be established to conduct the technical demarcation of the border in accordance with this Article. The procedures governing the work of this Commission are set forth in Annex X.
   ii. Any disagreement in the Commission shall be referred to the IVG in accordance with Annex X.
   iii. The physical demarcation of the international borders shall be completed by the Commission not later than nine months from the date of the entry into force of this Agreement.
5. Settlements
   i. The state of Israel shall be responsible for resettling the Israelis residing in Palestinian sovereign territory outside this territory.
   ii. The resettlement shall be completed according to the schedule stipulated in Article 5.
   iii. Existing arrangements in the West Bank and Gaza Strip regarding Israeli settlers and settlements, including security, shall remain in force in

each of the settlements until the date prescribed in the timetable for the completion of the evacuation of the relevant settlement.

iv. Modalities for the assumption of authority over settlements by Palestine are set forth in Annex X. The IVG shall resolve any disputes that may arise during its implementation.

v. Israel shall keep intact the immovable property, infrastructure and facilities in Israeli settlements to be transferred to Palestinian sovereignty. An agreed inventory shall be drawn up by the Parties with the IVG in advance of the completion of the evacuation and in accordance with Annex X.

vi. The state of Palestine shall have exclusive title to all land and any buildings, facilities, infrastructure or other property remaining in any of the settlements on the date prescribed in the timetable for the completion of the evacuation of this settlement.

6. Corridor

i. The states of Palestine and Israel shall establish a corridor linking the West Bank and Gaza Strip. This corridor shall:

a. Be under Israeli sovereignty.

b. Be permanently open.

c. Be under Palestinian administration in accordance with Annex X of this Agreement. Palestinian law shall apply to persons using and procedures appertaining to the corridor.

d. Not disrupt Israeli transportation and other infrastructural networks, or endanger the environment, public safety or public health. Where necessary, engineering solutions will be sought to avoid such disruptions.

e. Allow for the establishment of the necessary infrastructural facilities linking the West Bank and the Gaza Strip. Infrastructural facilities shall be understood to include, inter alia, pipelines, electrical and communications cables, and associated equipment as detailed in Annex X.

f. Not be used in contravention of this Agreement.

ii. Defensive barriers shall be established along the corridor and Palestinians shall not enter Israel from this corridor, nor shall Israelis enter Palestine from the corridor.

iii. The Parties shall seek the assistance of the international community in securing the financing for the corridor.

iv. The IVG shall guarantee the implementation of this Article in accordance with Annex X.

v. Any disputes arising between the Parties from the operation of the corridor shall be resolved in accordance with Article 16.

vi. The arrangements set forth in this clause may only be terminated or revised by agreement of both Parties.

Article 5—Security

1. General Security Provisions
   i. The Parties acknowledge that mutual understanding and co-operation in security-related matters will form a significant part of their bilateral relations and will further enhance regional security. Palestine and Israel shall base their security relations on cooperation, mutual trust, good neighborly relations, and the protection of their joint interests.
   ii. Palestine and Israel each shall:
      a. Recognize and respect the other's right to live in peace within secure and recognized boundaries free from the threat or acts of war, terrorism and violence;
      b. refrain from the threat or use of force against the territorial integrity or political independence of the other and shall settle all disputes between them by peaceful means;
      c. refrain from joining, assisting, promoting or co-operating with any coalition, organization or alliance of a military or security character, the objectives or activities of which include launching aggression or other acts of hostility against the other;
      d. refrain from organizing, encouraging, or allowing the formation of irregular forces or armed bands, including mercenaries and militias within their respective territory and prevent their establishment. In this respect, any existing irregular forces or armed bands shall be disbanded and prevented from reforming at any future date;
      e. refrain from organizing, assisting, allowing, or participating in acts of violence in or against the other or acquiescing in activities directed toward the commission of such acts.
   iii. To further security cooperation, the Parties shall establish a high level Joint Security Committee that shall meet on at least a monthly basis. The Joint Security Committee shall have a permanent joint office, and may establish such sub-committees as it deems necessary, including sub-committees to immediately resolve localized tensions.
2. Regional Security
   i. Israel and Palestine shall work together with their neighbors and the international community to build a secure and stable Middle East, free from weapons of mass destruction, both conventional and nonconventional, in the context of a comprehensive, lasting, and stable peace, characterized by reconciliation, goodwill, and the renunciation of the use of force.
   ii. To this end, the Parties shall work together to establish a regional security regime.
3. Defense Characteristics of the Palestinian State

    i. No armed forces, other than as specified in this Agreement, will be deployed or stationed in Palestine.

    ii. Palestine shall be a non-militarized state, with a strong security force. Accordingly, the limitations on the weapons that may be purchased, owned, or used by the Palestinian Security Force (PSF) or manufactured in Palestine shall be specified in Annex X. Any proposed changes to Annex X shall be considered by a trilateral committee composed of the two Parties and the MF. If no agreement is reached in the trilateral committee, the IVG may make its own recommendations.

        a. No individuals or organizations in Palestine other than the PSF and the organs of the IVG, including the MF, may purchase, possess, carry or use weapons except as provided by law.

    iii. The PSF shall:

        a. Maintain border control;

        b. Maintain law-and-order and perform police functions;

        c. Perform intelligence and security functions;

        d. Prevent terrorism;

        e. Conduct rescue and emergency missions; and

        f. Supplement essential community services when necessary.

        g. The MF shall monitor and verify compliance with this clause.

4. Terrorism

    i. The Parties reject and condemn terrorism and violence in all its forms and shall pursue public policies accordingly. In addition, the parties shall refrain from actions and policies that are liable to nurture extremism and create conditions conducive to terrorism on either side.

    ii. The Parties shall take joint and, in their respective territories, unilateral comprehensive and continuous efforts against all aspects of violence and terrorism. These efforts shall include the prevention and preemption of such acts, and the prosecution of their perpetrators.

    iii. To that end, the Parties shall maintain ongoing consultation, cooperation, and exchange of information between their respective security forces.

    iv. A Trilateral Security Committee composed of the two Parties and the United States shall be formed to ensure the implementation of this Article. The Trilateral Security Committee shall develop comprehensive policies and guidelines to fight terrorism and violence.

5. Incitement

    i. Without prejudice to freedom of expression and other internationally recognized human rights, Israel and Palestine shall promulgate laws to prevent incitement to irredentism, racism, terrorism and violence and vigorously enforce them.

    ii. The IVG shall assist the Parties in establishing guidelines for the implementation of this clause, and shall monitor the Parties' adherence thereto.

6. Multinational Force
   i. A Multinational Force (MF) shall be established to provide security guarantees to the Parties, act as a deterrent, and oversee the implementation of the relevant provisions of this Agreement.
   ii. The composition, structure and size of the MF are set forth in Annex X.
   iii. To perform the functions specified in this Agreement, the MF shall be deployed in the state of Palestine. The MF shall enter into the appropriate Status of Forces Agreement (SOFA) with the state of Palestine.
   iv. In accordance with this Agreement, and as detailed in Annex X, the MF shall:
      a. In light of the non-militarized nature of the Palestinian state, protect the territorial integrity of the state of Palestine.
      b. Serve as a deterrent against external attacks that could threaten either of the Parties.
      c. Deploy observers to areas adjacent to the lines of the Israeli withdrawal during the phases of this withdrawal, in accordance with Annex X.
      d. Deploy observers to monitor the territorial and maritime borders of the state of Palestine, as specified in clause 5/13.
      e. Perform the functions on the Palestinian international border crossings specified in clause 5/12.
      f. Perform the functions relating to the early warning stations as specified in clause 5/8.
      g. Perform the functions specified in clause 5/3.
      h. Perform the functions specified in clause 5/7.
      i. Perform the functions specified in Article 10.
      j. Help in the enforcement of anti-terrorism measures.
      k. Help in the training of the PSF.
   v. In relation to the above, the MF shall report to and update the IVG in accordance with Annex X.
   vi. The MF shall only be withdrawn or have its mandate changed by agreement of the Parties.
7. Evacuation
   i. Israel shall withdraw all its military and security personnel and equipment, including landmines, and all persons employed to support them, and all military installations from the territory of the state of Palestine, except as otherwise agreed in Annex X, in stages.
   ii. The staged withdrawals shall commence immediately upon entry into force of this Agreement and shall be made in accordance with the timetable and modalities set forth in Annex X.
   iii. The stages shall be designed subject to the following principles:
      a. The need to create immediate clear contiguity and facilitate the early implementation of Palestinian development plans.

> b. Israel's capacity to relocate, house and absorb settlers. While costs and inconveniences are inherent in such a process, these shall not be unduly disruptive.
> c. The need to construct and operationalize the border between the two states.
> d. The introduction and effective functioning of the MF, in particular on the eastern border of the state of Palestine.

> iv. Accordingly, the withdrawal shall be implemented in the following stages:
>> (a). The first stage shall include the areas of the state of Palestine, as defined in Map X, and shall be completed within 9 months.
>> (b). The second and third stages shall include the remainder of the territory of the state of Palestine and shall be completed within 21 months of the end of the first stage.

> v. Israel shall complete its withdrawal from the territory of the state of Palestine within 30 months of the entry into force of this Agreement, and in accordance with this Agreement.
> vi. Israel will maintain a small military presence in the Jordan Valley under the authority of the MF and subject to the MF SOFA as detailed in Annex X for an additional 36 months. The stipulated period may be reviewed by the Parties in the event of relevant regional developments, and may be altered by the Parties' consent.
> vii. In accordance with Annex X, the MF shall monitor and verify compliance with this clause.

8. Early Warning Stations
> i. Israel may maintain two EWS in the northern, and central West Bank at the locations set forth in Annex X.
> ii. The EWS shall be staffed by the minimal required number of Israeli personnel and shall occupy the minimal amount of land necessary for their operation as set forth in Annex X.
> iii. Access to the EWS will be guaranteed and escorted by the MF.
> iv. Internal security of the EWS shall be the responsibility of Israel. The perimeter security of the EWS shall be the responsibility of the MF.
> v. The MF and the PSF shall maintain a liaison presence in the EWS. The MF shall monitor and verify that the EWS is being used for purposes recognized by this Agreement as detailed in Annex X.
> vi. The arrangements set forth in this Article shall be subject to review in ten years, with any changes to be mutually agreed. Thereafter, there will be five-yearly reviews whereby the arrangements set forth in this Article may be extended by mutual consent.
> vii. At any point during the period specified above a regional security regime is established, then the IVG may request that the Parties review whether to continue or revise operational uses for the EWS in light of these

developments. Any such change will require the mutual consent of the Parties.

9. Airspace
   i. Civil Aviation
      a. The Parties recognize as applicable to each other the rights, privileges and obligations provided for by the multilateral aviation agreements to which they are both party, particularly by the 1944 Convention on International Civil Aviation (The Chicago Convention) and the 1944 International Air Services Transit Agreement.
      b. In addition, the Parties shall, upon entry into force of this Agreement, establish a trilateral committee composed of the two Parties and the IVG to design the most efficient management system for civil aviation, including those relevant aspects of the air traffic control system. In the absence of consensus the IVG may make its own recommendations.
   ii. Training
      a. The Israeli Air Force shall be entitled to use the Palestinian sovereign airspace for training purposes in accordance with Annex X, which shall be based on rules pertaining to IAF use of Israeli airspace.
      b. The IVG shall monitor and verify compliance with this clause. Either Party may submit a complaint to the IVG whose decision shall be conclusive.
      c. The arrangements set forth in this clause shall be subject to review every ten years, and may be altered or terminated by the agreement of both Parties.

10. Electromagnetic Sphere
    i. Neither Party's use of the electromagnetic sphere may interfere with the other Party's use.
    ii. Annex X shall detail arrangements relating to the use of the electromagnetic sphere.
    iii. The IVG shall monitor and verify the implementation of this clause and Annex X.
    iv. Any Party may submit a complaint to the IVG whose decision shall be conclusive.

11. Law Enforcement
    The Israeli and Palestinian law enforcement agencies shall cooperate in combating illicit drug trafficking, illegal trafficking in archaeological artifacts and objects of arts, cross-border crime, including theft and fraud, organized crime, trafficking in women and minors, counterfeiting, pirate TV and radio stations, and other illegal activity.

12. International Border Crossings
    i. The following arrangements shall apply to borders crossing between the state of Palestine and Jordan, the state of Palestine and Egypt, as well as airport and seaport entry points to the state of Palestine.

   ii. All border crossings shall be monitored by joint teams composed of members of the PSF and the MF. These teams shall prevent the entry into Palestine of any weapons, materials or equipment that are in contravention of the provisions of this Agreement.

  iii. The MF representatives and the PSF will have, jointly and separately, the authority to block the entry into Palestine of any such items. If at any time a disagreement regarding the entrance of goods or materials arises between the PSF and the MF representatives, the PSF may bring the matter to the IVG, whose binding conclusions shall be rendered within 24 hours.

  iv. This arrangement shall be reviewed by the IVG after 5 years to determine its continuation, modification or termination. Thereafter, the Palestinian party may request such a review on an annual basis.

   v. In passenger terminals, for thirty months, Israel may maintain an unseen presence in a designated on-site facility, to be staffed by members of the MF and Israelis, utilizing appropriate technology. The Israeli side may request that the MF-PSF conduct further inspections and take appropriate action.

  vi. For the following two years, these arrangements will continue in a specially designated facility in Israel, utilizing appropriate technology. This shall not cause delays beyond the procedures outlined in this clause.

 vii. In cargo terminals, for thirty months, Israel may maintain an unseen presence in a designated on-site facility, to be staffed by members of the MF and Israelis, utilizing appropriate technology. The Israeli side may request that the MF-PSF conduct further inspections and take appropriate action. If the Israeli side is not satisfied by the MF-PSF action, it may demand that the cargo be detained pending a decision by an MF inspector. The MF inspector's decision shall be binding and final, and shall be rendered within 12 hours of the Israeli complaint.

 viii. For the following three years, these arrangements will continue from a specially designated facility in Israel, utilizing appropriate technology. This shall not cause delays beyond the timelines outlined in this clause.

  ix. A high level trilateral committee composed of representatives of Palestine, Israel, and the IVG shall meet regularly to monitor the application of these procedures and correct any irregularities, and may be convened on request.

   x. The details of the above are set forth in Annex X.

13. Border Control

   i. The PSF shall maintain border control as detailed in Annex X.

  ii. The MF shall monitor and verify the maintenance of border control by the PSF.

Article 6—Jerusalem

1. Religious and Cultural Significance:

i. The Parties recognize the universal historic, religious, spiritual, and cultural significance of Jerusalem and its holiness enshrined in Judaism, Christianity, and Islam. In recognition of this status, the Parties reaffirm their commitment to safeguard the character, holiness, and freedom of worship in the city and to respect the existing division of administrative functions and traditional practices between different denominations.

ii. The Parties shall establish an inter-faith body consisting of representatives of the three monotheistic faiths, to act as a consultative body to the Parties on matters related to the city's religious significance and to promote inter-religious understanding and dialogue. The composition, procedures, and modalities for this body are set forth in Annex X.

2. Capital of Two States
The Parties shall have their mutually recognized capitals in the areas of Jerusalem under their respective sovereignty.

3. Sovereignty
Sovereignty in Jerusalem shall be in accordance with attached Map 2. This shall not prejudice nor be prejudiced by the arrangements set forth below.

4. Border Regime
The border regime shall be designed according to the provisions of Article 11, and taking into account the specific needs of Jerusalem (e.g., movement of tourists and intensity of border crossing use including provisions for Jerusalemites) and the provisions of this Article.

5. al-Haram al-Sharif/ Temple Mount (Compound)
i. International Group
a. An International Group, composed of the IVG and other parties to be agreed upon by the Parties, including members of the Organization of the Islamic Conference (OIC), shall hereby be established to monitor, verify, and assist in the implementation of this clause.
b. For this purpose, the International Group shall establish a Multinational Presence on the Compound, the composition, structure, mandate and functions of which are set forth in Annex X.
c. The Multinational Presence shall have specialized detachments dealing with security and conservation. The Multinational Presence shall make periodic conservation and security reports to the International Group. These reports shall be made public.
d. The Multinational Presence shall strive to immediately resolve any problems arising and may refer any unresolved disputes to the International Group that will function in accordance with Article 16.
e. The Parties may at any time request clarifications or submit complaints to the International Group which shall be promptly investigated and acted upon.
f. The International Group shall draw up rules and regulations to maintain security on and conservation of the Compound. These shall include lists of the weapons and equipment permitted on the site.

    ii. Regulations Regarding the Compound

        a. In view of the sanctity of the Compound, and in light of the unique religious and cultural significance of the site to the Jewish people, there shall be no digging, excavation, or construction on the Compound, unless approved by the two Parties. Procedures for regular maintenance and emergency repairs on the Compound shall be established by the IG after consultation with the Parties.

        b. The state of Palestine shall be responsible for maintaining the security of the Compound and for ensuring that it will not be used for any hostile acts against Israelis or Israeli areas. The only arms permitted on the Compound shall be those carried by the Palestinian security personnel and the security detachment of the Multinational Presence.

        c. In light of the universal significance of the Compound, and subject to security considerations and to the need not to disrupt religious worship or decorum on the site as determined by the Waqf, visitors shall be allowed access to the site. This shall be without any discrimination and generally be in accordance with past practice.

    iii. Transfer of Authority

        a. At the end of the withdrawal period stipulated in Article 5/7, the state of Palestine shall assert sovereignty over the Compound.

        b. The International Group and its subsidiary organs shall continue to exist and fulfill all the functions stipulated in this Article unless otherwise agreed by the two Parties.

6. The Wailing Wall

   The Wailing Wall shall be under Israeli sovereignty.

7. The Old City:

   i. Significance of the Old City

        a. The Parties view the Old City as one whole enjoying a unique character. The Parties agree that the preservation of this unique character together with safeguarding and promoting the welfare of the inhabitants should guide the administration of the Old City.

        b. The Parties shall act in accordance with the UNESCO World Cultural Heritage List regulations, in which the Old City is a registered site.

   ii. IVG Role in the Old City

        a. Cultural Heritage

           1. The IVG shall monitor and verify the preservation of cultural heritage in the Old City in accordance with the UNESCO World Cultural Heritage List rules. For this purpose, the IVG shall have free and unimpeded access to sites, documents, and information related to the performance of this function.

2. The IVG shall work in close coordination with the Old City Committee of the Jerusalem Coordination and Development Committee (JCDC), including in devising a restoration and preservation plan for the Old City.

b. Policing

1. The IVG shall establish an Old City Policing Unit (PU) to liaise with, coordinate between, and assist the Palestinian and Israeli police forces in the Old City, to defuse localized tensions and help resolve disputes, and to perform policing duties in locations specified in and according to operational procedures detailed in Annex X.

2. The PU shall periodically report to the IVG.

c. Either Party may submit complaints in relation to this clause to the IVG, which shall promptly act upon them in accordance with Article 16.

iii. Free Movement within the Old City

Movement within the Old City shall be free and unimpeded subject to the provisions of this article and rules and regulations pertaining to the various holy sites.

iv. Entry into and Exit from the Old City

a. Entry and exit points into and from the Old City will be staffed by the authorities of the state under whose sovereignty the point falls, with the presence of PU members, unless otherwise specified.

b. With a view to facilitating movement into the Old City, each Party shall take such measures at the entry points in its territory as to ensure the preservation of security in the Old City. The PU shall monitor the operation of the entry points.

c. Citizens of either Party may not exit the Old City into the territory of the other Party unless they are in possession of the relevant documentation that entitles them to. Tourists may only exit the Old City into the territory of the Party which they posses valid authorization to enter.

v. Suspension, Termination, and Expansion

a. Either Party may suspend the arrangements set forth in Article 6.7.iii in cases of emergency for one week. The extension of such suspension for longer than a week shall be pursuant to consultation with the other Party and the IVG at the Trilateral Committee established in Article 3/3.

b. This clause shall not apply to the arrangements set forth in Article 6/7/vi.

c. Three years after the transfer of authority over the Old City, the Parties shall review these arrangements. These arrangements may only be terminated by agreement of the Parties.

      d. The Parties shall examine the possibility of expanding these arrangements beyond the Old City and may agree to such an expansion.

  vi. Special Arrangements

      a. Along the way outlined in Map X (from the Jaffa Gate to the Zion Gate) there will be permanent and guaranteed arrangements for Israelis regarding access, freedom of movement, and security, as set forth in Annex X.

        1. The IVG shall be responsible for the implementation of these arrangements.

      b. Without prejudice to Palestinian sovereignty, Israeli administration of the Citadel will be as outlined in Annex X.

  vii. Color-Coding of the Old City

A visible color-coding scheme shall be used in the Old City to denote the sovereign areas of the respective Parties.

  viii. Policing

      a. An agreed number of Israeli police shall constitute the Israeli Old City police detachment and shall exercise responsibility for maintaining order and day-to-day policing functions in the area under Israeli sovereignty.

      b. An agreed number of Palestinian police shall constitute the Palestinian Old City police detachment and shall exercise responsibility for maintaining order and day-to-day policing functions in the area under Palestinian sovereignty.

      c. All members of the respective Israeli and Palestinian Old City police detachments shall undergo special training, including joint training exercises, to be administered by the PU.

      d. A special Joint Situation Room, under the direction of the PU and incorporating members of the Israeli and Palestinian Old City police detachments, shall facilitate liaison on all relevant matters of policing and security in the Old City.

  ix. Arms

No person shall be allowed to carry or possess arms in the Old City, with the exception of the Police Forces provided for in this agreement. In addition, each Party may grant special written permission to carry or possess arms in areas under its sovereignty.

  x. Intelligence and Security

      a. The Parties shall establish intensive intelligence cooperation regarding the Old City, including the immediate sharing of threat information.

      b. A trilateral committee composed of the two Parties and representatives of the United States shall be established to facilitate this cooperation.

8. Mount of Olives Cemetery

i. The area outlined in Map X (the Jewish Cemetery on the Mount of Olives) shall be under Israeli administration; Israeli law shall apply to persons using and procedures appertaining to this area in accordance with Annex X.

   a. There shall be a designated road to provide free, unlimited, and unimpeded access to the Cemetery.

   b. The IVG shall monitor the implementation of this clause.

   c. This arrangement may only be terminated by the agreement of both Parties.

9. Special Cemetery Arrangements

Arrangements shall be established in the two cemeteries designated in Map X (Mount Zion Cemetery and the German Colony Cemetery), to facilitate and ensure the continuation of the current burial and visitation practices, including the facilitation of access.

10. The Western Wall Tunnel

   i. The Western Wall Tunnel designated in Map X shall be under Israeli administration, including:

      a. Unrestricted Israeli access and right to worship and conduct religious practices.

      b. Responsibility for the preservation and maintenance of the site in accordance with this Agreement and without damaging structures above, under IVG supervision.

      c. Israeli policing.

      d. IVG monitoring

      e. The Northern Exit of the Tunnel shall only be used for exit and may only be closed in case of emergency as stipulated in Article 6/7.

   ii. This arrangement may only be terminated by the agreement of both Parties.

11. Municipal Coordination

   i. The two Jerusalem municipalities shall form a Jerusalem Co-ordination and Development Committee ("JCDC") to oversee the cooperation and coordination between the Palestinian Jerusalem municipality and the Israeli Jerusalem municipality. The JCDC and its sub-committees shall be composed of an equal number of representatives from Palestine and Israel. Each side will appoint members of the JCDC and its subcommittees in accordance with its own modalities.

   ii. The JCDC shall ensure that the coordination of infrastructure and services best serves the residents of Jerusalem, and shall promote the economic development of the city to the benefit of all. The JCDC will act to encourage cross-community dialogue and reconciliation.

   iii. The JCDC shall have the following subcommittees:

      a. A Planning and Zoning Committee: to ensure agreed planning and zoning regulations in areas designated in Annex X.

b. A Hydro Infrastructure Committee: to handle matters relating to drinking water delivery, drainage, and wastewater collection and treatment.

c. A Transport Committee: to coordinate relevant connectedness and compatibility of the two road systems and other issues pertaining to transport.

d. An Environmental Committee: to deal with environmental issues affecting the quality of life in the city, including solid waste management.

e. An Economic and Development Committee: to formulate plans for economic development in areas of joint interest, including in the areas of transportation, seam line commercial cooperation, and tourism.

f. A Police and Emergency Services Committee: to coordinate measures for the maintenance of public order and crime prevention and the provision of emergency services.

g. An Old City Committee: to plan and closely coordinate the joint provision of the relevant municipal services, and other functions stipulated in Article 6/7.

h. Other Committees as agreed in the JCDC.

12. Israeli Residency of Palestinian Jerusalemites
Palestinian Jerusalemites who currently are permanent residents of Israel shall lose this status upon the transfer of authority to Palestine of those areas in which they reside.

13. Transfer of authority
The Parties will apply in certain socio-economic spheres interim measures to ensure the agreed, expeditious, and orderly transfer of powers and obligations from Israel to Palestine. This shall be done in a manner that preserves the accumulated socio-economic rights of the residents of East Jerusalem.

Article 7—Refugees

1. Significance of the Refugee Problem
   i. The Parties recognize that, in the context of two independent states, Palestine and Israel, living side by side in peace, an agreed resolution of the refugee problem is necessary for achieving a just, comprehensive and lasting peace between them.
   ii. Such a resolution will also be central to stability building and development in the region.

2. UNGAR 194, UNSC Resolution 242, and the Arab Peace Initiative
   i. The Parties recognize that UNGAR 194, UNSC Resolution 242, and the Arab Peace Initiative (Article 2.ii.) concerning the rights of the Palestinian refugees represent the basis for resolving the refugee issue,

and agree that these rights are fulfilled according to Article 7 of this Agreement.

3. Compensation

   i. Refugees shall be entitled to compensation for their refugeehood and for loss of property. This shall not prejudice or be prejudiced by the refugee's permanent place of residence.

   ii. The Parties recognize the right of states that have hosted Palestinian refugees to remuneration.

4. Choice of Permanent Place of Residence (PPR)

   The solution to the PPR aspect of the refugee problem shall entail an act of informed choice on the part of the refugee to be exercised in accordance with the options and modalities set forth in this agreement. PPR options from which the refugees may choose shall be as follows;

   i. The state of Palestine, in accordance with clause a below.

   ii. Areas in Israel being transferred to Palestine in the land swap, following assumption of Palestinian sovereignty, in accordance with clause a below.

   iii. Third Countries, in accordance with clause b below.

   iv. The state of Israel, in accordance with clause c below.

   v. Present Host countries, in accordance with clause d below.

      a. PPR options i and ii shall be the right of all Palestinian refugees and shall be in accordance with the laws of the State of Palestine.

      b. Option iii shall be at the sovereign discretion of third countries and shall be in accordance with numbers that each third country will submit to the International Commission. These numbers shall represent the total number of Palestinian refugees that each third country shall accept.

      c. Option iv shall be at the sovereign discretion of Israel and will be in accordance with a number that Israel will submit to the International Commission. This number shall represent the total number of Palestinian refugees that Israel shall accept. As a basis, Israel will consider the average of the total numbers submitted by the different third countries to the International Commission.

      d. Option v shall be in accordance with the sovereign discretion of present host countries. Where exercised this shall be in the context of prompt and extensive development and rehabilitation programs for the refugee communities

   Priority in all the above shall be accorded to the Palestinian refugee population in Lebanon.

5. Free and Informed Choice

   The process by which Palestinian refugees shall express their PPR choice shall be on the basis of a free and informed decision. The Parties themselves are committed and will encourage third parties to facilitate the refugees' free choice in expressing their preferences, and to countering any attempts at interference or organized pressure on the process of choice. This will not prejudice the recognition of Palestine as the realization of Palestinian self-determination and statehood.

6. End of Refugee Status

   Palestinian refugee status shall be terminated upon the realization of an individual refugee's permanent place of residence (PPR) as determined by the International Commission.

7. End of Claims

   This agreement provides for the permanent and complete resolution of the Palestinian refugee problem. No claims may be raised except for those related to the implementation of this agreement.

8. International Role

   The Parties call upon the international community to participate fully in the comprehensive resolution of the refugee problem in accordance with this Agreement, including, inter alia, the establishment of an International Commission and an International Fund.

9. Property Compensation

   i. Refugees shall be compensated for the loss of property resulting from their displacement.

   ii. The aggregate sum of property compensation shall be calculated as follows:

      a. The Parties shall request the International Commission to appoint a Panel of Experts to estimate the value of Palestinians' property at the time of displacement.

      b. The Panel of Experts shall base its assessment on the UNCCP records, the records of the Custodian for Absentee Property, and any other records it deems relevant. The Parties shall make these records available to the Panel.

      c. The Parties shall appoint experts to advise and assist the Panel in its work.

      d. Within 6 months, the Panel shall submit its estimates to the Parties.

      e. The Parties shall agree on an economic multiplier, to be applied to the estimates, to reach a fair aggregate value of the property.

   iii. The aggregate value agreed to by the Parties shall constitute the Israeli "lump sum" contribution to the International Fund. No other financial claims arising from the Palestinian refugee problem may be raised against Israel.

   iv. Israel's contribution shall be made in installments in accordance with Schedule X.

   v. The value of the Israeli fixed assets that shall remain intact in former settlements and transferred to the state of Palestine will be deducted from Israel's contribution to the International Fund. An estimation of this value shall be made by the International Fund, taking into account assessment of damage caused by the settlements.

10. Compensation for Refugeehood
    i. A "Refugeehood Fund" shall be established in recognition of each individual's refugeehood. The Fund, to which Israel shall be a contributing party, shall be overseen by the International Commission. The structure and financing of the Fund is set forth in Annex X.
    ii. Funds will be disbursed to refugee communities in the former areas of UNRWA operation, and will be at their disposal for communal development and commemoration of the refugee experience. Appropriate mechanisms will be devised by the International Commission whereby the beneficiary refugee communities are empowered to determine and administer the use of this Fund.
11. The International Commission (Commission)
    i. Mandate and Composition
        a. An International Commission shall be established and shall have full and exclusive responsibility for implementing all aspects of this Agreement pertaining to refugees.
        b. In addition to themselves, the Parties call upon the United Nations, the United States, UNRWA, the Arab host countries, the EU, Switzerland, Canada, Norway, Japan, the World Bank, the Russian Federation, and others to be the members of the Commission.
        c. The Commission shall:
            1. Oversee and manage the process whereby the status and PPR of Palestinian refugees is determined and realized.
            2. Oversee and manage, in close cooperation with the host states, the rehabilitation and development programs.
            3. Raise and disburse funds as appropriate.
        d. The Parties shall make available to the Commission all relevant documentary records and archival materials in their possession that it deems necessary for the functioning of the Commission and its organs. The Commission may request such materials from all other relevant parties and bodies, including, inter alia, UNCCP and UNRWA.
    ii. Structure
        a. The Commission shall be governed by an Executive Board (Board) composed of representatives of its members.
        b. The Board shall be the highest authority in the Commission and shall make the relevant policy decisions in accordance with this Agreement.
        c. The Board shall draw up the procedures governing the work of the Commission in accordance with this Agreement.
        d. The Board shall oversee the conduct of the various Committees of the Commission. The said Committees shall periodically report to the Board in accordance with procedures set forth thereby.
        e. The Board shall create a Secretariat and appoint a Chair thereof. The Chair and the Secretariat shall conduct the day-to-day operation of the Commission.

iii. Specific Committees
   a. The Commission shall establish the Technical Committees specified below.
   b. Unless otherwise specified in this Agreement, the Board shall determine the structure and procedures of the Committees.
   c. The Parties may make submissions to the Committees as deemed necessary.
   d. The Committees shall establish mechanisms for resolution of disputes arising from the interpretation or implementation of the provisions of this Agreement relating to refugees.
   e. The Committees shall function in accordance with this Agreement, and shall render binding decisions accordingly.
   f. Refugees shall have the right to appeal decisions affecting them according to mechanisms established by this Agreement and detailed in Annex X.
iv. Status-determination Committee
   a. The Status-determination Committee shall be responsible for verifying refugee status.
   b. UNRWA registration shall be considered as rebuttable presumption (prima facie proof) of refugee status.
v. Compensation Committee
   a. The Compensation Committee shall be responsible for administering the implementation of the compensation provisions.
   b. The Committee shall disburse compensation for individual property pursuant to the following modalities:
      1. Either a fixed per capita award for property claims below a specified value. This will require the claimant to only prove title, and shall be processed according to a fast-track procedure, or
      2. A claims-based award for property claims exceeding a specified value for immovables and other assets. This will require the claimant to prove both title and the value of the losses.
   c. Annex X shall elaborate the details of the above including, but not limited to, evidentiary issues and the use of UNCCP, "Custodian for Absentees' Property", and UNRWA records, along with any other relevant records.
vi. Host State Remuneration Committee
   There shall be remuneration for host states.
vii. Permanent Place of Residence Committee (PPR Committee)
   The PPR Committee shall,
   a. Develop with all the relevant parties detailed programs regarding the implementation of the PPR options pursuant to Article 7/4 above.
   b. Assist the applicants in making an informed choice regarding PPR options.

c. Receive applications from refugees regarding PPR. The applicants must indicate a number of preferences in accordance with article 7/4 above. The applications shall be received no later than two years after the start of the International Commission's operations. Refugees who do not submit such applications within the two-year period shall lose their refugee status.

d. Determine, in accordance with sub-Article (a) above, the PPR of the applicants, taking into account individual preferences and maintenance of family unity. Applicants who do not avail themselves of the Committee's PPR determination shall lose their refugee status.

e. Provide the applicants with the appropriate technical and legal assistance.

f. The PPR of Palestinian refugees shall be realized within 5 years of the start of the International Commission's operations.

viii. Refugeehood Fund Committee

The Refugeehood Fund Committee shall implement Article 7/10 as detailed in Annex X.

ix. Rehabilitation and Development Committee

In accordance with the aims of this Agreement and noting the above PPR programs, the Rehabilitation and Development Committee shall work closely with Palestine, Host Countries and other relevant third countries and parties in pursuing the goal of refugee rehabilitation and community development. This shall include devising programs and plans to provide the former refugees with opportunities for personal and communal development, housing, education, healthcare, re-training and other needs. This shall be integrated in the general development plans for the region.

12. The International Fund

i. An International Fund (the Fund) shall be established to receive contributions outlined in this Article and additional contributions from the international community. The Fund shall disburse monies to the Commission to enable it to carry out its functions. The Fund shall audit the Commission's work.

ii. The structure, composition and operation of the Fund are set forth in Annex X.

13. UNRWA

i. UNRWA should be phased out in each country in which it operates, based on the end of refugee status in that country.

ii. UNRWA should cease to exist five years after the start of the Commission's operations. The Commission shall draw up a plan for the phasing out of UNRWA and shall facilitate the transfer of UNRWA functions to host states.

14. Reconciliation Programs

　　　i. The Parties will encourage and promote the development of coopera-
　　　　tion between their relevant institutions and civil societies in creating
　　　　forums for exchanging historical narratives and enhancing mutual un-
　　　　derstanding regarding the past.
　　　ii. The Parties shall encourage and facilitate exchanges in order to dissem-
　　　　inate a richer appreciation of these respective narratives, in the fields
　　　　of formal and informal education, by providing conditions for direct
　　　　contacts between schools, educational institutions and civil society.
　　iii. The Parties may consider cross-community cultural programs in or-
　　　　der to promote the goals of conciliation in relation to their respective
　　　　histories.
　　iv. These programs may include developing appropriate ways of commem-
　　　　orating those villages and communities that existed prior to 1949.

Article 8—Israeli-Palestinian Cooperation Committee (IPCC)

1. The Parties shall establish an Israeli-Palestinian Cooperation Committee
   immediately upon the entry into force of this agreement. The IPCC shall
   be a ministerial-level body with ministerial-level Co-Chairs.
2. The IPCC shall develop and assist in the implementation of policies for
   cooperation in areas of common interest including, but not limited to,
   infrastructure needs, sustainable development and environmental issues,
   cross-border municipal cooperation, border area industrial parks, exchange
   programs, human resource development, sports and youth, science, agriculture and culture.
3. The IPCC shall strive to broaden the spheres and scope of cooperation
   between the Parties.

Article 9—Designated Road Use Arrangements

1. The following arrangements for Israeli civilian use will apply to the designated roads in Palestine as detailed in Map X (Road 443, Jerusalem to
   Tiberias via Jordan Valley, and Jerusalem –Ein Gedi).
2. These arrangements shall not prejudice Palestinian jurisdiction over these
   roads, including PSF patrols.
3. The procedures for designated road use arrangements will be further detailed in Annex X.
4. Israelis may be granted permits for use of designated roads. Proof of
   authorization may be presented at entry points to the designated roads.
   The sides will review options for establishing a road use system based on
   smart card technology.
5. The designated roads will be patrolled by the MF at all times. The MF
   will establish with the states of Israel and Palestine agreed arrangements
   for cooperation in emergency medical evacuation of Israelis.

6. In the event of any incidents involving Israeli citizens and requiring criminal or legal proceedings, there will be full cooperation between the Israeli and Palestinian authorities according to arrangements to be agreed upon as part of the legal cooperation between the two states. The Parties may call on the IVG to assist in this respect.
7. Israelis shall not use the designated roads as a means of entering Palestine without the relevant documentation and authorization.
8. In the event of regional peace, arrangements for Palestinian civilian use of designated roads in Israel shall be agreed and come into effect.

Article 10—Sites of Religious Significance

1. The Parties shall establish special arrangements to guarantee access to agreed sites of religious significance, as will be detailed in Annex X. These arrangements will apply, inter alia, to the Tomb of the Patriarchs in Hebron and Rachel's Tomb in Bethlehem, and Nabi Samuel.
2. Access to and from the sites will be by way of designated shuttle facilities from the relevant border crossing to the sites.
3. The Parties shall agree on requirements and procedures for granting licenses to authorized private shuttle operators.
4. The shuttles and passengers will be subject to MF inspection.
5. The shuttles will be escorted on their route between the border crossing and the sites by the MF.
6. The shuttles shall be under the traffic regulations and jurisdiction of the Party in whose territory they are traveling.
7. Arrangements for access to the sites on special days and holidays are detailed in Annex X.
8. The Palestinian Tourist Police and the MF will be present at these sites.
9. The Parties shall establish a joint body for the religious administration of these sites.
10. In the event of any incidents involving Israeli citizens and requiring criminal or legal proceedings, there will be full cooperation between the Israeli and Palestinian authorities according to arrangements to be agreed upon. The Parties may call on the IVG to assist in this respect.
11. Israelis shall not use the shuttles as a means of entering Palestine without the relevant documentation and authorization.
12. The Parties shall protect and preserve the sites of religious significance listed in Annex X and shall facilitate visitation to the cemeteries listed in Annex X.

Article 11—Border Regime

1. There shall be a border regime between the two states, with movement between them subject to the domestic legal requirements of each and to the provisions of this Agreement as detailed in Annex X.

2. Movement across the border shall only be through designated border crossings.
3. Procedures in border crossings shall be designed to facilitate strong trade and economic ties, including labor movement between the Parties.
4. Each Party shall each, in its respective territory, take the measures it deems necessary to ensure that no persons, vehicles, or goods enter the territory of the other illegally.
5. Special border arrangements in Jerusalem shall be in accordance with Article 6 above.

Article 12—Water: still to be completed

Article 13—Economic Relations: still to be completed

Article 14—Legal Cooperation: still to be completed

Article 15—Palestinian Prisoners and Detainees

1. In the context of this Permanent Status Agreement between Israel and Palestine, the end of conflict, cessation of all violence, and the robust security arrangements set forth in this Agreement, all the Palestinian and Arab prisoners detained in the framework of the Israeli-Palestinian conflict prior to the date of signature of this Agreement, DD/MM/2003, shall be released in accordance with the categories set forth below and detailed in Annex X.
   (a) Category A: all persons imprisoned prior to the start of the implementation of the Declaration of Principles on May 4, 1994, administrative detainees, and minors, as well as women, and prisoners in ill health shall be released immediately upon the entry into force of this Agreement.
   (b) Category B: all persons imprisoned after May 4, 1994 and prior to the signature of this Agreement shall be released no later than eighteen months from the entry into force of this Agreement, except those specified in Category C.
   (c) Category C: Exceptional cases - persons whose names are set forth in Annex X—shall be released in thirty months at the end of the full implementation of the territorial aspects of this Agreement set forth in Article 5/7/v.

Article 16—Dispute Settlement Mechanism

1. Disputes related to the interpretation or application of this Agreement shall be resolved by negotiations within a bilateral framework to be convened by the High Steering Committee.

2. If a dispute is not settled promptly by the above, either Party may submit it to mediation and conciliation by the IVG mechanism in accordance with Article 3.
3. Disputes which cannot be settled by bilateral negotiation and/or the IVG mechanism shall be settled by a mechanism of conciliation to be agreed upon by the Parties.
4. Disputes which have not been resolved by the above may be submitted by either Party to an arbitration panel. Each Party shall nominate one member of the three-member arbitration panel. The Parties shall select a third arbiter from the agreed list of arbiters set forth in Annex X either by consensus or, in the case of disagreement, by rotation.

Article 17—Final Clauses

Including a final clause providing for a UNSCR/UNGAR resolution endorsing the agreement and superceding the previous UN resolutions.
The English version of this text will be considered authoritative.

Notes

Foreword

1. Régis Debray, "Les États-Unis d'Occident, tout va bien . . . ," *Marianne*, Paris, juin 14, 2004.

2. Bob Woodward, *State of Denial Bush at War*, III, 2006.

3. Henry Kissinger, *A World Restored: Metternich, Castelreagh and the Problem of Peace, 1812–1822*, New York: Houghton Mifflin, 1957.

4. F.A.O. *L'État de l'insécurité alimentaire dans le monde*, Rome, 2005.

5. Normal nourishment stands for 2,700 calories per day for an adult person.

6. Emmanuel Kant, *Kritik der Vernunft*, Gesamtausgabe, Preussische Akademie, 1902, vol. II, chap. IV.

7. Ibid.

Chapter 1

1. Hannah Arendt, *On Violence*, New York: Harcourt, Brace & World, Inc., 1969, p. 35.

2. See Max Weber's definition of the state as "the rule of men over men based on the means of legitimate, that is allegedly legitimate violence." in *Politics as a Vocation*, Philadelphia, PA: Fortress Press, 1965.

3. Karl von Clausewitz, *On War*, New York: Penguin Classics, 1968.

4. For documents, beginning in the eighteenth century, consult The Avalon Project, Yale Law School, New Haven, CT.

5. See C. Wright Mills, *The Power Elite*, New York: Oxford University Press, 1956, p. 171.

6. See Jean-Paul Sartre's "Introduction," in Franz Fanon's *The Wretched of the Earth*, New York: Grove Press edition, 1968.

7. See Max Weber, *On Charisma and Institution Building*, Chicago: University of Chicago Press, 1968.

8. 40,000 dead and 40,000 wounded. Public Record Office, Kew, Richmond, Surrey, United Kingdom, document reference ZHC2/873.

9. For an original, preliminary conservative estimates of casualties from these bombings stand at 300,000 dead, 760,000 wounded and 7,500,000 homeless. Fire Raids on German Cities, United States Strategic Bombing Survey, Physical Damage Division, January 1945. Supporting Document No. 34 et seq.

10. Hiroshima, 66,000 dead, 69,000 wounded, Nagasaki, 39,000 dead and 25,000 wounded (http://www.atomicarchives.com).

11. Huigh DeGroot, *De Jure belli ac Pacis*, 1625.

12. For a complete collection of international agreements on the laws of war and peace see Yale's University's collection: The Avalon Project, op. cit.

Chapter 2

1. G.M. Gilbert, *Nuremberg Diary*, New York: Farrar, Straus and Company, 1947, pp. 278–279.

2. See Tom Regan, "Does Britain new antiterror act goes too far," in *csmonitor.com*, posted October 4, 2005, 11:30 A.M.

3. Thomas Donnelly, et al., *Rebuilding America's Defenses—Strategy, Forces and Resources for a New Century*, Washington, DC: Project for the New American Century, 2000.

4. See Tom Regan's "Studies: War radicalized most foreign fighters in Iraq" in *The Christian Science Monitor*, available at www.csmonitor.com/2005/0718/dailyUpdate, who reported that many observers and studies published in the United States, the United Kingdom, and elsewhere have asserted that the Iraq war has vastly contributed to the scores of young people flowing into Iraq to confront the "invading infidels."

5. Douglas R. Burgess Jr., "The Dread Pirate Bin Laden: How thinking of terrorists as pirates can help win the war on terror," in *Legal Affairs*, June 23, 2005.

6. Ibid.

7. Ibid.

8. Ibid.

9. Ibid.

10. Terror is a method of human interaction as old as humanity itself. It is used currently in the daily life, in the business sphere, by the various gangs and mafias, by income tax and debt collectors, in many conjugal relations, by some parents, by teachers in some schools, in the maintenance of security and justice, etc. Much of it is well meaning, or at least has a positive objective; some of the most evident cases of this are Robin Hood, Zorro, and the like, who terrorized rich and powerful for the benefit of the downtrodden.

11. See Ariel Merari's "Terrorism as a strategy of insurgency," in *Terrorism and Political Violence*, no. 4 (Winter 1993), pp. 213–251, London: Frank Case, London, UK.

12. This study is mainly concerned with political terror, and recognizes the existence of a much wider taxonomy on terrorism.

13. R. Ernest Dupuy and Trevor N. Dupuy, *The Encyclopedia of Military History, From 3500 BC to the Present*, Revised edition, New York: Harper & Row Publishers, 1977, p. 9.

14. The first instances of international terrorism were in fact carried out two decades earlier by Zionist terrorists organizations, particularly the Irgun Zvai Leumi and the Stern Gang during the struggle to establish a Jewish State in Palestine: among these the 1944 Assassination of Lord Moyne, the British High Commissioner in Cairo, the 1946 bombing of the British Embassy in Rome, the 1947 killing of two British sergeants taken as hostages in retaliation to the execution of two alleged Jewish terrorists, and the 1948 assassination of Count Bernadotte, the Special United Nations Envoy to Palestine.

15. See "General Assembly Adopts Convention on Nuclear Terrorism," available at www.un.org/News/Press/docs/2005/ga10340.doc.

16. "UN Adopts Nuclear Terrorism Convention; Treaty Seven Years in the Making," The Arms Control Association, 1150 Connecticut Avenue, NW, Suite 620, Washington, DC 20036.

17. Burgess, "The Dread Pirate Bin Laden."

18. See particularly the discussions on the draft of the Preamble and of Arts. 2bis and 18 in the working document of the United Nations Ad Hoc Committee on Terrorism.

19. The Lavon Affair, referred to in Israel as "*esek bish*," a terrorist attack carried out by Israel's Intelligence Service in 1954 against the United States Information Office, and British targets, in Alexandria, Egypt, designed to surreptitiously implicate the Egyptian Regime and turn the United States and the United Kingdom against Egypt fits the definition of International Terrorism.

20. Consider the political intimidation resulting from the perverse use of "unpatriotic" by the George W. Bush administration concerning political dissent. Or the persistent pejoration implied in the references to the "BIG L" beginning with President Regan's Administration?

21. See Alan Cowell, "Britain Assails Critical Report on Role in Iraq," *The New York Times*, July 19, 2005, A11.

22. "Stunning Cost of 9/11," *The New York Post*, January 28, 2002.

23. Robert Looney, "Economic Cost to the United States Stemming from the 9/11 Attacks," *Strategic Insights*, 1 no. 6 (August 2002), available at www.nps.navy.mil/si/aug02/homeland.asp.

24. "Compensating the Victims of 9/11," Rand Institute for Civil Justice, Rand Corp., November 8, 2004 (www.rand.org/publications/RB/RB9087/).

25. See Matthew Clark's, "Britain struggles with how to prevent terror legally," *The Christian Science Monitor*, available at www.csmonitor.com/2005/0810/dailyUpdate.

Chapter 3

1. See Amin Maalouf, *Les croisades vues par les Arabes*, Editions J'ai lu, 1983. 75007, Paris, France.

2. See Henri Laoust, *Essai sur les doctrines sociales et politiques de Takï-d-Dïn Ahmad b. Taimïya*, Cairo, 1939, for fundamentalist Islamic doctrinal development from Ibn Hanbal and Ibn Taymiyya to Ibn Abd-al-Wahhab.

3. See Fawaz Gerges' brilliant study, *The Far Enemy: Why Jihad Went Global*, New York: Cambridge University Press, 2005.

4. Ayman al-Zawāhiri, *Knights under the Prophet's banner*, as reported by *Al-Sharq al-Awsat*, London, December 2, 2001.

5. Wole Soyinka, *Climate of Fear: The Quest For Dignity in a Dehumanized World*, New York: Random House, 2005.

6. Mohammad Habash, *Islam's Fanatical 1 per cent*, Project Syndicate 2005, www.project-sundicate.org, Damascus, Syria: Islamic Studies Center, 2005.

7. Soyinka, op. cit.

8. Interestingly, this perception is not too dissimilar from the Christians who anticipate general enlightenment and salvation in the Second Coming, at the end of the world.

9. Barry Rubin and Judith Colp Rubin have reported in *Anti-American Terrorism and the Middle East*, Oxford, UK: Oxford University Press, 2002, p. 36, the following statement by Shaykh Mohammad Sayyed Tantawi, the Rector of the Cairo *Al-Azhar*, the flagship university of mainstream Sunni Islam: "Suicide bombers are legitimate self-defense. Those who say it is forbidden [terrorism] should ask what motivate it."

10. http://en.wikipedia.org/wiki/Ayman_Zawahiri

11. loc. cit.

Chapter 4

1. For the whole interview see "Mayor Blames Middle East policy," BBC News, UK edition, Wednesday, July 20, 2005, available at www.bbc.co.uk.

2. See *The Diaries of Theodor Herzl*, edited and translated with an introduction by Marvin Lowenthal, The Universal Library, Grosset & Dunlap, New York, 1962. The Jewish Colonizing Association or ICA was founded in 1891, by Baron Maurice de Hirsch to settle East European Jews in Argentina, but later in Palestine.

3. See Benny Morris, *The Birth of the Palestinian Refugee Problem*, New York: Cambridge University Press, 1989.

4. See Hussein Agha and Robert Malley, "Camp David: The Tragedy of Errors," *The New York Review of Books*, August 9, 2001; Dennis Ross, *The Missing Peace—The Inside Story of the Fight for Middle East Peace*, New York: Farrar, Straus and Giroux, 2004.

5. For a candid assessment on the brutality of Israeli occupation, see the documentary, "Yoman Masa," (Diary of a Journey), on the colonization of the West Bank, by Haim Yavin, Israel's most celebrated news analyst and founder of that country's Ch. 1 Television channel. Steven Erlanger reported in "Israel 'Mr. TV' Assails Occupation of West Bank," that the documentary is "pessimistic, angry and intensely personal, He quotes Yavin as saying that the occupation is a real "Greek tragedy," in the course of which, "Since 1967, we have been brutal conquerors, occupiers, suppressing other people. . . . The settlers are so strong. In a way, they run the country, or run the agenda of the country. I don't see anyone undoing what they've done" in combination with Israeli governments, which is "an annexation of land that goes against a viable state for the Palestinians." *The New York Times/International Herald Tribune*, of June 1, 2005.

6. cf. John J. Mearsheimer, University of Chicago's director of the Program on International Security Policy, and Stephen M. Walt, Dean of Harvard's Kennedy School of Government, "For the past several decades, and especially since the Six-Day War in 1967, the centerpiece of U.S. Middle Eastern policy has been its relationship with Israel. The combination of unwavering support for Israel and the related effort to spread 'democracy' throughout the region has inflamed Arab and Islamic opinion and jeopardized not only US security but that of much of the rest of the world." "The Israeli Lobby," in *London Review of Books*, 28, no. 6 (March 23, 2006).

7. For a recent, candid appreciation of despair and terrorism, see statement by Jenny Tonge, a Liberal British MP, in Sky News reports, News24.com, January 29, 2004. [Suicide bombers are] "born out of desperation from minor things to major things their life does not

feel like it is their own. I do not condone suicide bombers. No one can condone them but I do understand why people out there become suicide bombers.... It is out of desperation and I guess if I was in their situation, with my children and grandchildren, and I saw no hope for the future at all, I might just think about it myself."

Chapter 5

1. For the full text, see J.C. Hurewitz, *Diplomacy in the Near and Middle East, Vol. II: A Documentary Record: 1914–1956*, Princeton, NJ: D. Van Nostrand Company, Inc. 1956.

2. Ahad Ha'am, quoted in "Zionism—Definition and Early History," www.mideastweb.org/zionism.htm.

3. See also, Aharon Cohen, *Israel and the Arab World*, New York: Funk and Wagnalls, 1970.

4. See the definitive study of Justin McCarthy, *The Population of Palestine: Palestinian History and Statistics of the Late Ottoman Period and the Mandate*, New York: Columbia University Press, 1990.

5. See former Knesset member Uri Avneri's article, "Death of a Myth," in *Gush Shalom*, pob 3322, Tel-Aviv 61033, Israel, otherisr@actcom.co.il, May 13, 2005, 2:51 P.M.

6. Richard L. Rubenstein, *After Auschwitz: Radical Theology and Contemporary Judaism*, Indianapolis, IN: Bobbs Merrill, 1966.

7. For a thorough discussion of this issue, see Norman G. Finkelstein, *Beyond Chutzpah: On the Misuse of Anti-Semitism and the Abuse of History*, Berkeley: University of California Press, 2005.

8. Reference is made here to the controversy surrounding the article of John Mearscheimer and John Walt, "The Israel Lobby," *The London Review of Books*, 28, no. 6 (March 23, 2006). See also Norman Solomon's rebuttal of media attacks labeling Mearscheimer and Walt, two outstanding scholars, as anti-Semites, in "The Lobby and the Bulldozer: Mearscheimer, Walt, and Corrie," in *Truthout Perspective* of April 13, 2006 (www.truthout.com)

9. See also, Kristine McNeil, "The War on Academic Freedom," *The Nation*, November 1, 2002. A specific example of harassment has been his campaign against professors of Middle East subjects at Columbia University, NY, which made a big splash in the Media, in the Spring of 2005.

10. *Theodore Herzl, Complete Diaries*, Vol. I, ed. Raphael Patai, trans. Harry Zohn. New York: Herzl Press, 1960, p. 88.

11. Joseph Weitz, *Diaries and Letters to Children*, Tel-Aviv, 1965, 2:181.

12. Chaim Weizmann, *Trial and Error: The Autobiography of Chaim Weizmann*, London: Hamish Hamilton, 1949.

13. Yitzhak Rabin, *The Rabin Memoirs*, Berkeley, CA: University of California Press, 1961.

14. Benny Morris, *The Birth of the Palestinian Refugee Problem*, New York: Cambridge University Press, 1989. "We had only five days left ... until May 15, 1948. We regarded it as imperative to cleanse the interior of the Galilee, and create Jewish territorial continuity in the whole of Upper Galilee." (Allon). See pp. 122–125.

15. Martin Buber raised his voice against the Zionist emulation of the Nazis in harboring and executing a plan for the extermination of a people. He also cautioned, as did Dr. Judah Magnes, founder and first President of Jerusalem's Hebrew University that

creating a strictly Jewish State against the will of the Palestinians is not only un-Jewish, it would require endless violence and warfare.

16. Letter from Albert Einstein to Chaim Weizmann, November 25, 1929, Albert Einstein Archives, pp. 33–411, Jewish National & University Library, Jerusalem.

17. Read Felicia Langer's Deposition before the Special Investigative Committee on Israeli Practices Affecting Human Rights on the Population of the Occupied Territories, in *Sionisme et droits de l'homme*, Association Suisse-Palestine, Lausanne, C.H., February, 1977.

18. "Ever since the 1967 occupation, the military and political elites ... deliberated over the question of how to keep maximum land with minimum Palestinian population.... But a simple solution of annexation of the occupied territories would have turned the ... Palestinians into Israeli citizens and this would have caused what has been labeled the 'demographic problem'—the fear that the Jewish majority could not be preserved. Therefore two basic conceptions were developed. The Allon Plan consisted of annexation of 35–40% of the territories.... This plan originated with those who thought that it is possible to repeat the 1948 'solution' of mass expulsion.... The second view, whose primary spokesman was Sharon, assumed that it is possible to find more acceptable and sophisticated ways to achieve a 1948 style 'solution'—it is only necessary to find another country for the Palestinians.... This was part of Sharon's global world view by which Israel can establish 'new orders' in the region." Dr. Tanya Reibhart, *Yediot Aharonot*, June 10, 2001 (trans. From Hebrew edition.)

19. Perhaps the most vocal critic of Israel on this issue is Ben Gurion University Professor of History, Benny Morris; see his article in *The New York Times Review of Books*, April 8, 2004. See also his authoritative book, *Righteous Victims—A History of the Zionist-Arab Conflict, 1881–2001*, New York: Alfred A. Knopf, 1999.

20. "The thesis that the danger of genocide was hanging over us in June 1967, and that Israel was fighting for its physical existence is only a bluff which was born and developed after the war.... To pretend that the Egyptian forces massed on our frontiers were in a position to threaten the existence of Israel, constitutes an insult not only to the intelligence of anyone capable of analyzing this sort of situation, but above all an insult to the Zahal" General Matityahu Peled, as quoted in *Haaretz* of March 19, 1972.

21. See text in Appendix.

22. See text in Appendix.

23. a.k.a., Hugh Foot, Baron Caradon.

24. Uri Avneri, *Paved With Bad intentions*, Gush Shalom, pob 3322, Tel-Aviv 61033 www.gush-shalom.org/, March 26, 2005; and *From the Mind of Sharon*, op. cit., January 8, 2005, and the other article in *Haaretz* on the issue.

25. Loc. cit.

26. See Meron Benvinisti, et al., *West Bank and Gaza Data Base Project*, Interim Report, Jerusalem, The West Bank Data Base Project, 1982. See also David K Shipler, "Israel Dramatically Changing Face of the West Bank," *The New York Times*, September 12, 1982.

27. By the end of FY2002, The total United States amount of aid to Israel stood at $84,854,827,200.00 and counting, approximately three plus billions per year; with the routine waiving by Congress of the loan guarantees, the total cost to US tax payer stood then at $134,791,507,200.00 (*Source*: Washington Report on Middle East Affairs, Washington, DC), http://www.WRMEA.com.

28. Admiral Moorer quoted by Richard Curtis in *A Changing Image: American Perceptions of the Arab-Israeli Dispute*, Washington, DC: American Educational Trust, 1986.

29. See Yuri Avneri's article in www.gush-shalom.org, 01,22,2005. "The relationship between the United States and Israel is difficult to define. The USA has no official mandate over our country. It is not a normal alliance between two nations. Neither is it a relationship between a satellite and the master country. Some people say, only half in jest, that the United States is an Israeli colony. And, in many respects, it looks like that. President Bush dances to Ariel Sharon's tune. Both Houses of Congress are totally subservient to the Israeli right wing—much more so than the Knesset. It has been said that if the pro-Israeli lobby were to sponsor a resolution on Capitol Hill calling for the abolition of the Ten Commandments, both Houses of Congress would adopt it overwhelmingly. Every year Congress confirms the payment of a massive tribute to Israel.

But others assert the reverse: that Israel is an American colony. And that is also true in many respects. It is unthinkable for the Israeli government to refuse a clear-cut request by the President of the United States. America forbids Israel to sell an expensive intelligence-gathering plane to China? Israel cancels the sale. America forbids a large-scale military action, as happened last week in Gaza? No action. America wants the Israeli economy to be managed according to American precepts? No problem: an American (circumcised, to be sure) has just been appointed as Governor of the Central Bank of Israel.

As a matter of fact, both versions are right: The USA is an Israeli colony and Israel is an American colony. The relationship between the two countries is a symbiosis, a term defined by the Oxford Dictionary as "an association of two organisms living attached to each other or one within the other (from the Greek words for "living" and "together"). Much has already been said about the origins of this symbiosis. American Christian Zionism preceded the founding of the Jewish Zionist organization. The American myth is almost identical with the Zionist Israeli myth, both in content and symbolism. (The settlers fleeing from persecution in their homelands, an empty country, pioneers conquering the wilderness, the savage natives, etc.) Both are countries of immigration, with all that this implies for good or ill. Both governments believe that their interests coincide. On Independence Day in Israel, many American flags are to be seen next to the Israeli ones—a phenomenon that is without parallel in the world." (Permission to reproduce granted by Uri Avnery)

30. See Ami Eden's Op-Ed, "Playing the Holocaust Card," *The New York Times*, January 29, 2005, criticizing Jewish organizations ultimately counterproductive use of the label "anti-Semitic" to silence any opposition of Israel; see also Jewish reader's support of Eden's argument in relevant letters-to-the-Editor, op. cit. February 2, 2005.

31. See Israel Shahak, "Relations between Israel and the Organized American Jews," *Middle East Policy*, No. 40, 2 (3) (1993).

32. George W. Bush, "State of the Union Address," 2003.

33. See Charles Siebert, "An Elephant Crackup. Attacks by elephants on villages, people and other animals are on the rise. Some researchers are pointing to a species-wide trauma and the fraying of the fabric of pachyderm society." *The New York Times Magazine*, October 8, 2006, section 6.

34. See, Benny Morris, *Righteous Victims: A History of the Zionist-Arab Conflict, 1881–1999*, London: John Murray, 2000.

35. Menachem Begin, Yitzhak Shamir, Moshe Aren, and other leaders of these terrorist organizations went on to become respected statesmen.

36. See Rachel Corrie's Memorial website, www.rachelcorrie.org.

37. Expropriations continue unabated, in Jerusalem and elsewhere, even as Prime Minister Abbas attempts to reach an agreement with Palestinian extremists in Gaza for a cease fire. See *The New York Times*, Greg Myre's article "Palestinians Fear East Jerusalem Land Grab," January 24, 2005, A/4. See also BBC Daily e-mail of January 25, 2005, "Land Grab Fears For Jerusalem," reporting that Israel is using a 1950 law on "absentee landowners," in East Jerusalem. Owners live across the "wall," in Bethlehem. The wall is built on Palestinian land, also expropriated, not on Israeli land.

38. Seldom a day goes by without tanks or bulldozers are called in to demolish civilian dwellings. Israeli Human Rights Organizations, Gush Shalom, Peace Now, and the US Campaign to End Israeli Occupation have organized demonstrations against Caterpillar, products that are used in the razing of civilian homes.

39. The 1947, U.N. General Assembly Resolution 181, on the Partition of Palestine was carried by 33 in favor (Australia, Belgium, Bolivia, Brazil, Byelorussia, Canada, Costa Rica, Czechoslovakia, Denmark, Dominican Republic, Ecuador, France, Guatemala, Haiti, Iceland, Liberia, Luxembourg, Netherlands, New Zealand, Nicaragua, Norway, Panama, Paraguay, Peru, Philippines, Poland, Sweden, Ukraine, Union of South Africa, USSR, USA, Uruguay, Venezuela) to 13 against (Afghanistan, Cuba, Egypt, Greece, India, Iran, Iraq, Lebanon, Pakistan, Saudi Arabia, Syria, Turkey, Yemen), and 10 abstentions, (Argentina, Chile, China, Colombia, El-Salvador, Ethiopia, Honduras, Mexico, United Kingdom, and Yugoslavia). It is notable that the United Kingdom, the Mandatory power in Palestine and victim of Zionist terrorism, was among the abstaining states.

40. Harry S. Truman, *Memoirs,* Vol. I and II, Garden City, New York, Doubleday, 1955, 1956.

41. See various reports available on www.hrw.org and www.amnesty.org/usa.

42. cf. Zeev Sternhell, *The Founding Myths of Israel*, Princeton, NJ: Princeton University Press, 1999.

43. See Gershom Goremberg's *The Accidental Empire: Israel and the Birth of the Settlements*, New York: Times Books, 2006; and his Op-Ed, "Israel's Tragedy Foretold," *The New York Times*, March 10, 2006.

44. The "benign occupation" has long since turned into a brutal and ugly regime of oppression. The prophecy of Professor Yeshayahu Leibowitz, that the occupation would corrupt us through and through and turn us into a people of exploiters and secret-service men, has come awfully true. Nothing has remained of the "beautiful Eretz Israel" but a cloying nostalgia . . ." Uri Avneri, former member of the Israeli Knesset and peace activist, in "Death of a Myth," in an article published by the International edition of *Gush Shalom*, as he looked back in anger on the occasion of the 38th victory anniversary of the Six Days War. Gush Shalom, pob 3322, Tel-Aviv, 61033, Israel. (June 2005).

45. For a copy of the text, see:www.usip.org/library/pa/israel_plo/oslo_09131993.html.

Chapter 6

1. "I failed in finding out how many unauthorized outposts exist in Judea, Samaria and Gaza, since the source for the data is the Infrastructure Dept. of the Civil Administration, which has not delivered all the necessary information. I was informed that gathering the information requires much work and takes time," (Talia Sasson). For the complete report of the former Attorney General of the State of Israel, check www.mideastweb.org/sassonreport. htm.

2. Ben Lynfield, "Israel Aid to Illegal Settlers," *The Christian Science Monitor*, March 10, 2005.

3. See Seymour M. Hersh. *The Samson Option: Israel's Nuclear Arsenal and American Foreign Policy*, New York: Random House, 1991. See also Alfred G. Gerteiny, "The Threat of Peace in the Middle East," *World Review*, 10, no. 1 (March 1971), pp. 12–19, The University of Queensland Press (published under the auspices of the Australian Institute of International Affairs, Queensland Branch).

4. See Uri Avneri's column "How the Hell Did This Happen" (Sharon Inside out) of January 8, 2005, www.gush-shalom.org, Gush Shalom, pob 3322, Tel-Aviv 61033, Israel. Gush Shalom is an Israeli Organization that endorses a just peace and coexistence with an independent Palestine. It has endorsed the Geneva Agreement. For the Hebrew original, go to: www.geocities.com/keller_adam/Avnery_heb.

5. For a text of the Convention on the Prevention and Punishment of the Crime of Genocide, see: www.preventgenocide.org/convention/text.htm.

6. "Law making treaties ... such as the Genocide Convention ... are in principle binding only on the parties, but the number of parties, the explicit acceptance of rules of law, and in some cases the declaratory nature of the provisions produce a strong law-creating effect at least as great as the general practice considered sufficient to support a customary rule." I. Brownley, *Principles of Public International Law*, Oxford: Clarendon Press, 1973, p. 12.

7. United Nations General Assembly, 78 UNTS 277 (1951).

On 7 April, 2004, on the occasion of the 10th anniversary of the Rwanda Genocide, United Nations Secretary General Kofi Annan announced an Action Plan to Prevent Genocide which calls for the appointment of a Special Advisor on Genocide Prevention.

8. Ibid.

9. Ibid.

10. Ibid.

11. Raphael Lemkin, *Axis Rule in Occupied Europe*, New York: Carnegie Endowment for International Peace, 1944, p. 79.

12. Richard Aren, ed., *Genocide in Paraguay*, Philadelphia, PA: Temple University Press, 1976, p.137.

13. Op. cit. General Rabin's memoirs. This author also recalls the excited narratives, in Paris, of an Arabic speaking Israeli friend, Ted Bental, and former Hagganah fighter who, during the War of 1948, using a bullhorn atop a lorry, rushed the Palestinian inhabitants in many towns and cities to "leave town or risk massacre." He proudly confessed that the "trick" was routinely used by commanders to empty the area of the native inhabitants, to make room for Jewish immigrants.

14. For a discussion of the relationship between "deculturation' as mentally damaging, see Stephen Goroye's "Mental Harm in the Genocide Convention," *Washington University Law Quarterly*, 1951, 17.

15. Chaim Shatan, "Genocide and Bereavement," in *Genocide in Paraguay*, loc. cit. p. 116.

16. See D. Davies, *The Last of the Tasmanians*, London: Trinity Press, 1972; B. Bethlehem, "Individual and Mass Behavior in Extreme Situations," *Journal of Abnormal and Social Psychology*, 38 (1943), 417; C. Bendy, "Problems of Internment Camps," ibid., 453.

17. Ibid.

18. Aren, op. cit. p. 138. See also A.H. Crisp and R.R. Priest, "Psychoneurotic Status During the Year Following Bereavement," *Journal of Psychosomatic Research*, 16 (1973), 351.

19. Genocide Watch, P.O. Box 809, Washington, D.C., 20044, USA.

20. See George H. Stanton, *The Eight Stages of Genocide*, a paper presented at the Yale University Center for International and Area Studies, in 1998, on the net, info@genocidewatch.org.

21. See Gad Becker, *Yehodiot Ahronot*, April 13, 1983, and *The New York Times*, April 14, 1983.

22. Shatan, loc. cit.

23. For a history of Israeli massacres and other acts of inhumanity against the Palestinian peoples, see Benny Morris, *The Birth of the Palestinian Refugee Problem*, New York: Cambridge University Press, 1989. Morris methodically covers how each city, town and village in Palestine was emptied during the 1948–1949. It is an important and valuable work, because Morris works almost entirely from primary sources and manages to demonstrate that the flight of the Palestinian refugees was a complex process, and differed in circumstance from region to region. The book is written from an Israeli perspective . . ." (Review). See also, *1948 and After: Israel and the Palestinians*. Oxford: Clarendon Press, 1994, by the same author.

24. Stanton op. cit.

25. Example of Internet campaign to boycott U.S. newspapers who reported on the massacre of Jenin: "Don't get mad, get even. Cancel your subscription to the L.A. Times. Call 1-800-252-9141," www.pmwatch.org/pmw/cast/jenindistortions.asp.

26. See "What Is Genocide," info@genocidewatch.org.

27. Benny Morris, op. cit.

28. Loc. cit, "Key terms."

29. Several massacres of Palestinians are alleged to have taken place during and after 1948, among them El-Tantura, Deir Yassin, Jenin, Raffah, and Beit Hanoun. The settlements in the Occupied Territories are the result of expropriations and are exclusively for Jews.

Chapter 7

1. See "Bush was Set on Path of War: Memo by British Advisor Says," by Don Van Natta, *The New York Times*, March 27, 2006. Among the publications supporting this point of view see, Patrick J. Buchanan, *Where the Right Went Wrong: How Neo-Conservatives Subverted the Reagan Revolution and Hijacked the Bush Presidency*, New York: Thomas Dunn Books, September 2004; Paul O'Neil's interview, in Ron Suskind, *The Price of Loyalty: George W. Bush, the White House and the Education of Paul O'*, New York: Simon & Schuster, January 2004; Michael Scheuer, *Why the West is Losing the War on Terror,* Brassy's, Inc., 2002; Richard A. Clarke, *Against All Enemies: Inside America's War on Terror,* Free Press, a Div. of Simon & Schuster, 2004. Reference is made here also to statements on the matter by Senator Ernest Fritz Hollings of South Carolina, before his retirement, the columnist Robert Novak, and various retired generals, including former U.S. Marine Commander and Special George W. Bush's Special Envoy to Israel/Palestine, General Anthony Zini.

2. See John Mearsheimer and Stephen Walt, "*The Israeli Lobby And US Foreign Policy*," Faculty Research Working Paper, no. RWP06, John F. Kennedy School of Government, Harvard University.

3. The authenticity of the document, released during Prime Minister Tony Blair's electoral campaign and widely reported in the United States media during the week of May 16, 2005, without much brouhaha, was not repudiated by the British Authorities. See, among other newspaper the *Christian Science Monitor*, May 17, 2005.

4. See Michal Smith's article "R.A.F. Bombing Raids Tried to Goad Saddam into War," *The Sunday Times—Britain*, May 29, 2005, www.timesonline.co.uk/article/0,2087-1632566,00.html.

5. *The Christian Science Monitor*, loc. it., on the British Government document leaked to *The Sunday Times of London* specifying that the United States had decided to remove Saddam Hussein and that "intelligence and facts were being fixed around the policy."

6. Donnelly, Thomas, et al. *Rebuilding America's Defenses—Strategy, Forces and Resources for a New Century*, Project for The New American Century, 1150 Seventeenth Street, N.W., Suite 510, Washington, D.C. 20036.

7. Literally, "the ass rubs the ass," the saying refers to individuals who agree and support each other, as a matter of course.

8. Project for The New American Century, op. cit.

9. William Kristol is on the Board of Advisors of The Foundation for the Defense of Democracy; with Lawrence Kaplan, he coauthored. *The War over Iraq: Saddam's Tyranny and America's Mission*, Encounter Books, 2003, a New York Times best seller that advocated war on, and a change of regime in Iraq.

10. Donnelly et al., *Rebuilding America's Defenses*.

11. The Pentagon's *Quadrennial Defense Review,* of May 1997, and the *Report of the National Defense Panel*, of December 1997.

12. Donnelly et al., *Rebuilding America's Defenses*.

13. Ibid.

14. Ibid.

15. *Tacitus: The Life of Gnaeus Julius Agricola.* "They have created a desert where they said they brought peace." Phrase attributed to Galgacus, the Caledonian hero, contrasting derisively the ravages wreaked by the Roman conquerors, with their specious claim of bringing civilization.

Bibliography

Aaronson, Geoffrey. *Israel, Palestinians, and the Intifada: Creating Facts on the West Bank.* London: Keegan Paul, 1990.

Abukhalil, As'ad. *Bin Laden, Islam and America's "New War on Terrorism."* New York: Seven Stories Press, 2002.

Al-Zayyat, Montasser. *The Road to Al-Qaeda: The Story of Osama Bin Laden's Right Hand Man*, Sara Nimis (ed.), Ahmad Fekri (trans.). North Melbourne, Victoria: Pluto Press Australia, 2004.

Aren, Richard (ed.). *Genocide in Paraguay.* Philadelphia, PA: Temple University Press, 1976.

Arendt, Hannah. *On Violence.* New York: Harcourt, Brace & World, Inc., 1969.

Avalon Project, Yale Law School, New Haven, CT.

Ball, George W. and Douglas B. *The Passionate Attachment: America's Involvement with Israel, 1947 to the Present.* New York: W.W. Norton and Company, 1992.

Bard, Mitchell. "Israeli Lobby Power." *Midstream*, 33, no. 1 (January 1987).

Bass, Warren. *Support Any Friends: Kennedy's Middle East and the Making of the US-Israeli Alliance.* New York: Oxford University Press, 2003.

Beit-Hallahmi, Benjamin. *Original Sins: Reflections on the History of Zionism and Israel.* New York: Olive Branch, 1992.

Bell, J. Bower. *Terror Out of Zion: The Fight for Israeli Independence.* New Brunswick, NJ: Transaction Publishers, 1996.

Benn Aluf. "Background: Enthusiastic IDF Awaits War in Iraq." *Haaretz* (February 17, 2002).

Benvinisti, Meron. *Conflicts and Contradictions.* New York: Random House, 1986.

———. *Intimate Enemies: Jews and Arabs in a Shared Land.* Berkeley, CA: University of California Press, 1995.

———. *Sacred Landscape, The Burried History of the Holy Land, Since 1948*, Maxine Kaufman-Lacusta (trans.). Berkeley, CA: California University Press, 2000.

Benvinisti, Meron. *West Bank and Gaza Data Base Project*, Interim Report, Jerusalem, The West Bank Data Base Project, 1982.

Bergen, Peter, L. *Holy War Inc.: Inside the Secret World of Osama Bin Laden*. New York: Free Press, 2001.

Besser, James, D. Most Muscle? Its NRA, then AIPAC and AARP, *Chicago Jewish Star* (March 11–24, 2005).

Brenner, Lenni. *The Iron Wall: Zionism Revisionism from Jabotinsky to Shamir*. London: Zed Books, 1984.

Brisard, Jean-Charles, et Dasquié, Guillaume. *Ben Laden: La Vérité Interdite*. Paris: Editions Denoel, 2001.

Carey, Roane (ed.). *The New Intifada: Resisting Israel's Apartheid*. London: Verso, 2001.

Chomsky, Noam. *The Fateful Triangle: The United States, Israel and the Palestinians*. Cambridge, MA: South End Press, 1999.

Clarke, Richard, A. *Against All Enemies: Inside America's War on Terror*. New York: Free Press, a Division of Simon & Schuster, 2004.

Clausewitz, Karl von. *On War*. New York: Penguin Classics, 1968.

Cohen, Aharon. *Israel and the Arab World*. New York: Funk and Wagnalls, 1970.

Curtis, Richard. *A Changing Image: American Perceptions of the Arab-Israeli Dispute*. Washington, DC: American Educational Trust, 1986.

Davies, D. *The Last of the Tasmanians*. London: Trinity Press, 1972.

Davis, Uri. *Israel: An Apartheid State*. London: Zed Books, 1987.

Dayan, Moshe. *Story of My Life*. New York: William Morrow, 1976.

DeGroot, Huigh. *De Jure belli ac Pacis*, 1625, Fanon, Franz *The Wretched of the Earth*. New York: Grove Press edition, 1968.

Dershowitz, Alan. *The Case for Israel*. Hoboken, NJ: John Wiley & Sons, 2003.

Dupuy, Ernest, R. and Trevor Dupuy. *The Encyclopedia of Military History, From 3500 BC to the Present*, Revised edition, New York: Harper & Row Publishers, 1977.

Eden, Ami. "9/11 Commission Finds Anger at Isreal Fueling Islamic Terrorism Wave," *Forward* (July 30, 2004).

Finkelstein, Norman G. *Image and Reality of the Israel-Palestine Conflict*. London: Verso, 1995.

———. *Beyond Chutzpah: On the Misuse of anti-Semitism and the Abuse of History*. Berkeley, CA: University of California Press, 2005.

Flapan, Simha. *Zionism and the Palestinians*. New York: Barnes & Noble Books, 1979.

———. *The Birth of Israel, Myths and Realities*. New York: Pantheon, 1987.

Gaines, Robert. "The Battle at Columbia University," *Washington Report on Middle East Affairs*, April 2005.

Gerges, Fawaz. *The Far Enemy: Why Jihad Went Global*. New York: Cambridge University Press, 2005.

Gilbert, G.M. *Nuremberg Diary*. New York: Farrar, Straus and Company, 1947.

Goldberg Jeffrey. "Real Insiders: A Pro-Israel Lobby and an FBI Sting." *New Yorker*, 81 (July 24, 2005).

Goldmann, Nahum. *The Jewish Paradox*, Steve Cox (trans.). New York: Grosset and Dunlap, 1978.

Gordon, Neve and Ruchama Marton. *Torture: Human Rights, Medical Ethics and the Case of Israel*. London: Zed Books, 1995.

Goremberg, Gershom. *The Accidental Empire: Israel and the Birth of the Settlements*. New York: Times Books, 2006.

Graff, James A. *Palestinian Children and Israeli State Violence*. Toronto: NECEF, 1991.

Green, Stephen. *Living by the Sword: America and Israel in the Middle East 1968–87*. Brattleboro, VT: Amana Books, 1988.

Grossman, David. *Sleeping on a Wire: Conversations with Palestinians in Israel*. New York: Farrar, Straus and Giroux, 1993.

Habash, Mohammad. *Islam's Fanatical 1 percent*, Project Syndicate 2005, Islamic Studies Center, Damascus, Syria, 2005.

Heller, Joseph. *The Stern Gang: Ideology, Politics and Terror, 1940–1949*. London: Frank Cass, 1995.

Hersh, Seymour. *The Samson Option: Israel's Nuclear Arsenal and American Foreign Policy*. New York: Random House, 1991.

Huggler, Justin. "Israel Imposes "Racist" Marriage Law." *Guardian* (August 1, 2003).

Hurewitz, J.C. *Diplomacy in the Near and Middle East, Vol. II: A Documentary Record: 1914–1956*. Princeton, NJ: D. Van Nostrand Company, Inc., 1956.

Kagan, Donald, Gary Schmitt, and Thomas Donnelly. *Rebuilding America's Defenses—Strategy, Forces and Resources For a New Century*, Project For The New American Century, 1150 Seventeenth Street, N.W., Suite 510, Washington, DC 2000.

Karon, Tony. "How Israel's Hamas Killings Affects the US." *Time* (March 23, 2004).

Khalidi, Walid. "Why Did the Palestinians Leave Revisited." *Journal of Palestine Studies*, 34, no. 2 (Winter 2005).

Khromchenko Yulie. "Suvey: Most Jewish Israelis Support Transfer of Arabs." *Ha'aretz* (June 22, 2004).

Kimmerling, Baruch. *Politicide: Ariel Sharon's War Against the Palestinians*. London: Verso, 2003.

Koestler, Arthur. *The Thirteenth Tribe*. New York: Random House, 1976.

Kristol, William and Lawrence, Kaplan. *The War over Iraq: Saddam's Tyranny and America's Mission*. New York: Encounter Books, 2003.

Kronfeld, Ami. "Avneri on Ethnic Cleansing and a Personal Note." *Jewish Peace News* (March 17, 2003).

Langer, Felicia. *Sionisme et droits de l'homme*, Association Suisse-Palestine, Lausanne, C.H., 1977.

Laoust, Henri. *Essai sur les doctrines sociales et politiques de Takï-d-Dïn Ahmad b. Taimïya*, Cairo, 1939.

Lemkin, Raphael. *Axis Rule in Occupied Europe*. New York: Carnegie Endowment for International Peace, 1944.

Lilienthal, Alfred M. *The Zionist Connection: What Price Peace?* New York: Dodd, Mead and Company, 1978.

Lowenthal, Marvin. (ed. and trans.) *The diaries of Theodor Herzl*. New York: The Universal Library, Grosset & Dunlap, 1962.

Maalouf, Amin. *Les croisades vues par les Arabes*, Editions J'ai lu, 1983, 75007, Paris, France.

Mallison, W. Thomas and Sally V. *The Palestine Problem in International Law and World Order*. Essex, UK: Longman Group Ltd., 1986.

Margalit, Avishai. "The Violent Life of Yitzhak Shamir." *The New York Review of Books* (May 14, 1992).

Masalha, Nur. *Expulsion of the Palestinians: The Concept of "transfer in Zionist Political Thought," 1882–1948*. Washington, DC: Institute for Palestinian Studies, 1992.

McCarthy, Justin. *The Population of Palestine: Palestinian History and Statistics of the Late Ottoman Period and the Mandate*. New York: Columbia University Press, 1990.

McGreal, Chris. "Snipers with Children in their Sight." *Guardian* (June 28, 2005).

McNeil, Kristine. "The War on Academic Freedom." *Nation* (November 11, 2002).

Mills, C. Wright. *The Power Elite*. New York: Oxford University Press, 1956.

Morris, Benny. *The Birth of the Palestinian Refugee Problem*. New York: Cambridge University Press, 1989.

———. *Israel Border Wars, 1949–1956*. New York: Oxford University Press, 1997.

———. *Righteous Victims: A History of the Zionist-Arab Conflict, 1881–1999*. New York: Alfred Knopf, 1999.

Netanyahu, Benjamin. "The Case for Toppling Saddam." *Wall Street Journal* (September 20, 2002).

Nussbaum, Paul. "Israel Finds an Ally in American Evangelicals." *Philadelphia Inquirer* (November 17, 2005).

Patai, Raphael (ed.) and Harry Zohn (trans.). *Theodore Herzl, Complete Diaries*. New York: Herzl Press, 1960.

Podhoretz, Norman. "Israel isn't the Issue." *The Wall Street Journal* (September 20, 2001).

Popper, Nathaniel. "Pro-Israel Groups: Campuses Improving." *Forward* (June 24, 2005).

Quandt, B. William. *Peace Process: American Diplomacy and the Arab-Israeli Conflict since 1967*, 3rd ed. Washington, DC: Brooking Institution Press, 2005.

Rabin, Yitzhak. *The Rabin Memoirs*. Berkeley, CA: University of California Press, 1961.

Reeve, Simon. *The New Jackals: Ramzi Yousef, Osama Bin Laden and the Future of Terrorism*. Boston, MA: Northeastern University Press, 1999.

Rokach, Livia. *Israel's Sacred Terrorism: A Study based on Moshe Sharett's Personal Diary and Other Documents*. Belmont, MA: Association of Arab-American University Graduates, 1986.

Ross, Dennis. *The Missing Peace—The Inside Story of the Fight for Middle East Peace*. New York: Farrar, Straus and Giroux, 2004.

Rubenstein, Richard L. *After Auschwitz: Radical Theology and Contemporary Judaism*. Indianapolis, IN: Bobbs Merrill, 1966.

Rubin, Barry and Colp, Judith. *Anti-American Terrorism and the Middle East*. New York: Oxford University Press, 2002.

Said, Edward and Christopher, Hitchens (ed.); *Blaming the Victims: Spurious Scholarship and the Palestinian Question*. London, NY: Verso, 1988.

Said, Edward. *The Politics of Dispossession: The Struggle for Palestinian Self Determination 1969-1994*. New York: Pantheon Books, 1994.

Said, Edward. *The Question of Palestine*. New York: Vintage Books, 1979.

———. *The Politics of Dispossession: The Struggle for Palestinian Self Determination 1969–1994*. New York: Pantheon Books, 1994.

Said, Edward and Christopher, Hitchens (ed.); *Blaming the Victims: Spurious Scholarship and the Palestinian Question*. London: Verso, 1988.

Scheuer, Michael. *Why the West is Losing the War on Terror*. Washington, DC: Brassy's, Inc., 2002.

Shamir, Shlomo. "US Jews: Sharon is 'Worried' by Terrorism Distinction." *Haaretz* (September 18, 2001).

Shonfeld, Reb Moshe. *The Holocaust Victims Accuse: Documents and Testimony on Jewish War Criminals.* Brooklyn, NY: Neturei Karta of U.S.A., 1977.

Spiegel, L. Steven. *The Other Arab-Israeli Conflict: Making America's Middle East Policy from Truman to Reagan.* Chicago, IL: Chicago University Press, 1985.

Sternhell, Zeev. *The Founding Myths of Israel.* Princeton, NJ: Princeton University Press, 1999.

Suskind, Ronald. *The Price of Loyalty: George W. Bush, the White House and the Education of Paul O'.* New York: Simon & Schuster, 2004.

Swisher, E. Clayton. *The Truth About Camp David: The Untold Story about the Collapse of the Peace Process.* New York: Nation Books, 2004.

Telhami, Shibley. *The Stakes, America and the Middle East.* Boulder, CO:, Westview Press, 2002.

Timerman, Jacobo. *The Longest War: Israel in Lebanon.* New York: Alfred A. Knopf, 1982.

Tivnan, Edward. *The Lobby: Jewish Political Power and American Foreign Policy.* New York: Simon and Schuster, 1987.

Urquhart, Conal. "Israeli Soldiers Tell of Indiscriminate Killings by Army and a Culture of Impunity." *Guardian* (September 6, 2005).

Weber, Max. *Politics as a Vocation.* Philadelphia, PA: Fortress Press, 1965.

———. *On Charisma and Institution Building.* Chicago, IL: University of Chicago Press, 1968.

Weitz, Joweph. *Diaries and Letters to Children.* Massada, Israel: Ramat Gan, 1965.

Weizmann, Chaim. *Trial and Error: The Autobiography of Chaim Weizmann.* London: Hamish Hamilton, 1949.

Wole, Soyinka. *Climate of Fear: The Quest For Dignity in a Dehumanized World.* New York: Random House, 2005.

Woodward Bob. *Bush at War.* New York: Simon and Schuster, 2002.

Yoffie, Eric. "Reform the Conference." *Forward* (August 2, 2002).

Young, Ronald J. *Missed Opportunities for Peace: U.S. Middle East Policy 1981–86.* Philadelphia, PA: American Friends Service Committee, 1987.

Zogby, John. *The Ten Nations Impressions of America Poll.* Utica, NY: Zogby International, 2004.

Index

Magnes, Judah, 68, 73
Mahdi. *See Shī'i;* Twelvers
Mandate for Palestine, 59, 79, 82
Mandatory power, 144n39
Maquisards, 20
Martyrdom, 42, 78; asymmetric retaliation fueling, 36
Massacre: in Palestine, 95; by suicide, 31
McCarthy, Joseph, 21, 22
Media: American, 73, 98; attention benefiting terrorists, 29; corporate, 9; indifference toward oppressed, 9
Meier, Golda, on Palestinians, 69
Middle East: sources of oil, 88; U.S. policy for, 35–36, 100–104
Military, 5; doctrine, 5, 16; law, 75; occupation, 78
Mills, C. Wright, on violence, 4
Minorities, persecuted, 5
Mission Civilisatrice, 102
Mossad, 75
Mubarak, Hosni, 44, 98
Muslim(s): born-again, 52; humiliation sensed among, 53, 65; intolerance among, 49; lesser, 48
Muslim Brotherhood. *See* Society of Muslim Brotherhood
Muslim countries: dissent in, 34; fundamental progress lacking in, 66; insurgencies in, 53
Muslim culture, 35
Muslim intellectuals, 39
Muslim modernists, 45, 47; theocratic forces threatening, 37
Muslim reformers, 39, 47; loss of confidence in, 40
Muslim traditionalist(s), 66
Mutual Assured Destruction, 31

Nagasaki, 9–10, 31. *See also* Bombings; State terrorism; Weapons
Nasser, Gamal Abd'ul, 44–45,
National liberation movements, 7, 9, 23, 30; birth of, 7; motivating self-immolation, 42; status of, 6; struggles of, 17. *See also* Insurgencies; Oppressed

National security, 3, 14; ensuring, 21, 29; used to coerce popular support, 14
Nations: colonial/former colonial, 13, 23; emerging, 12–13; Eurogenic, 23; hegemonic, 23; negotiating with terrorists, 13; possessing thermonuclear weapons, 23. *See also* State(s)
Navy Seals, suicidal missions of, 8
Nazi, 3, 7, 9–10, 17, 19, 21, 31, 58, 71, 80, 91–92
Nazi Germany, 21. *See also* France; Holocaust; Jews; Kristall Nacht; Maquisards; State terrorism; Yellow star
Neocon(s), 101–3; fantasy, 105; manipulating terrorism factor, 98
New Dark Age, 37, 54
New York. *See* 9/11 attacks; World Trade Center
New York Post, 98
New York Times, 72, 77
9/11 attacks, xiii, 24, 41, 50; additional consequences of, 29; scope of impact of, 28; U.S. hubris following, 98–99; world's empathy for U.S. following, 97
Nobel Peace Prize: Arafat, 60–61; Cassin, 17; Peres, 71; Rabin, 71
Nuclear-free Middle East, 76. *See also* Israel
Nuclear terrorism, 23. *See also* Mutual Assured Destruction; Weapons
Nuremburg Trials, 14. *See also* Gilbert, G.M; Goering, Hermann

Objective(s): of insurgencies, 7; of Islāmists, 52; of terrorists, 25, 29; of war, 5; Zionism's, 72–73
Occupation, 79; check-points, 81, 90; curfews, 22, 60, 80–81, 91; of France, 20; laws, 86; of Lebanon, 105; military, 78. *See also* Caterpillar; Military, Law(s); Palestine; Settlements; Wall of separation
Occupied Territories. *See* Israel-Palestine; Palestine; Settlements
Oil: controlling Middle East sources of, 88; revenues of Sa'udi Arabia, 41

About the Author

ALFRED G. GERTEINY has long been a student of the Middle East and of Islam. As a Professor of History and International Relations (recently at the University of Connecticut in Stamford), he has, over nearly four decades, offered undergraduate and graduate courses, conducted research, and lectured in many universities around the world. Beginning in 1973, following the terrorist attack on the Israeli Olympic team in Munich, he designed and led seminars on terrorism. He has been a longtime media commentator on the Middle East, Africa, terrorism, and U.S. foreign policy. His previous publications include *Mauritania* (1967) and *Historical Dictionary of Mauritania* (1981).